Ritual and Capital

Published by Bard Graduate Center and Wendy's Subway

While designing Bard Graduate Center's Spring programs in 2017, I wanted to consider new ways to activate the gallery space by moving outside of the confines of traditional exhibition-making. It was clear that the upcoming shows on view that season, *New York Crystal Palace 1853* and *Design by the Book: Chinese Ritual Objects and the Sanli tu*, while not conceived as a pair, yielded productive tensions through their juxtaposition within our galleries. With this in mind, I enlisted Wendy's Subway as a collaborator in considering the relationship between these two geographically and temporally disparate shows. Together we decided upon an organizing thematic focus at the intersection of ritual and capital, and through their ongoing Reading Room project, they assembled a collection of artists' books, periodicals, and other publications to interrogate, expand upon, clarify, and complicate the field that lay between the two exhibitions.

Books, installed in a space conceived for reading and study, provided a perfect proposal for this public space, which unifies many of the values of the institution in which research is always at the forefront. The Wendy's Subway Reading Room was animated with live readings given by contemporary poets and writers considering these themes, many of whom contributed work to this collection, in addition to works selected from an open call. While the writings in this book do not address either exhibition directly, they expand upon the theme "Ritual and Capital," speaking to our contemporary experience in an increasingly consumerist global culture and the impact that has on our habits, our thoughts, and our everyday lives. This volume gathers all of these contributions into four discrete, though interrelated sections, which each open with a note authored by the editorial committee. Rather than describe any single approach, genre, or subject, each section comprises a heterogeneous range of texts and artworks. Considered together, they address the inseparability of ritual and capital from the organization and experience of daily life, refracted by sites and places, expressed through gestures and movements, embedded in objects and fetishes, and embodied in the social or the spiritual.

This volume was motivated in part by a desire to somehow capture and expand some of the conversations occurring during the live readings and on the gallery floor—I had not expected the conversations I was having with visitors to reverberate through into the live readings, but they did. Standing in the gallery surrounded by maps and lithographs of America's first World's Fair, visitors talked to me about how they've watched the New York of their childhood disappear; or, referencing the ritual robe displayed in our *Design by the Book* exhibition, they described the personal rituals they hold on to to help them break out of the quotidian grind. Our open call was a way to bring that conversation out into a larger community.

This book is the first in the BGCX series, a publication series designed to extend the learning period around time-based programming so that it may continue after the events themselves have ended. Taking the spontaneous alchemy of conversation, performance, and hands-on engagement as their starting points, these experimental publishing projects provide space for continued reflection and research in a form that is particularly inclusive of artists.

— Emily Reilly, Bard Graduate Center

What habits and practices do we form to subvert, subsist, survive? Is there refuge in ritual? How might ritual practices endow objects and artifacts with qualities that resist their assimilation within the market? What function can movement rituals have for embodying practices of healing and care? How does ritual strengthen and solidify communities? In what ways have ritual practices turned the landscape of the everyday into a playground for consumption, where ritual enables the reproduction of structures of capital? What is the function of ritual as it challenges or facilitates the activities of capital in everyday life, whether globally or locally? What are your rituals?

Wendy's Subway is open to submissions including, but not limited to, poems, essays, inventories, inquiries, protocols and instructions, reading lists, journals, pillow books, found texts, fiction, and desiderata on the topics of ritual and capital.

— Ritual and Capital Open Call, Wendy's Subway, Summer 2017

I

12 Note
13 DJ Ashtrae
22 Jeremy Hoevenaar
28 Rebecca Keith
32 Matthew Kosinski
40 Krystal Languell
46 Cameron Quan Louie
52 Devin N. Morris
59 Daniel Poppick
64 Josh Silver
70 Celina Su
84 Deirtra Thompson

II

98 Note
99 Justin Blinder
114 Jackie Clark
121 Shou Jie Eng
126 Josef Kaplan
153 Matt Longabucco
163 Sarah Passino
175 Danniel Schoonebeek
180 David Whelan
186 Rachael Guynn Wilson

III

194 Note
195 Catherine Chen
200 Ted Dodson
222 Mia Kang
240 Jeff Alessandrelli and Amy Lawless
250 Feliz Lucia Molina
260 Laura Mullen
268 Judah Rubin
279 Shelby Shaw

IV

286 Note
287 Mitch Anzuoni
290 Future Host
302 Miranda Mellis
308 Cam Scott
321 Maya Sisneros in conversation with David Bowles, Rodney Gomez, Emmy Pérez, José Antonio Rodríguez, and Veronica Sandoval aka Lady Mariposa
328 Eirik Steinhoff
349 Takáts Márk
351 Matthew Whitley

355 Contributors

I

The African Burial Ground is located in Lower Manhattan, where less than half a square acre of the site was designated as a national monument, although the burial ground occupies nearly six acres. The part of the burial ground that which lies beyond in the half acre monument has been developed. This land now holds U.S. Federal Buildings. Trinity Church barred all Africans—free and enslaved—from being buried in the city during the late 17th century. At the time, New York City ended at Chambers Street, and the African Burial Ground was officially outside city limits. An estimated 15,000 African people were buried on the site between the 1690s and the 1790s.

I first heard about the burial ground on the radio. I hadn't known it existed, even though I was less than ten blocks away. Even when I took classes in American History and African American Studies near the city, the site never came up. I didn't even happen upon it when I researched New York's urban planning and how it annexed what society deemed "Other." The monument is rarely, if ever, listed among any museums of the city's history, while less than a mile away, the 9/11 Memorial and Museum averages 9,000 visitors a day. It is a mass grave of nearly 3,000 people. The museum itself holds a repository of unidentified remains.

Union Square is built on top of a former paupers' grave from the 18th century. Even though I know this part of the city's history, I don't remember it. If I'm transferring trains at the subway station underneath or sitting in the park above, the people buried in the ground are not in my thoughts. I forget what the site once was. There is a disconnect between the people who remain in a place and those just passing through.

I forget often that Manhattan is an island. Overlooking the New York Harbor, taking my lunch break in Battery Park, I assume I'm on a part of land which is connected to the rest of the country. I forget entirely that the city is built on an archipelago. There are islands nearby at any given moment wherever you are in New York City. Staten Island. Long Island. Governors Island. Liberty Island. Fire Island. Roosevelt Island. Coney Island. Ellis Island. Rikers Island.

—Editors

DJ Ashtrae

GAY LOVE SONG

fire powered smoothies are
for the imp in a halter top he licks illegally
tho he's not 24, 25.

sunburnt coyotes, you know that love
is foolish, gives me all this
gold I don't know what
to do with

fortune befalls the doll
rather than shock
kissing drooling charcoal rolling dolly bees
whose hot sauce
is open to hunger

when we have each other
our frenzy runs like shampoo
when we have each other

AM / FM

Up for the ultimate alignment, ushered
Out for wanting cheap
Kawala. Women in black bandanas watch me Yearn.
¡Fear the Monkey King!
You pose for $2 with a Torus mask in the commuter nerf.
Explanations of eras end in seconds,
Trifectas withering
Bouquets,
Pure and carnal measures. People fill their glasses.
Area slushes.
zzzzzzzzzzzzzzzzzzzzzzzzzzzzzzzzzzzzzzzzzzzzzzzzzzzzzzzzzzzzzzzzzzz
Yucca leaves behind its scary-ass past.
Gangstresses skate over our souls.
Muse puts her key in the ignition.
¡Whales wash Manhattan!
Release America's unicorns! ¡The radio tower has a
City, has an ear, has a tangerine shirt!
sssssssssssssssssssssssssssssssssssssssssssssssssssssssssssssssssssss
Duet, assume Anna Gabriel all afternoon, Technicolor roses bore Morningside
qqqqqqqqqqqqqqqqqqqqqqqqqqqqqqqqqqqqqqqqqqqqqqqqqqqqqqqq
June rain #9
Less thirst, less fetish, fewer monitors, less ridicule, more puddles
Imps passionately demonstrate death across this mesa.
xxxxxxxxxxxxxxxxxxxxxxxxxxxxxxxxxxxxxxxxxxxxxxxxxxxxxxxxxxxxxxxxxxxxxxxx
Naked lightning in the 80's, fissure feast, Tezcatlipoca sings. They
Vanish.

STRIKE

Warm eyes with something to do, on a couch turning down the TV. Dogs outside sip Mexican soda. I was young and never sent to a cave of snakes, but the wind wound up at funerals. Chest red in a grove of oranges, in this volcano, a special blend of chili fries and denial. Lips for breath. Effort for money. His legs are mushrooms and nopales. Mini-miseries painted red and yellow, by minions. Tnozlitli lies across the 405, loroco, stadium small, I am only x and have ate Lucifer's cereal, he would love to make love, he shows me his aisle of heroes, the silver laser, this place whose fade is forgiving, in 20 or 30 years you will be dead to society whose freedoms are recyclable, in halves and twisted, technotonic, easternbloc of crushed red, reading more than driving more than sleeping more than screaming, hair and juice, alchemy and wilt, color the walls, chili chili, language says nightmares are where love comes from but we know otherwise. I want a future. Every chingona gets a free bicicleta, painted purple.

HIT ON A MU$E

Fungus Fungus Fungus
Vacancy Vacancy Vacancy
Sex Sex Sex
Naranja Naranja Naranja
Tweet Tweet

WNYC

I'm lying in bed high while it rains.
If I do anything tonight, I'd be so evil.
I'm not high on drugs or life.
There's lightning.
I don't know what I'll do tonight,
Maybe something perfect.
I'll tell those voices of doubt a lie,
And go back to being dirty.

Nobody asks about what you're doing when it rains.

POBLANO

Imp boomerang she, snack hammer, the clearing of the wolf,
As we both wear reflective sneaks
Soaking
In the river.
22 with brown eyes and never confused
Purpose still tuned out
With most of the pixels blown up
In a walnut pyre of their making I am still impossible I was hooked on the
Emerald vroom
Inflected southwest
Stuck in the Resident reds and doubling
Accidents of foam
Yelling at sticks in the rattle

And dying until we found the gangs of papaya melted takes helix noons
Ciphering

We crash
If we want
We need more iced tea We roost

We spill and stain
Lucky and dangerous

We spill and stain
Lucky and dangerous

We spill and stain
Lucky and dangerous

yellow all night with a jealous and gross boyfriend, his other half, running away into circumambulation, as rubber as knowledge, a monster, until he made me cum he was based in Paris, I flex and burn and resist shock, gooey, we are usually too pretty to ride with each other, d is for spice as in d spice, dance kitten gnaws my ear at the bar in the twilight of my fun, during the 69 nap club I remember where I am, all over my chest, he tells me not to leave as he showers me, my back against his chest, his hands down my pants is so hot as I ready to leave, and he kisses me before I leave him to his Mexica cassettes and candle water, if all our lovers could lie together, not retro molecular, or in backlit wars without any affiliations, steps out of the ego and looks back to a sleeping reality, he asks if I can rail, bound by instruction, that ready evil, that grog, warehouse in dirt fields, again and again, the past slips into its own vast, either way I eat the seeds beat up thief action, green shorts numberless hard work, sour weight perpendicular to the vistas, at the tip of twelve tragedies, of a mage's hot rage, cold moon in and out of telegraph, transit on nudity, skating plainshirted with pale tongued Manhattan, with an 80's mastermind that is the source of my love, of my nightmares, mayhem, easily, so avenue sad with dust and wings, 18 19 20 poké genius, lucky and cash nice, freakish huffing is a turn on for the scary and possessed, we just don't seek out dogs but glow-in-the-dark palms, jackfruit, ridiculous hours, scripts and scripture chili, x is a nation that stands for nothing, her pink and blue triangles, his unicorn has a black eye, spiked with pineapple, we should watch the blockbuster that ends with everyone on drugs, morsels of teenage penance and fame, for the fourth time tonight, luxury falls out of his back pocket into mine, I am no lover but a fool and mistress, hot for carpet, as rigid and schematic as bingo, washed out with the neoprene armada who throughout various takes in the burning reels of San Francisco survives

Jeremy Hoevenaar

UNDER OUR INSOLVENCY

1. *On the compassion train**

It's no big secret
I'm sure but still
the resolve to find
and sustain a consistent
median level of compassion
for ourselves has remained
doggedly elusive up until
this point. We'd just
moved from an old
large space and into
a new small space.
Subsidized housing, new construction.
We are quietly astonished

*The first line of a poem in a series of poems I started writing at the time described above, late 2011. My partner Dee Dee and I had been living in Baltimore for about a year. I was having a hard time finding steady work and loan payments were looming. It occurs to me now, in 2017, that a whole other life is hiding inside those poems.

by how the dark
wood cabinets and buttery
floors generate and gently
expend warm wavelengths of
yellow light. Everything's on
smooth hinges, moves with
a slow easy heaviness,
quality resists slightly, feeds
back deliberately and at
a reasonable volume.* The
dishwasher has never been

*I can remember with an uncanny clarity how the volume control and tuning dials felt on my father's stereo system when I was a kid—a memory I can feel in my hands. There was a weight to the silver dials, a counterbalanced or cantilevered feeling, an exertion required to shift sonic parameters. A physics feeling: momentum, inertia, an earthy metallic heft. Turning the knobs was a serious business. I have always associated this feeling of weight in interface, of slight resistance in feedback, with quality. Mostly now we make listening choices and raise the volume on our devices by pressing plastic keys or buttons with less of a sense of effort and consequence. Frivolity steadily leaks in and my ears ring, never stop, the residual tone in my head a tiny continuous thread and sonic monument to my mismanaged or abused interfaces, my many small impulsive appetites over time for a bigger noise to stick my head into while trying to make my body disperse and recombine in an expanded field of increased loudness. Incidentally, my body presents as more real to me now than it used to, more low tech, despite (or maybe because of) the prosthetic extension of all of today's common interfaces. The old heavy dial versus the more contemporary plastic key or button is a little like the difference between older handmade horror movie effects and contemporary CGI as seen, for instance, in the vast qualitative difference between Rob Bottin and Stan Winston's shockingly grotesque (and heavy! real!) creations in John Carpenter's *The Thing* and the limp and soupily efficient newfangled CGI iterations of the same creature seen in the 2011 prequel. Degraded quality. The air is thinner in the now's future. The monsters look like screensavers. A sign at my local post office states: *due to a National technical issue we are currently working in a degraded mode. Thank you for your patience and understanding.—Management.* But it's all about the rituals of impatience and misunderstanding. Lines, grumbling, shuffling, shouting. When I was a teenager in the early '90s I could point a remote control at my plastic stereo console and watch the volume dial turn as I depressed the volume button, spooky action at a distance, the physics of quality eclipsed by invisible threads of infrared magic.

used and releases a
waft of new plastic-
ness when first opened.
But all of our
weird piles* are here,
our provisional solutions, our
dusty hacks and track
records and broken shit
in bags we steered
down the street on
an enormous rusting hand-
truck and our cat
reclining there in a
stretched shape of sunlight
breathing and throwing off
clouds of white hair
like lazy spores into
the spotless conditioned air.
We build desks into

*How is it we have so many chairs? And why is everything always so dusty? We carry luan walls with us every time we move, set them up and create divisions that miraculously seem to increase the area of whatever space we put them in. It's a ritual for us to move them around, test how they bend a room, crease the light and change its emotional tone. The right spot and the apartment spreads, increases in value, holds more possibility. Space contains more of itself than it seems to. We find a thin but serviceable autonomy in these self-cultivated options.

our two closets, side
by side, less to
save space than to
delineate and keep safe
a zone for a
special kind of thinking
we aspire to and
occasionally achieve and even
document. We experiment with
several smoking cessation methods
and sample various tinctures
to cleanse and calibrate,
perform the odd guided
meditation white sitting or
lying upon the glossy
floor forcing pinched points
of awareness through the
tunnels of our limbs
and into our twitching
extremities and tighten and
loosen and breathe and
early to bed.* In
the building lobby there's

a bulletin board palimpsested
with signup sheets for
quasi-optional tenant "community"
events, classes, jobs, stuff
for sale, trade, etc.
One flyer states: Artists
with legal questions wanted.
I try to think
of some tough ones.

*To get to bed early is still difficult. I've resisted sleep at night for as long as I can remember and always want to nap during the day. Is this a ritual grounding or a habitual avoidance? So many social and familial isms webbed together to create the complex rituals of my childhood nights. There was real artifice and analysis in my apotropaic elaborations of movement and thought, an admirable ability to sync complex mental machinations with systems of gesture and focused attention to various internal spaces. The feeling of the inside of my hands and the feeling of the outside of my hands. Swallow to divert or imprint an image. Litany, taxonomy. Nightly labors. Is capital responsible? Magic is the medium we live in now, as in we live within metaphor, alchemies of language, invisible forces moving our eyes, feet, and fingers. What is it we are calling *ourselves*? We're trained early in magical thinking. Perhaps I felt the need to interface with that magic in order to exert control over local circumstance. So I learned deep secret keeping early, too. No one knows how we really expend most of our energy. Is alcoholism responsible? My dad worked in finance, at the New York Stock Exchange, later at Goldman Sachs. Did the pressure contribute to his drinking? Did his drinking contribute to my OCD? There's a causal chain or smoky lace of influence over- and under-laying these figures of family, addiction, co-dependency, capital, control. Ritual consumption and avoidance, styles of attachment and intimacy. I can remember when—but not why—4 replaced 3 as the number of personal salvation. More efficient? I see 4 as blue/green, 3 as yellow/orange. A shift from ocean to sunset? Who's not afraid of what menaces the ocean depths? Capital is down there, so large and so deep down its scale renders it imperceptible. I was most afraid of brain tumors and blindness, uncontrolled growth and aphasia, the body as barely contained riot or self-contradiction. I was compelled to cocoon myself in blankets in order to protect my body from malign external influence. Interior and exterior were in league against me, so what space was there for me to inhabit? A small opening for my face, for air. 4 became anathema. I still don't trust it. I do have compassion for this version of myself now.

Rebecca Keith

REGULATIONS MAY SHIFT BETWEEN TAKE-OFF AND LANDING: Q + A WITH THE TSA

Neither the passenger nor the baby or toddler will be asked to test or taste breast milk or formula. Our Security Officers will not test or taste formula or breast milk.

—Transportation Security Administration regulations (September, 2006)

Neither mother nor father nor security officer will be required to taste the baby. The baby or toddler will not be asked to taste him or herself.

All inspections will be carried out in a timely, professional manner. All liquids must be in containers of three ounces or less and packaged in a quart-size, clear plastic, zip-top bag. The fewer liquids you require, the better.

KY Jelly is a situation that will be evaluated case-by-case. Best to have sex in the airport before boarding the aircraft. If said act results in baby, be prepared for spot checks of breast milk or formula.

Other bodily secretions will not be permitted aboard the aircraft. If you have to use the facilities, hold it. Your urine may be plotting an act of terror.

If medications are in containers of three ounces or less, they may also be included in the quart-size, zip-top bag with other items—as long as it all comfortably fits.

You may not all fit comfortably on the aircraft, but if your liquids are secure, everything will be ship-shape, squared away, zip-locked. Liquid babies must be contained in a child safety bottle, preferably soundproof.

Step over here, I believe you have not followed the instructions. That appears to be a *gallon-size* clear plastic, zip-top bag rather than a *quart-size*, clear plastic, zip-top bag. We'll let you through this time, but on the return flight I guarantee they won't be so lenient.

If the name on the prescription medication label does not match the name of the passenger, the passenger should expect to explain why to our Security Officer.

Legitimate excuses include:

1. Recent marriage. (You should have kept your maiden name.)
2. Selling your roommate's Ritalin, Adderall, Ambien, Ativan, Xanax, Valium, vintage Quaaludes.

FAQ:

What is the TSA's policy if a passenger comes to the screening checkpoint with multiple clear plastic, quart-size, zip-top bags?

We encourage you to travel light.

What if a passenger develops a rash from passing through the screening checkpoint?

Such are the hazards of air travel. Prolonged exposure may lead to unpleasant side effects such as hacking cough, wheezing, racial profiling, skin irritation, dehydration, and in rare cases, shingles.

Are there any changes to the policy regarding gel-filled bras and similar prosthetics?

Only gel-filled bras will be allowed aboard the aircraft. Security officers may be required to inspect gel-filled bras, or any suspect bras, especially those with lace or animal prints. Any gel-filled bras that appear to be lactating will activate an immediate code red. Red is worse than orange.

There is no custom I understand anymore.

In the event of catastrophe, we hope you will still enjoy.

Matthew Kosinski

RITUAL IN THE EVENT THAT LOVE IS NOT ENOUGH

Place your hair in the sink and

[You worry, but there is time.]

the offer letters of the
financiers, as you would a
communion wafer or breath
mint, on your tongue.

[They don't dissolve into air.
We were wrong about that
part.
It turns out things persist
far beyond the expected sublimation point.]

Open the tap. Chew
until you feel ill.

[By now the neighborhood
has revealed its battleground nature;
the island has announced its fortress self.]

Disgorge your payload
into the municipal water supply.

[I see you tremble; the clock panics you.
You have the righteous sense that a vague window is

closing. But listen:

Armageddon is a mountain;
it will be there when we're
done.]

EXTINCTION-LEVEL EVENT, *AFTER MARBAS*

I admit I
have been passing my
days in a strange
manner.
My problems
were not too serious
until the radiologist
yelled at me for breathing.
Now our galaxy's magnetic
field is all askew, and Google
has censored the
photographs.
Our top minds are on it
when they are not
hacking celebrities' phones.
One day all our nudes
will be in the public domain.
The stage magician
bears his assistant who
agrees
to bear her midriff
because the ticket price
is high.
Her head disappears inside a
box.

Come out, child with hair. The Lord calls you to light.

This next call will
be the disaster
call, like pushing
a nose
through someone's
face in a failed
attempt at self-
defense.
What about a garlic
skin shell? What about the
ACLU? Oh, sure, selling
your labor power is
common sense
but tell everyone you cast
a healing
spell for the two-year-old
with rhabdomyosarcoma
and you're the bad
guy?
Nine in ten theorists
agree: when it's time to
rally support for the New
World Order they'll stage
first contact,
but we've already had it.

AS IF LOOKING UP, *AFTER GAAP*

My president's
name is
Gaap.
His office is
to make
men
ignorant
and
insensible.
Following
my
endoscopy
the nurse
wheeled me
into the
recovery
bay. Gaap
climbed onto
my gurney
and put his
ear to my
stomach.
No, no,
Gaap said.
I'm afraid it's
all inflamed.
This
conflicted
with my
doctor's
report.
I looked
up as if
from a
shallow firepit.

He
conducts
himself
in a human
shape.

This bed is very small. For both of us to fit, we must cradle one another.

Fact-
check your
tongue. Is
that an
apple seed
or cyanide?
The answer
is usually
the worse
one.
Fact-
check your
haptics.
Whose body
is under
yours and
how did they
get there?
Eminent
domain
doesn't
count. Fact-
check your
tax
documents.
When
the armored
truck rolls
through your
ward, ask for
a rebate.
Terminate
the contract.

DISGRACE MAGIC, *AFTER RAUM*

What follows is:
I fall upon the
(t)horns of life; I
poke a finger at the
gash; my whole
hand slips in. I sink
up to my elbow in
myself. This is the field
of action dominates
you.
This is whittling a tiny
Solomon figurine
to deposit in the
gash. This is
smuggling that
figurine
through a hole
in the fence.
This is removing that
figurine from your
gut and igniting it.
This is lobbing that
figurine through a
window.
This is maybe it
detonates. This is who
is the target?

Acceptable forms of disgrace
magic and news feed contents 1/29/17:

Smoking organic
cigarettes while you practice
energy healing.

Gunking up your computer
brain with J-pop dance
routines.

Military raid in which
an eight-year-old child
dies.
Her red tutu spills out of her
neck to configure the seal
of Raum.

[The creator gave us certain
dignities by rendering us in
his image.]

Wolfing pickles before
bed and rubbing salt on your
lips but you still can't astral
project.

[Is it any wonder in this climate?]

It has become inborn and your body is sensitive.
Has the world not ever been bloody?

When it turns
midnight
commercials
talk to us like
angels from the
Bible: Our
beautiful water
bottles
will save the
world. We are
that rich and
more important
than usual. I
directly
unloaded our
bank account
into the mouth
of the waiter
who upsold us
on
the
champagne
because it
was a
compliment.
That's New
Year's Eve.
Let's give her
great reviews.
Tasteful
drapery wallows in her
plundered
firmament.

And red was the snake of our first heredity, that coiled forth as the tortured road;
the blood-cord of Lilith's blessing to all children of the moon.

One
rare animal
squalls its
mating call
into the
avaginal
thicket of
iron and rock:
no face but
the gaze
of
handlers
who
shovel its
shit back
into its pit.
The other
feverbeasts
become
like
mirrors:
silver chines,
glass hyoids.
Materials for
an orgy: one
thirst hollow
enough to
require this
much water;
one organ
starved
enough to
hallucinate
this much
flesh.

CRUSH AND GIFT, *AFTER ASMODAY*

Dragons are
convenient until we let
them do
all the work for us.
Throw the cloak;
find a machine. One
man ordered another
to pull the lever.
He did and the lights
went out across
Kentucky.

The texts say
nothing of us. Still,
the land reaches its
fever pitch. Compare
the melthaze cast
upward by
hot tar in August.

I never asked for
this phossy jaw, but I
earned its greenwhite
smolder.

Blessed with the sight to see beyond the mask,
to walk the wilderness and embrace the banishment.

You and I have a treasure
which
comprises a
field of empty
crosses
adjacent
the New Jersey Turnpike.

We are meant to thread them
with
grapevines because
grapes remain
useful regardless

of how we treat them.
When you
crush a grape beneath your
bootheel, give it time and
fungus.
Call it by another name.

(Stick
that in your
utopia and
smoke it.)

Krystal Languell

POEM FOR MY FRIEND IN OHIO

I am glad you were not found in a
pit this morning or any other morning
beneath the shed of a troubled white man
in your state. I am glad that we, you and I,
only get groped on the street or
masturbated at on the NJ Transit bus,
that we are alive and not buried and
not buried alive, at least not by dirt,
a shed, that man.

POEM FOR MY FRIEND IN PROVIDENCE

Do you sometimes feel as if motherhood
is wielded against us? What used to gird me
changed. The big lightbulbs—one, two three—
foreground honeycomb tiles. I wake up
with a start & nothing is wrong. A field is no
place to panic. The amulet of clarity you gave me:
what am I doing with it? Congratulations
never last. An amethyst at the beach. Your
needle & thread. We can die trying.

POEM FOR MY FRIEND IN MONTREAL

Escalator. When carrots still taste sweet,
I know my tongue is clean. It's official.
The paternoster at the Ministry spun
on its chain & I was too afraid to enter
its open compartments. Its beauty—
the frequency with which one can leap
off, cease rising (or descending). A
stomachache at Middlesex Guildhall.
A pause: English lavender with maple
& charcuterie on your terrace. A grief.

POEM FOR MY FRIEND IN MAINE

To agree, we say "Correctol 44," which
is an anti-diarrheal that's been taken off
the market. To scold, we say "Very poor!"
At Olive Garden my language got stuck
& I ticced. The rabbits we liberated from
your father lived a number of years. I found
your letters from Spooner, but I didn't open
them because almost nothing is worth
reliving, certainly not your first banishment.
Tucked in with postcards my mother sent
from the Mayo Clinic. This must be another
woman's life: wild greens & Icelandic yogurt
by the jar, the trucker barreling toward Acadia.

POEM FOR MY FRIEND IN CHICAGO

Not a pedestal but a kind of chaise
longue of the gut, where love's bile
just wants to relax. We were trying
& I told that creep he got *himself*
thrown out. You can hug this cactus
I got you while your kid is away, if
you feel sad. We wish to half-recline
with our fellow travelers. We gasp
about some chore & either get up
or don't. Settle into a relational
aesthetic: experiential Pyrex & velvet.
I'd take an elective course on that.

Cameron Quan Louie

THE PERFECT EMPLOYEE

A brick is composed of shale and clay,
molded and left alone for a while
in 2000°F conditions.

Anything is going to transform that way.
Anything is remarkable as it's being made,
especially when it's being made by a machine.

A brick is a kind of inexhaustible machine.
For good reason, some people are worried
about machines taking our jobs.

I'm one of those people
who has never had a job
a machine couldn't do,

because every job is customer service,
and customer service is being left alone
to transform under thermal dynamics.

The brick looks forward to being framed
by other bricks. Tomorrow at work, I will do
just enough to show that I am inexhaustible.

THE GARDEN OF EDEN

Got excited about noon today
on the way out to buy fresh
½ & ½ from the market
nearby with overpriced
everything. A can of regular
beans for three dollars. Some
bread called *batard*. Even eggs
laid by miserable birds are
six bucks. I love it there.
I love the disappointing
produce selection, the small
displays of affection: a hand-
written sign, a few free slices
of orange on a plate by the till.
Most beautiful are the careful
piles of expensive cheese, rising
like a white & yellow ziggurat
towards the compact glow
of fluorescent lights above.

CATALOGUE

we are garbage
sitting for afternoons

in our own baked tofu
skin smell

wood-malt aroma
couched in comfort

you interrupt me reading
to claim

with one thrust
fork-ownership

over what remains
of this take-out

*

we scoffed at efficient
white chairs online

then they arrived
we marveled

at how they fit in
touched all our heirlooms

with that careless
kind of present

oily fingertip
on the glass of memory

*

that hot mom
in the Ikea ad

looks frightened
of her children

gemming the new
polish of the table

with young spit
many flecks

of dinner decorating
the lacquered

corrugations of the wood
that's time improved

*

but what long leaves!
around which future

guests can gather
what will they be like

when they grow up
her children

civilized and barely
aware of the leaves

folded inside just
above their small knees

and the old table
too bulky to get rid of

Devin N. Morris

RITUAL

The road was easy to travel as only 5 passengers boarded the bus tonight. I kiss the gold crowned boy who saw me off at the bus station. There's rarely a car in sight.

Baltimore looms 4 hours in the distance. Due to the lack of traffic the trip will probably exhaust itself within 3 hours. Almost running, I hastily exit my office for the elevator and make my way across 32nd street to 8th avenue. My subway train exits the station at 6:03. Terry suggests we leave work early in hopes of making the subway. Hurrying down the stairs to the train platform I locate my card in my wallet, voilà! I'm in. I release a breath of thanks, the scene is full of folk gazing with anticipation at the express train's vacant tracks. We have not missed the subway. A rat plays blindly below us.

A carnival of funeral bound mobiles cut a stunning line along the curve of the road's edge. Wind caught in a tunnel running through a black chiffon ocean we wind and profess allegiance to the departed. We follow the black family limousines united in fluorescent rectangular crests stamped F U N E R A L.

The praises went up as the tears came down. A sea of praise, mourning in tsunami waves, the hallelujahs rise up from those congregated. Woe pulses through the room where amber-tinted sun washes over the mourners. Swaying in mahogany pew foundations, with each bellow of sorrow we brace ourselves in an effort to support thou whose heart is punctured most. Inflicted we are all a miserable bunch hunched under the white ceiling of some funeral home. Legs don't fail me, please don't fail me, a veil hangs above the open casket shading the blow that is soon to come when viewing my departed, my heart. No matter the distance of family the heart aches when our blood relation is ended in the physical. I wear you lace shroud. An autumnal sunset of your memory follows me from the time I wake until when I rest. I feel so far away from you, I know my eyes are only a painting, a memory, a myth as nothing is real to you at this moment but the question, why? Why mother? Why brother? And you mr preacher you tell me to be assured that I will feel pain, can you assure me that I will sustain because I don't know what life is anymore, again.

"Family we love you, we pray for you, we will be there for you in the hours, days, weeks, and months to come."

I knock on the concrete door and ask if this is where the fathers are kept. Mine was killed a few years back and I can't find him so is he here, is this where you take all my fathers and lock them away. The lodging provided causes cancer. The ground shakes too often and meals are hard to attain. Look at us, going outside to sell what you brought here for me to use. I'm making money now and then my freedom is taken. Why did you lock him behind sixteen thousand vacant doors? He gon' drown in those depths. I can't hear his call because Concrete grit fills the window sills and thresholds. How is he gonna carry my mother over this threshold following their marriage that never happened because he sold drugs and was slain at night. I don't blame his killer.

The bricked up vacant house exists as pool of life sealed off away from those who planted seed into this fertile soil. Home is grown only to be closed off again.

We marched in 2 by 2, the family does. On display, the receiving line, the funeral car line, the nervous smiles and loves through the roof.

Within the muck she screams, stumbles, and is supported by her husband and the funeral home staff.

A woman sings "take me to the king," in a handsome loud screech that is not ethereal but elegant and authoritative. Her mouth curls in a howl, her head goes up and her mouth's arch mimics that of the curve of the windows and wall fixtures. A round portal pointing upward thrusting healthy blows as she leads the choir.

In contrast to the pale tones of the hospital's decor this funeral home is lined with burgundy carpet, sage green walls, a beige mid wall, and honey wood beams ascend to an octagonal light fixture above, shadow box. Muted jewels are offered for death.

Oval windows, rounded windows, the movement leads the eye upward.

The pucker of a pink rose shoots above white and pink carnations all fighting to overpower the fragrant baby's breath.

He asks, "can we still trust God, can we still serve God?"

Two strips of white fluorescent lights choke the tunnel's nape, where ceiling meets wall. White opalescent pearl strands whip around turns and curves, beaming, all guests who pass through this bosom glow from their brilliance.

The Sun rises east and I lay on that coast. I wake before you, brother west.

Hollow is the mind consumed by thoughts of a relation laid ill. Thoughts reverberate like echoes and all who greet you find a blank stare answering their smiles and hugs. Bare thine relation's back lays on the wisp of hospital cover-up and somber goes the beeps, and LED lit screens. Tubes flow from wither and tither. You lay weighted and unconscious of the still terror, like a lake before rain. I await the word of some anonymous individual who now occupies the hearts and minds of the family who has come to share in this sacred ritual. Laughter echoes through these empty halls and like spring you blossom as a stray family member passes you on your way to the bathroom or to get coffee in the family kitchen/lounge that is appointed with enough sugar and cream to smooth the murky black liquid.

Here we are again, sitting in wait as the injured lays in wake. We hope he awakes at the end of this ride.

"Oh, you are here now. It is so good to see you. Your mother told me you were coming down."

"How is it in the big city?"

"Boy I haven't seen you since you were just a little thing. You remember me? I'm cousin..."

The affectations of greeting enter the psyche as a murmur. A murmur is all I muster in response and allude to the grandeur of a life lived in a city other than but not greater than. Nonetheless the presence of so many family members soothes to a feeling akin to excitement, one realizes they are happy to be seen, received. I decide to lay my head upon the shoulder sitting closest to me, who owns this shell makes no difference as the occasion removes any deference or need to question who I am near. We are all here in support of one another and most importantly slowly building a foundation to hold up the mother of the affected.

The hallways are washed white porcelain cadavers, eerily still and flecked with pale greens, butter yellow banisters with floating pastel nurse and staff. The furnishings in the waiting area are appointed with Kandinsky like abstract woven textiles in muted jewel tones. Playing a sound of calming elevator music to the ear I look out into this sea only to see and no seat for me. I stand by the window and look out over those whose lives continue without pause or alarm. How is it that I'm having trouble breathing and coping with the stop gap that is she asks in a loud tone, "are there any Deltas on this train," after her first stomp. She screams again, "Delta Sigma Theta, are there no black violets on this train?" Wearing an unzipped oversized hoodie, black skinny 3-stripe shiny Adidas sweats that puddle into black smoky UGG boots stained with the white water remains from a salty snow bath. She whispered, "I'll go away and when I come back I'll be like you, again." Using half expressed hand gestures as if she wants to reach out but stops as she thinks what for, why now, how? She sat behind me and removed a green apple from her pocket. I worried that she might use the object as a projectile. Her temperament being very unsettled. She pulls the hood from her head unveiling a half composed mass of half done braids and two inches of curly afro above. The braids are beautifully made of black yarn. I compliment her on the style. She smiles. She asks, to the window in front of her I'm assuming, if it preferred her hair as it now or as it were before. You like my hair now? Under the black hoody she wears a plum purple sports bra.

A fellow rider reminds her, "Don't let it take you so far that you can't find yourself in all that you are."

Daniel Poppick

RUMORS

For some months now I've been returning to this one night from late last year. We were at Kristen's. She had received this jigsaw puzzle as a housewarming gift and had enlisted me and Ariel to help her finish. It wasn't the traditional picture of a waterfall or dew-drenched fawn. In fact there was no figuration at all—just a gradient that swept between a tropic green into a hospital blue. It was a week after she had moved in to her new place. I was excited to see it. She had saved up for almost two decades to buy it. The first home I'd ever entered owned by a friend. Property is the syntax of the reddening horizon. There we were, splashed on just this or that side of thirty, surgically reassembling a color so cool it was really closer to a cry than a hue. She hadn't yet completely unpacked the blank room we sat at the end of, and it was cavernous—a kitchen that bled seamlessly into a living room. What would she hang on the walls, she wondered. A spidery beat lilting from the laptop on the floor. The lamplight looked smaller than it had in her old place, it didn't quite reach all the way to the ceiling. I sipped my Sazerac and felt symphonic, like a smooth, dumb stone over which cool water rolls. I listened intently to the playlist as it flowed by. The music was so cool and I hated it so much, and I noted how sweet it felt to hate cool music; it was the beginning of the end our youth, a tipping point I've marked at least once a month for the last five years, and it feels real each time because in fact so far it always is. A siren went by outside. It was November. An enormous pile of books stood teetering against the wall as Kristen's cat batted the blinds. We were making no progress on the puzzle. I love to dance but I hate games—I love to hate them. These rainy day exercises people use to be together when they have nothing to say. Why can't we just talk or not talk? Was it even raining? No, the stars were out. The only games I like negate competition. I wonder what I mean by that. "I think a piece is loose—see how it wobbles?" Kristen laid her hand flat on the table and shifted them minutely back and forth, tectonically, and the surface rippled. She took a rip off her tiny bong and passed it to me over the table. She and Ariel have a bond that runs on its own idiom, but we've all three built a harmony of shit-talking these last years that I've come to cherish. We share a sense of premature nostalgia—that a moment always ends too early, a gold thread spun from the straw of what's already happened stitching the future into the present tense. Kristen grew up on a farm in Wisconsin and is the only person I know who seems genuinely energized by living in Brooklyn in 2017. We were neighbors in Iowa City but we didn't really properly meet until we both moved east. She was designing books and I was working at a bookstore. The first time we hung out I found her on the street in front of the bar where we were meeting, on her phone, yelling at someone about a font. She saw me, smiled, held her finger up, turned around, and continued yelling. Ariel held cardboard shards up to the light to determine the precise shade of blue or green so we could place them accurately inside the lily pad of this crooked frame that was looking more and more, as the evening wore on, like a reflection of selfhood itself, Narcissus staring through the pieces of the pond—a surface soft as planetary id that no one who names himself "one" could love. Were I it I'd do what it did. Distant music echoed off the building. I squinted and tried to make my eyeballs, awash with pleasure but not industry, articulate the difference between "aqua" and "teal." Even in the moment it seemed like a pretty tidy parable for going insane. But maybe that's the industry of heaven, getting over its wall so your reflection can speak to you directly. At one point I realized we were all staring at our hands. We were in no shape for this game, but we went on. It was November, but what "it" was we could no longer say. The air was getting chill, not quite freezing over, and somewhere to the west of us a wave of rage was washing up on the machinery of the season. Ariel pushed a bright little knob of blue perfectly into its hollow. I paused the playlist I loved to hate and in its stead put on *Rumours*. As "Second Hand News" started up a cozy silence settled in between us, and a creaturely interruption spilled across the room. We worked for a while and made no progress. Ariel and I have known each other a bit longer. We first met at a Labor Day barbeque about seven years ago in Iowa City and I asked her about her writing, trying to make small talk. She looked past me over my shoulder and her face flattened and rescheduled itself into a glyph that said, in the universal language of inward narration, "Now I am dealing with a moron." It's not uncommon for writers to assume you're an idiot if you're friendly. So I didn't attempt conversation with her again for another couple of years. She now claims to have no memory of this interaction, and I have no memory of when we picked up the thread from there, but we gradually followed it into the present tense. She's prone to excessive narrativization, an affliction and a gift. She insinuates all the possibilities along the way, one thing that I think makes her writing crackle. "I love spreading rumors about myself," she said tonight as we walked up her frozen street. Back at Kristen's house, staring into this oceanic jigsaw piece, I wondered how or if my friends would recount this evening to one another at some later date; who would remember things correctly as they happened, and what we would all get wrong; and if we would ever verify it accurately among one another, being our only witnesses, before we slowly melted down to be sipped up by worms, the whole scene as we remembered or forgot it blown away and buried in the architecture of our dust. This is the only game I can get behind: what do you run from in writing? A sentence turns to you in the starlight and stares into you with an amiable cruelty that only art achieves. I'm delaying my point. After what seemed like a long time Kristen cut through the music and said that back home on her family's farm in Wisconsin something was wrong with the chickens: they had developed a taste for insulation. "A taste for insulation?" I said. Yes. One day in September when her mother opened the latch to feed the chickens as she always did, she noticed that their mood had shifted. They swarmed around with an unprecedented, dark enthusiasm and started pecking at the coop's outer edge. They were going after the pink fluff that lined the structure, the stuff that kept them warm. *Never going back again*. I recognized my life plotted in dim shapes on the other side of the high and naked ceiling. An alien geometry installed itself along the surface of an ink so vast and silent that I remembered a poem I'd never written with it, and pitch black words streamed through me. It was almost artless. Ariel said, "Are you serious?" Yes,

pink fiberglass leaked
between the warped wooden beams
and they ate it all

Josh Silver

FOUR EXERCISES FOR THE ORDINARY

1: ELEVATORS

Keep track of the floors chosen in the elevator and the order in which they are chosen. The number of people in the elevator will become the number of poem stanzas. The floor at which each person leaves will become the number of syllables in their stanza. The order in which each person enters the elevator is important. The title is developed from the number of people in the elevator (e.g.: three people becomes three words). Execute at every elevator journey.

An example:
Three people
Floors 6, 13 and 17
Structure: 13/6/17

Tender as Flash
Renegade left-overs
Crossed,
Star-crossed?
Or quiet.

A constellation,
No.

A flash,
Hold-out from passageways of
What became a place
(imagined?)

2: SIGNS

As you travel any distance, keep track of the signs. Choose one for your project. Split the sign into syllable groups. The number of syllables will be the number of stanzas and the number of line in each stanza. Each letter will be used to start each word on each line, a "rolling tautogram." The title is of your choice.

An example:
Sign: Wholesome Market
Syllable and letter order: WHOLE SOME MAR KET
Structure: 5/4/3/3 (X4)

Make, Either
What had once left everywhere
Should once more end.
Make a restive
Kaddish, either twist.

Where happenings offer low elegies,
Saddened orders, medial exits
Make a ready
Kaddish, either tea.

Who holds one laconic element?
So? One must excavate
Make a rendered
Kaddish, either tenderness.

Wandering heraldry or lofted exegesis?
Soft operations made effigies.
Make a relation,
Kaddish, either turn.

3: STOREFRONTS

Choose a building. Choose a storefront in the building. List the objects viewed within. These will become the beginning of a short story or flash fiction or plot concept or book, movie, play or video. Form a story that connects each object to the next. The title is your choice.

An example:
The list:
- Four Mannequins
- A pair of black boots
- Two pairs of pump heels
- A white shirt
- A pair of Greek-style sandals
- A poster

Plot Sketch for: Missed Connections

A person goes into a store after seeing A POSTER marking a huge sale. There are other people in the store, four of which our main character finds especially attractive. Our main character loudly tries on a series of shoes to try and impress the four shoppers. First, a pair of slick, BLACK LEATHER BOOTS. These were polished to an intense sheen. Our main character parades around the store in these boots, yet the four shoppers do not notice or even turn around. Next, a pair of PUMP HEELS. THEN A SECOND, DIFFERENT PAIR. Each of these breeds no reaction from the four shoppers. Last, a pair of SANDALS, HELD TO THE LEG WITH LEATHER THONGS. With these too, no reaction is imminent. In a last ditch attempt, our illustrious and unhappy main character approaches one of the shoppers, one in a WHITE SHIRT only to find that the figures were each only MANNEQUINS.

4: ODOUR

Take an inventory of smells over a set period (one hour, ten minutes, a subway ride, a bus ride, a class, a shift, an entire day). Take notes on the quality of the smells, memories, things that stand out. Use these smells and their notes as the form of a story or book or piece of flash fiction or movie or drama. The title is your choice.

An example:
The list:

- Perfume: fruity floral with a pointed snap; it occupies space.
- Cigarillo smoke: it lingers; a memory of teen boys smoking grape ones in secret.
- Stale air: heavy scentless and warm, a baseline.
- Pastry: vaguely sweet in the background. Only noticeable in a flash.
- Meat: turkey or ham cold cuts; layers on the pastry.
- Outside air: cold and scentless.

The Accidental Meeting

X, on their way to buy a GIFT for a friend's upcoming birthday runs into an old school acquaintance. He has taken over his father's tobacconist shop, which specializes in Havanas. He sells ILLEGAL TOBACCO on the side to cover his EXPENSIVE EATING HABITS; the contraband is kept in a back room. The SHOP SMELLS OF STALE TOBACCO AND FLOOR POLISH (the flooring is antique hardwood and must be carefully and regularly polished). This old acquaintance is balding, but has grown a thick dark moustache, which turns up slightly at the corners. There is, apparently, no wax or oil involved, however. The only escape for X is a hasty excuse, an insistence that the errand is pressing.

A BREATH OF RELIEF OUTSIDE.

Celina Su

NOTES ON THE SHAPE OF ABSENCE

We trace the dust lines left behind from the appliances, fumble for the brick foundations between the steel beams, peer at serrated stairlines where the wall paints stopped. Reincarnated. Tenement apartments become dance spaces without barres or mirrors, in the dank basement of a bank on Market Street, in anonymous green-carpeted rooms on Mott Street.

The first time I met WM, she told me,

> *There were three main theaters that my family and I would go to: the Music Palace on Bowery, the Sun Sing on East Broadway, and the third one by the Manhattan Bridge whose name I've since forgotten and which is now a Buddhist temple...*
>
> *All of them played martial arts movies, ghost stories, and soft-core porn (there was some kind of two-for-one ticket thing to do with the latter).*

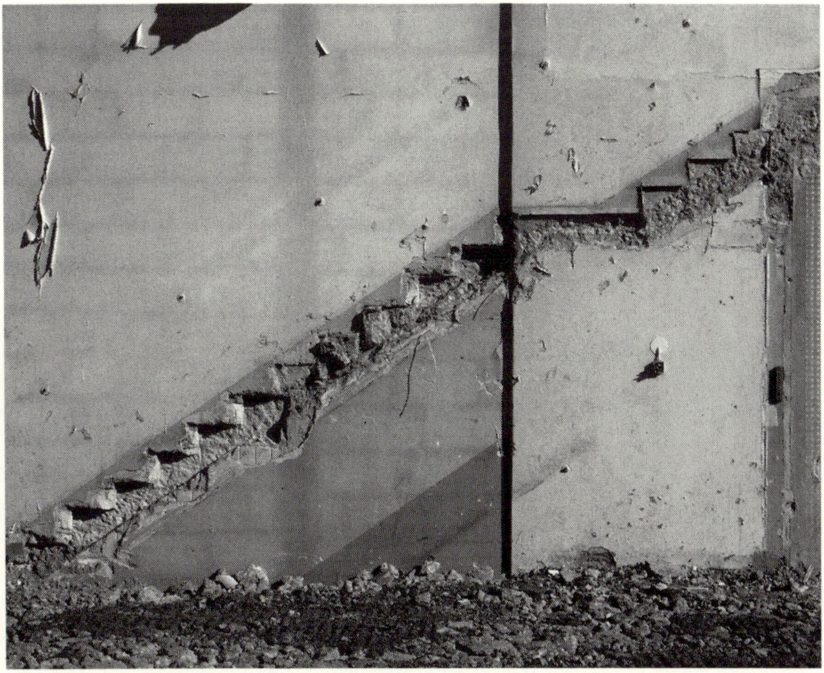

I found a *Life Magazine* spread about Sun Sing. It started off as the Florence New Strand Theatre in 1921, hosting Yiddish-language vaudeville.

In 1940, a professional opera troupe from Hong Kong arrived. World War 2 broke out, so the troupe got stranded here. They took over the theater and performed every night. Death, resurrection, applause. I try to imagine what Claude Levi Strauss thought as he sat in the audience, draw a causal pathway between these events.

In 1942, the same year as that *Life Magazine* spread, the company changed the theater's name to New Canton, and made its last appearance.

New Canton became a cinema and was renamed Sun Sing Theatre again in 1950. In the late 1970s and early 1980s, more non-Chinese folks showed up, with Chinese-language subtitles on top and English-language subtitles on the bottom.

In 1993, Sun Sing closed. *Enter the Wu-Tang (36 Chambers)*, featuring English dub audio samples from *Shaolin and Wu Tang* (1983) and *The 36th Chamber of Shaolin* (1978), hit stores. In *The 36th Chamber*, Yude becomes San Te, learning kung fu in each of the Shaolin temple's 35 chambers. Later, after helping his hometown defeat a brutal Manchurian general, he establishes the eponymous chamber, where the sacred can become a popular art form of resistance.

Last I checked, Sun Sing had been demolished to make room for a shopping mall peddling cell phone accessories. (At night, the dim sum palace across the street hosts dance parties, replete with fog machine.)

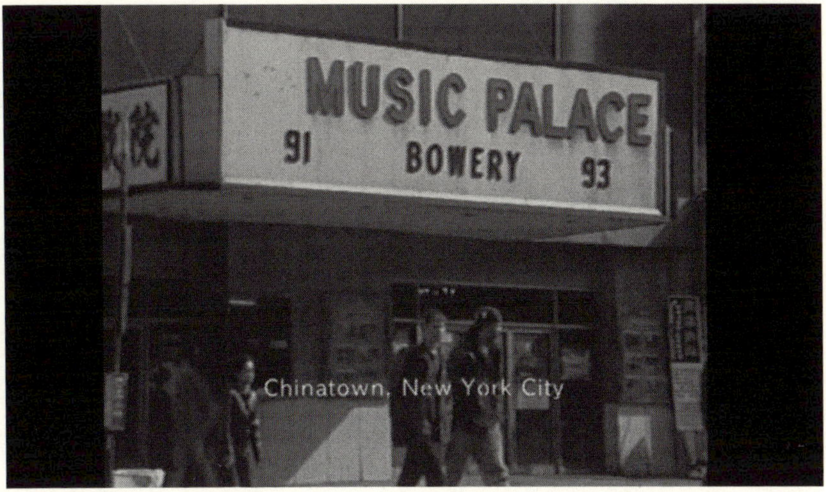

Haunted Karaoke. Fascination Amour. Kickboxer's Tears.

In 1998, the top-grossing feature films in the US were *Saving Private Ryan*, *Armageddon*, and *There's Something About Mary*. Cheap DVD knock-offs made it easy for immigrants to gain access to Hong Kong movies in the comfort of their own homes. The Music Palace closed.

It's a lonely job, but it's a nice job. I like being the guy up in the booth.

In the past, no seats were available. You had to stand to watch. We probably had one thousand people at a time.

A Vitasoy is 75 cents.

When you are here alone, without your family, you either rest or go to work, working overtime. You just have to buy one ticket, and you can stay here all day.

The Pagoda became an HSBC bank branch, the Sun Sing became a mall. One of the Music Palace's new owners told *Sing Tao Daily* in 2005 that he found and put aside between 400 and 500 old film reels before the building was demolished. The 18-story Wyndham Garden hotel replacing the Music Palace also displaced 50 low- and moderate-income residents next door.

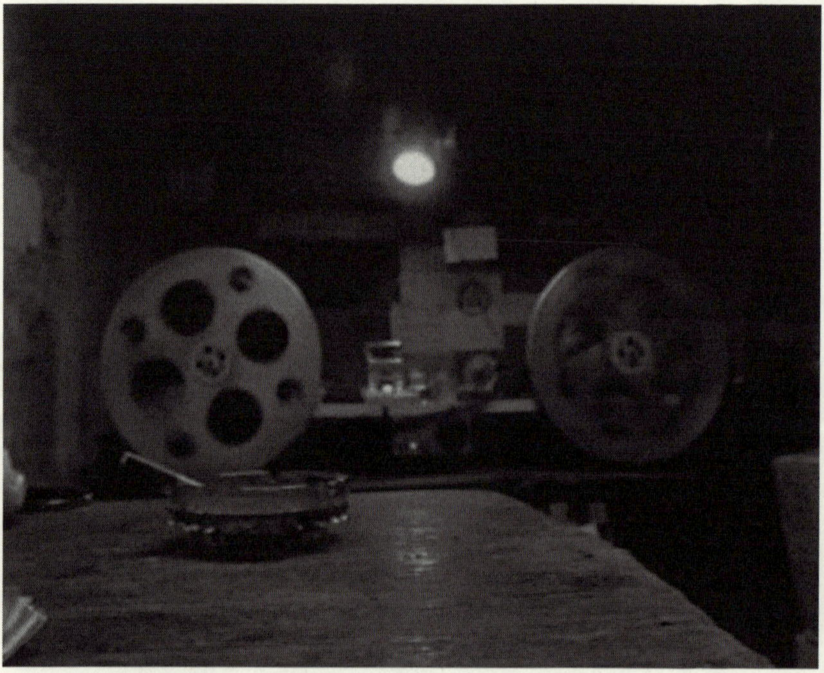

Our routine was to buy a packet of watermelon seeds and eat the entire bag while watching the films, and the seed husks would crunch beneath our feet when we left. Mom spent most of the time chasing me throughout the theater because I wouldn't sit still. One movie that's stayed with me was of Sally Yeh being gang-raped and then exacting a total and utter martial-arts revenge on the gang. (I think she fails at the first attempt, gets assaulted again, and then rises up again and finally kills them all.)

In real life, I am told, my mother was not a phoenix, for phoenixes do not exist.

It is not as if we spoke each Sunday evening, so that I could properly miss her then. Her absence is not conspicuous. There is no definition, I cannot define it, *i.e.*, I am at a loss for meaning. I constantly play a personal *Mad, Mad Libs*: I am living for (noun, verb). I cannot think of loss without falling into platitudes, specificities, Bishop's elusive art. When rhythms provide a cooing, a rocking back and forth, tendėr pain a painful tenderness, traipsing across the board at 45-degree angles, telling it slant.

Officially, we pay tribute when it is clear and bright: the paulownia begins to bloom, voles transform into quails. Somehow, with eerie consistency, we stand under low cloud cover, winds chilling us to our bones, despite the mild temperatures. Rainbows begin to appear.

Each evening, I sink into my bed, contemplating what I did not accomplish today.

She told me to build a shrine to my jaw, that which I whittled away, ground to arthritis. Lying like a biological pile of carpenters' off-cut, the width of that marked line that always curls to the ground. This irrepressible feeling, a primordial pyrrhic catarrh. It flares along borderlands, only in between. (An Elean paradox, every moment I am nearly, I am merrily, I am alive.)

And so, our hands are long. But she called narratives Sisyphian. Each time I pause typing, my chair rolls backward on the sloped floor. In a moment of magic, I thought that she simply withheld authorial power.

The facts do not change,
for they are constantly rewritten.
The ghostly Gowanus roofline I admired, now a Whole Foods store,
complete with rooftop garden,
atop a Superfund site. What remains
seeps into the soil, and our veins.

Hydrogen, carbon, and oxygen spin flashbacks into gray entrails, weaving lines of spice into the air. When the capricious gases are irascible enough, the social ties break apart, and the atoms breathe again to turn wet, to exhale carbon dioxide. In other words, they burn. Charred sweet, the carbs sometimes turn to cakey nostalgia, but more slowly. This is why shish kebabs from Brazil linger on the mind's tongue.
Carbon atoms emit air.
(But this only works when you dream that you are dreaming of nostalgia, or fire.)

In Thailand, in a corner of each plot of land, the owners build spirit houses to appease the spirits who once dwelled there. Figurines overflow from the opulent ones.

The simplest, built by Burmese refugees on the edge of the forest, or those in more isolated environments, strike me hardest.

In ancient Rome, similar houses were built for *Lares Familiares*. Our dead mothers live there, but when we seek greener pastures, higher offices, they stay put.

If we could have miniatures on every block of the homes,
say, that the Atlantic Yards Barclay's Center replaced, or
those that Robert Moses demolished to make way for the Cross-Bronx Expressway, with overpasses too low for public buses to pass under, so that Jones Beach could remain white.

I read that this was once the home of—

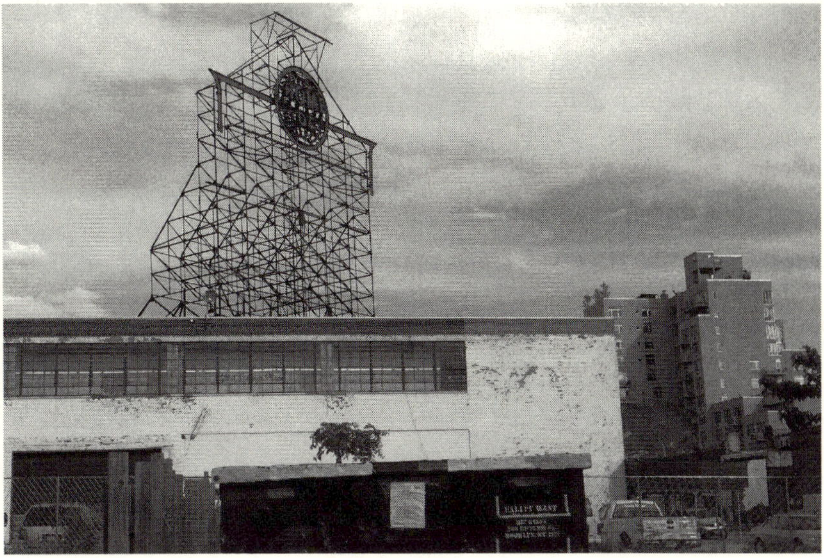

I cannot differentiate the homage from the lament. As I resign, I surmise. More often than not, via whitewashing or semiotic deconstruction, the erasure.

Sometimes, these virtual landscapes feel realer than

Were we to name names alongside black rectangles to symbolize
our mourning

Were we to   combat the mundane ferocity that prefigures the rough ride
                                        (He testified to his 22-month-old self)
                          he testifies to his   (knowing)
                                        The windows, paint was peeling off the windows.

        I mull and articulate too slowly. By then,
everyone else has covered the essential angles.
        I summon my voice to join the outrage,

Tangential weapon, ersatz activism with
        the bend of an index finger.   I   "like"   it
        because I am exhausted,   because I long for
                polyphonic   song

                This is not yet sacrifice
                        yet resistance
                        abolition
                        a refrain
                        from
                                    Each of us slumps forward
                                    tracing parallels.

Mothers at altitude
Mothers in solitude
Mothers as platitude
Mothers in spring

Mothers ashamed and Ablaze and clear
At the end
As they are
As they almost all are, and then
Mothers don't come around
Again in spring
—from *Red Doc>* by Anne Carson

But what is clear is invisible.
What is weightiest remains intangible.

The difference is not that I do not know,
but that I never will. I track most carefully what I cannot see.
Opening one's eyes wide is not seeing,
but believing. No witnessing to bear and hold up on my fingertips
to the window, the low blue light and long shadows of early spring.

As if I could listen to the silence (for silence

assumes the cadence of one's last gasping breaths,

synesthetic roar),

inadequate morphine, we succumb to negative space, stoop lower with each breath.

When I was younger, I dreamt of shine.
In my mind's eye, I glittered,
an optical illusion nearing the truth, more truthfully an alluring asymptote.

I refracted, proffered all

these shards of glass.

NOTES

Some of the italicized stanzas are excerpts from an oral history with Wah-Ming Chang, conducted with the Asian American Writer's Workshop Open City initiative. Some of the italicized lines are quotes by the staff of the Music Palace (lines transcribed from Eric Lin's short documentary, *Music Palace*)—Ho Ying Pang (manager), Jian Bang Wang (assistant manager), Dave Butterman (projectionist).

The line "The windows, paint was peeling off the windows" is by Freddie Gray, killed by hypervisible, fast violence in a "rough ride." In this poem, I am thinking also of Rob Nixon's notion of slow violence, from *Slow Violence and the Environmentalism of the Poor*, and how Gray himself worked to address this slow violence, gradual and often invisible killings, by testifying in his 2008 lawsuit regarding lead poisoning in his housing, against his absentee landlord. Scientists state that blood lead levels of 5 micrograms per deciliter cripple cognitive development, decrease IQ, impair memory. In June 1991, when Gray was 22 months old, his blood carried 37 micrograms. I first read these details in "Freddie Gray's Life a Study on the Effects of Lead Paint on Poor Blacks" by Terrence McCoy, published in the *Washington Post*, April 29, 2015.

IMAGES (IN ORDER OF APPEARANCE)

Untitled photo by Eva the Weaver.

Still from *Music Palace*, 2005, directed by Eric Lin (2005). 35mm, 9 min, B&W.

Still from *Music Palace*, 2005, directed by Eric Lin (2005). 35mm, 9 min, B&W.

Untitled photo by Celina Su.

Deirtra Thompson

Traveling by train from a place named by people accustomed to traveling by foot, I was heading north from High Point, North Carolina, back to the Takoma Park neighborhood of Washington D.C. when I smelled Bergamot for the first time. It was 1995 and I was 20 and sleepless after a week working at a trade show of home decor goods and furniture and trying to distract myself from smoking by splurging on an attractive Earl Grey tea bag that smelled like black pepper and citrus.

This was an early attempt at aromatherapy to modulate the physical discomfort of post-traumatic production syndrome—which is a form of emotional dysregulation experienced by cultural production workers—art handlers, caterers, film crew—who become traumatized while trying to stage an environment that simultaneously creates a feeling of calm or intrigue while commodifying the target audience of buyers under impossible deadlines and often under the thumb of a tyrant. It's like being a carnie without the freedom, without the self-direction.

I was hired to set up, arrange, and dismantle a trade show booth that appeared to mimic a Moroccan medina, crowded alongside other booths overstuffed with mid-90's metabolically-challenged furniture made of bloated leather stretched and colored to resemble Crayola crayons in suspicious fleshy hues, prophetic designs that seem to have predicted future health outcomes. I staged metalwork, hand-knotted wool rugs, tagines and metal lanterns in the mode we recognize today as "globally sourced" and marketed ethnic abundance. Pier 1 Imports, Anthropologie, Pottery Barn, Crate and Barrel;

these stores trade on the simulation of another culture's art as emotional artifact, but maintain a patriotic fidelity in their absence of African (with the exception of its northern triadic tip), Afghani, Iraqi, Cambodian, or Vietnamese-inspired products in their stores, unless you count manufacturing labels, which I do.

A year earlier I'd been to Morocco with another company as a buyer of rugs, textiles, and jewelry. While buying cassettes in Marrakech I learned they'd never heard of Elvis or Michael Jackson but the 17-year-old wife of our state-appointed guide had a New Kids on the Block poster in her bedroom.

The merchandise I was being paid to stage in High Point was hand-picked and globally-sourced by a reddish-blonde and middle-aged Englishman named John (who I later found out was surprised that I possessed a sense of humor), loaded into trucks in the Mid-Atlas mountains by locals, packed into a shipping container and set outbound on a cargo ship from the port of Casablanca to be delivered to Washington D.C. by tractor trailer about 6 weeks later.

Decades before Airbnb, the people of High Point, the descendants of Quakers and German immigrants, customarily rented out their homes, modest and responsible 1950's one level ranchers to furniture buyers and wholesalers from the around the world who attended the trade show known as the high point market, making 3-4 times the cost of their monthly mortgage in a single week. I imagined these families, the children and grandchildren of furniture craftsman following a seasonal protocol for this bi-annual event:

Hide self-help books in empty suitcases.

Refresh acrylic toilet seat liner and matching floor hugger. Remove any signs of sexual deviancy, including family photos.

These houses are the former homes of the highly-skilled workers of High Point's furniture industry, an economy which would peak as the furniture capital of the world in the early 1990's but fall into decline a decade later when Ikea and Asian imports would occupy most of the American market. My room had a queen-sized waterbed with a heavy wooden headboard and thick brindle carpeting. Framed footprints in the sand.

My mother prefers furniture that has trapped within its design a Cronenbergian biological impulse. She's never seen Lucian Freud's painting *Benefits Supervisor Resting*, but it's a terrific inversion of what she looks for in home furnishings: girthy, well-fed, and lethargic. My parents' first waterbed arrived the same year as my first memory of my mother's drug use, both facts occasionally prompting a garden hose to snake through our home. My mother would take Dramamine on flights, suffered from car sickness, and disappeared daily into a heavy load of prescription narcotics and opioids. Retreating to a silky Chinese-inspired bedroom, she would sink into the belly of the rippling floatilla, emerging sometimes when my father got home. I hate sleeping on waterbeds but I can understand her desire to be suspended in a gel-like fluid. By this time, she had suffered the loss of two children, one born a few years before me and one born after. My mother's chain-link of grief, loss, illness, and addiction extended her parents' addicted and avoidant coping strategies in an effort to subvert the post-traumatic vulnerability from war, poverty, and abuse. I suspect her love of waterbeds has to do with a desire to return to an amniotic state and start again, for herself and her missing children.

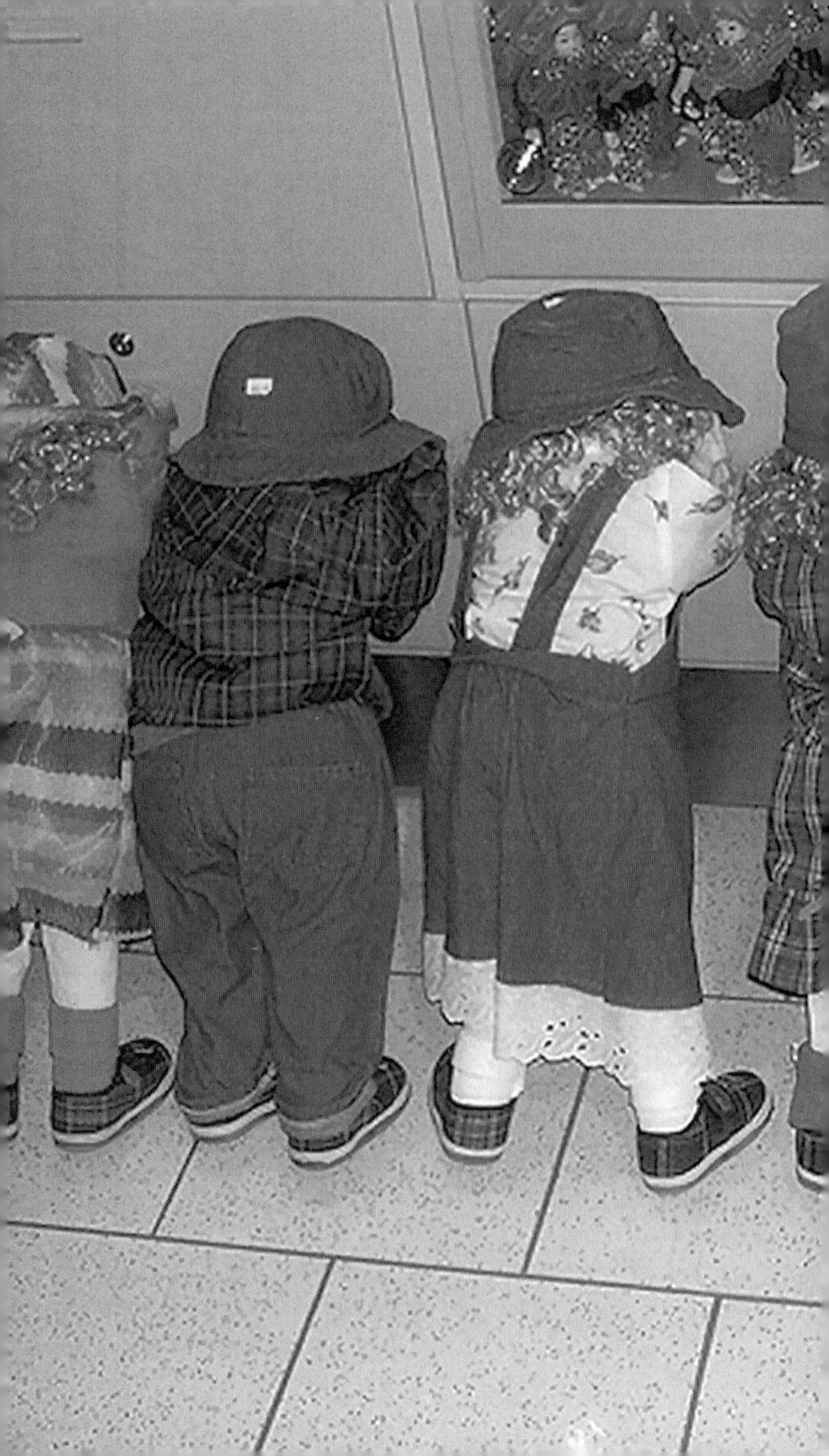

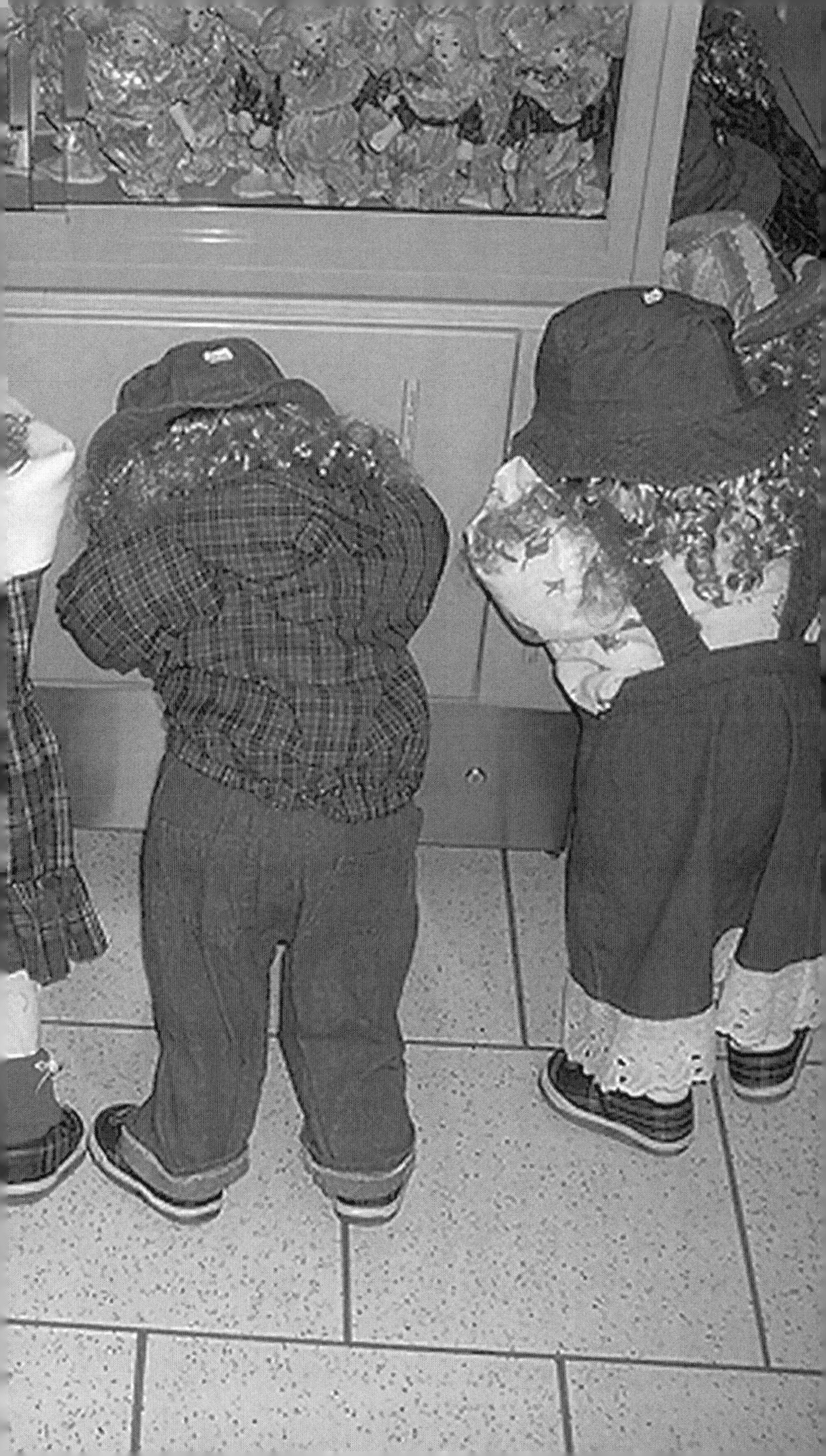

Back in High Point, across from the waterbed, in a dim corner next to the dresser, I was alarmed to find what appeared to be a tiny janitor inspecting the grooves in the wood paneling. His backwards baseball cap and oversized blue work shirt hung low on his stiffened body and he appeared to bristle as I poked him with his own tiny broom. When I swung him around, I was horrified to find that this janitor had no face and his arms had been sewn together above his head in a posture that suggested he'd been frozen while defending himself from a fatal blow.

Back then as now, I startled easily, partially because of the ever-present reminder that I'd been a "miracle baby," my birth sandwiched between two dead children (who were apparently not miraculous enough and who certainly sought revenge) and partially because of my mother's German brownie hobgoblin logic; the idea that there is a name for the small things seen from the corners of one's eyes. Was this what a house brownie looks like further down south? The dolls punctuated the corners of every room. I found a mini-ranch hand, a biker with toast-sized chaps, and a mail carrier, all frozen in a permanent state of time out. I was fascinated by this collection of prisoner of war placeholder kids but so terrified of them coming to life beside my bed that I would force myself to stay awake until I'd finally collapse into sleep an hour or so before I needed to be at work.

In the 1990s, fashion, food, fragrances, and craft below the Mason-Dixon line lingered about ten years behind. What you saw and smelled in New York you'd be hard-pressed to find in Savannah five years later. This is no longer the case but pre-internet much of our southern aesthetic was brought north by summer family reunions. Fashions may travel south but the

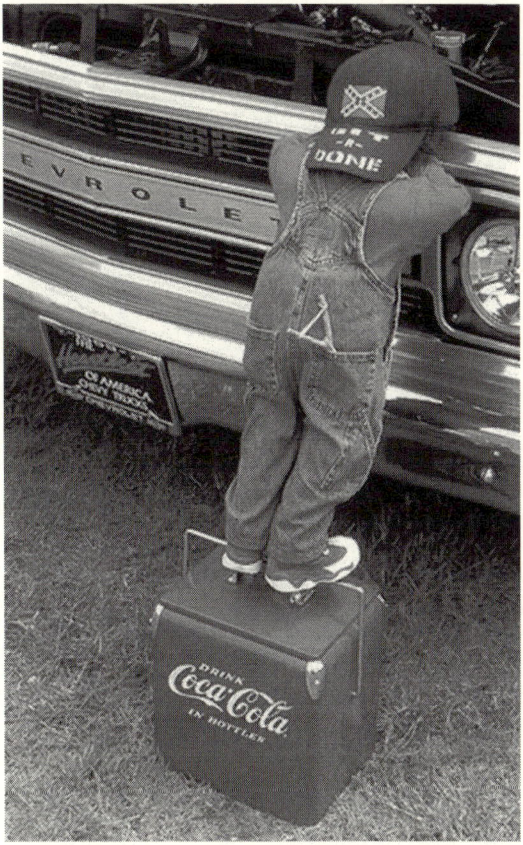
DRINK
Coca-Cola
IN BOTTLES

origins and artifacts of traumatic craft production travel north. These southern crafts traveled north and never left. Thousands of southern white women made patterns and sewed hoods for the Klan: the caption from Birth of a Nation boasts that thousands of hoods were sewn and "not one secret was betrayed." Florida and Delaware are exempt, or more accurately, immune to the logic of this trend exchange, both states buffered by the strangeness of their primordial origins.

A few years later, I would drive from my home in Baltimore City to rural northeastern Maryland to visit my family for a birthday party. My sisters are identical twins and like the dolls back in High Point, they embody all of the occupational stereotypes—a lifetime of cloned outfits, an indecipherable and insular shared language, one sees dead people while the other empathizes, and so on. After cake, the relational alienation I felt when around my family became clear to me when I found a tiny blonde shepherdess without any sheep cowering in the corner by my sister's fireplace.

According to the beloved and radical therapist John Bradshaw, dysfunctional families maintain secrecy by adopting roles that project the illusion of well-being. Bradshaw's roles often overlap but fall into these five categories—The Hero—the perfectionistic overachiever who shoulders the burden of making the family appear good; The Scapegoat—the trouble-making rebel who the family can hold accountable for all of its problems; The Lost Child—the withdrawn and preoccupied member who becomes attached to material possessions instead of people; The Mascot—who distracts from the family pain at their own expense using humor and avoidance as coping tools; and The Chief Enabler—whose responsible and self-righteous martyring behavior the chemically-dependent member depends on to survive.

My sister's shepherdess, whose shame and trauma was so clearly lived out right in the open, was a resourceful and magical form of self-medication. The unknown creator of these dolls, often called Time-Out Dolls, effectively translated the sorrows of the modern work place and the inner child within every employee, by fashioning cut remnants of leftover canvas into a loose pattern of a faceless occupational toddler, whose life will be lived propped and forever on the job-into a purely American mode of emotional self-defense through voodoo, a DIY therapy doll similar to a witch's poppet.

Reflecting back on the unbearable hypervigilance I originally experienced around these dolls, I now feel comforted when I see them. But there is one area of hypervigilance in my life that I'm still working through, and that's with smell. Hyperolfactoryvigilance.

Smell, like the craft trends of the 1990's, also seems to travel North and South via interstate I-95. Sometime around early 2015 I noticed affluent women in Williamsburg and Soho began to smell like sweetened mildew and salt water, in August of 2017 women in Savannah, Georgia will smell like it too, but by then, the women of Williamsburg will have moved on to smelling like copper pennies laced with notes of smoky cordite.

In 2015 Donald Trump introduced a cologne called Empire, a follow-up to his signature fragrance, Success. If we know through many scientific studies that the more wealth a person has, the less developed the areas of their brain responsible for

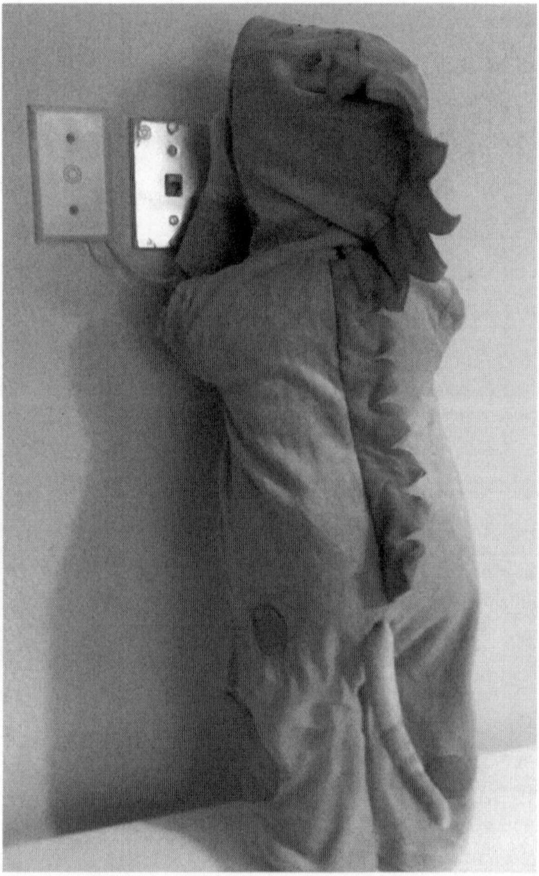

empathy, then I'm trying to locate the empathy of women, especially white women, perfuming themselves with the odors of trauma from a decade earlier. Like vitamins, does the topical application of a painful scent increase overall concentration in the body?

Trauma fragrance, these memes, smemes, are becoming compressed, so a trend that once took two years to atomize geographically arrives now in 1 year or less. But let's look back to a few historical markers of this smell-as-memorial phenomenon:

Silent Night—a toilet water with the base note of tuberose formulated at the end of 1945 and released in 1947.

Poison—with a base note of Opponax and a top note of Coriander—introduced in 1984, two years after the Tylenol cyanide murders.

Opium, not surprisingly, my mother's favorite perfume—with top notes of mandarin orange, bergamot, and lily of the valley—introduced in 1977 two years after the end of the Vietnam war.

And now, in 2017, when being held prisoner by the opioid addiction is the leading cause of death for Americans under 50, a fragrance company called Pharmacia's copy reads: inspired by the effortless confidence of a chic European woman, Pharmacia crafts fragrances reminiscent of a stroll through a castle garden.

II

Philosopher and media theorist Vilém Flusser construed gesture broadly, as a "movement of the body, or tool of the body, for which there is no satisfactory causal explanation." This postulate, of a tool without an obvious purpose, may appear contradictory, but perhaps it is on account of this indeterminacy that gesture becomes a vehicle of ritual behavior, in which formality precedes particular content. Serving as prelude, accompaniment, and punctuation, it is necessarily outward facing, performative, and finds its final cause in its reception.

We might even suggest that the ritual sequencing of gesture confers a plausible causality to otherwise discrete moments, or movements, in analogy to the integration of the human sensorium. Much as intentionality directs motion, and desire enlists the slightest stirrings in its course, Flusser's phenomenology is already keenly social—gesture is a micro-institution of the expressive body, and a thrilling articulacy consists in the most basic feats of kinesthesia, which is never entirely self-referential.

Gesture is motion-as-communication, and this description presumes a dynamic relationship of self and other, transparency and secrecy, inside and out. This could describe navigating cities, or interacting with algorithms; the intentionality of meditation, or the intensity of a fervent plea.

This motile ideal stands to considerable complication here, as well. For gesture can be injurious, habitual, and all the more deleterious, exhausting or violent in its repetitions. For that matter, capital itself consists in motion, and its occult causality effaces the occasions and bodies it includes. Gesture is formally ambivalent, a vehicle conveying anything from fondness to offence, and the texts and images in this section differ greatly, embodying this ambivalence, each relating in their own ways to the trouble of habit and the generosity and openness of gesture.

—Editors

Justin Blinder

The texts I am submitting were not written by me. Rather, I solicited them and compiled them as part of a larger conceptual art project:

In 1973, while on his deathbed, Pablo Neruda penned 316 questions, as 74 poems posthumously published in *The Book of Questions*.

My submission consists of excerpts from *The Book of Answers*, an anthology of responses to each of Neruda's poems (as translated by William O'Daly). *The Book of Answers* is an art project investigating the internet's prevailing political economies, especially how everyday practices simultaneously reify and resist the commodification of labor.

The enclosed response poems were written by anonymous workers. I compiled them using Amazon's Mechanical Turk, a utility that allows anyone to submit jobs to a global online workforce. I embedded each of Neruda's questions in a different menial survey answered by online workers, and I have collected answers from over 150 workers thus far. On Mechanical Turk, many laborers appear to answer hundreds of surveys a day for income, but others complete, say, a dozen before breakfast, in almost ritualistic ways. Regardless, they earn a small amount per survey completed.

What happens when this ritual is suddenly disrupted—with a very different sort of question embedded in each survey? The project explores not only small online tasks and surveys as a form of ritual, but also engagement with poetry as a deeply personal rite. What happens when these two very different practices collide, in an online marketplace? What sorts of answers do we get to Neruda's questions? Do we get quick and perfunctory answers, the ones that will get them paid quickly, or is there suddenly a disruption, a kink in the Mechanical Turk? When, in the midst of menial labor, do we find poetry?

I was struck by how the response poems echo the "alone together" dynamics of the internet, somewhat in conversation with Neruda, but also serving as haunting poems unto themselves. Anonymous workers from around the globe engaged with Neruda's questions in a myriad of ways; some workers answer literally and quickly. Others grow pensive, or pen witty retorts. Their answers compel us to more closely examine the intimate relationships between personal practices and capitalist ventures online.

(As these excerpts comprise less than 10% of Neruda's *The Book of Questions*, they can be published free of copyright infringement.)

—Justin Blinder

Tell me, is the rose naked or is that her only dress?

Why do trees conceal the splendor of their roots?

Who hears the regrets of the thieving automobile?

Is there anything in the world sadder than a train standing in
the rain?

Her dress, and I love to undress her one petal at a time.

They don't, branches mirror the roots.

The poor tires who have to haul it around.

A convertible with its top down in the rain.

What are you guarding under your hump?
    said a camel to a turtle.

And the turtle replied: What do you say to oranges?

Does a pear tree have more leaves than Remembrance of
    Things Past?

Why do leaves commit suicide when they feel yellow?

A devious secret and a hollow heart.

Peel my fine fruit, peel.

No, our memory tree has more leaves.

Some humans do it when they feel blue.

With the virtues that I forgot could I sew a new suit?

Why did the best rivers leave to flow in France?

Why does it not dawn in Bolivia after the night of Guevara?

And does his assassinated heart search there for his assassins?

Do the black grapes of the desert have a basic thirst for tears?

No, most modern virtues are too thin and don't drape well.

Ahh my, Cherie, surely you have no need to ask.

It's not that there is no dawn, it's just that no one is awake to see it.

No. It's under the floor, with the others from Poe.

Yes, but sadly there are not many to be found, and they slowly wither away and turn into raisins.

To whom does the ragged condor report after its mission?

What do they call the sadness of a solitary sheep?

And what happens in the dovecote if the doves learn to sing?

If the flies make honey will they offend the bees?

To a higher power.

Wooly melancholy.

There's a choir of angels.

No, they will cash in their IRAs and retire.

When I see the sea once more will the sea have seen or not seen me?

Why do the waves ask me the same questions I ask them?

And why do they strike the rock with so much wasted passion?

Don't they get tired of repeating their declaration to the sand?

There is no sea without the see in me.

Alan Watts once philosophized, “Bring me a wave separate from the ocean and I will show a human being separate from the universe.”

The rocks mock them by being on the beach.

Each grain of sand is a world of its own but there is no beginning or end or repeating.

Who can convince the sea to be reasonable?

What's it get from demolishing blue amber, green granite?

And why so many wrinkles and so many holes in the rock?

I came from behind the sea, now where do I go when it cuts
me off?

Why did I close the road, falling into the sea's trap?

The sky. It's the only thing that the sea reflects on.

Particles of dust.

That's what it looks like when you get abused and just sit there and take it instead of fighting against it.

The sky.

You are like the rocks, you like to be abused by the sea.

Jackie Clark

When I was a child I wanted to be an altar boy. Nevermind that I was a girl. I went to church each week with my mom and watched boys my age, cloaked in priest-like robes, walk in at the beginning of mass with the priests. I watched them help prepare communion, retreating behind the curtain to the left of the altar to retrieve cloth napkins and gold bowls of water. Their purpose triggered by specific lines in the mass, a script that I knew by heart, the Catholic mass being one of the first texts I was intimate with, though I didn't learn it by reading it but rather by hearing it. Week after week, I sat near the front of the church with my mom, preferring the side of the church where the wine and the communion hosts were waiting on a small table with a deep red table cloth. I loved the part of the mass when they were brought to the priest by the altar boy. While I understood the symbol of communion, that the host becomes the body of christ, I was more taken by the ceremony. Whether or not christ had actually existed was secondary to me. What I desired was the pleasure that comes from knowing what comes next, the verbal cues and intonation, when to stand up and when to kneel, the deep comfort of ritual.

*

Sofia Coppola's film *Marie Antoinette* details the high of hedonistic and aesthetic ritual as a cure to officious, political ritual. On their wedding night, the king's court is there to see Antoinette and her husband Louis XVI off to sleep in their private bedroom. The women of the court arrive every morning to help Antoinette with her morning toilette, Antoinette waiting in the nude for the most senior woman to come and drape her in her robe, the custom of the court stripping her of her right to do so alone and in private. Antoinette and her husband seated aside one another morning after morning for breakfast while the court stands behind them and looks on. The night-time ritual of laying in bed with her husband who merely endows her with a simple kiss goodnight before rolling over. Antoinette's response changes over time, growing from shock and self-consciousness, to amusement at the consistent and predictable, to finally a deeply suffocating and abject boredom. It is after this time that Antoinette begins to exercise her buying powers that focus on the pleasures of the body, both the physical adornment of the body, depicted through beautiful montages of exotic colors and fabrics, shoes and dresses, and her oversized le pouf hairdo, ornately decorated with flowers and jewels, and the physical hedonic hunger of the body, unsatisfyingly satisfied by plate upon plate of fresh fruit and exquisite pastries: pain au chocolat, macarons, petit fours, all while the French people were starving. She has the capital to do so, at least for a while. She is able to partake in these sublimated rituals because of the fortune at her fingertips. She becomes interested in these acts of commodifiable culture because the veil of the political and royal rituals leave her dead inside. Lacking the ability to actually disrupt the political she side steps and subverts. She fashions a reward system for having to endure her boring privilege, a gift that only money could buy.

*

Despite my great desire to participate in mass, in the 1980s a young girl was not able to be an altar boy. The patriarchy of the Catholic church would not allow it. I know that I felt hurt by this exclusion, but really the main thing that it caused me to do was reject the ritual in sum. If I was not able to participate in the way I desired then something must be wrong with the system, I concluded, an early feminist, but really mostly someone who thought highly of herself—if they don't want me then there must be something wrong with them. So I let that ritual go. But the space I held for ritual was never abandoned and has been hard to fill, mostly for the comfort it provides, the inherent instruction embedded in its structure. When there is ritual there is instruction. When there is instruction there is purpose. And when there is purpose there isn't depression, something that even from an early age found me at multiple turns. It was like being lost and then found and then lost again.

*

I've gravitated to yoga studios that have a "focus" every month, instructional concepts of how to better live one's life. Each class beginning with chanting and a dharma talk. Each class ending in meditation. Though the script of the class varies the vernacular remains the same. You will always spend five breaths in each posture. The instructor will always count off those breaths for you. You can always rely on that count.

*

I think of Coppola's Antoinette a lot because I want to understand why we work so hard for money. I want to understand the roots of our desires. The architecture of our society is reliant on money, both the making of it and the spending of it.

There are no other options. The delight Antoinette experiences in the moments of her hair dressing and cake eating have a sort of pure absoluteness. In the movie, you can see the delight and satisfaction radiate from Antoinette when Monsieur Léonard, the royal hairdresser, first completes the le pouf she becomes known for. Antoinette's back to the camera while her face is reflected back to us through the mirror she holds in order to admire her own style and beauty. The luxury to experience an immediate pleasure. Money holds the potential of buying immediate pleasure. If I am bored and lonely on a Saturday afternoon I can go shopping for new clothes or a new pair of shoes and let that buying satisfaction fill me up for a little while. The buying being a short cut to pleasure or purpose, something we increasingly believe we deserve, both the short cut and the pleasure. We have ritualized our capital and have built our entire modern global structure around it. If we didn't fetishize commodities or spend over half of our life working to earn money to live what would our lives mean? I am scared of the answer to this question. Globally, the ritual of capital instructs, it gives purpose and reason, only there is no parity between purpose and reason. There is only luck and location, the rest of your life conforming.

*

In the spin class I take on my lunch hour at the YMCA on 14th Street, the music we listen to harnesses these powers. Even if I didn't know from experience that the chorus of Shawn Mendes' "Stitches" is when the instructor is going to tell you to pick up the pace during your hill climb I would be able to intuit it. I can feel the beat winding up, the quickening rhythm, until it launches in a quick burst, a timed upbeat that maintains the higher pace for a short duration before returning to the original pace. I love choreographing our jumps to the beat of a song. The White Stripes. Lady Gaga. Justin Bieber. Pushing through each chorus in third position until the instructor counts backwards from five to one and we return to the saddle. Predicting the beginning and the ending of these pushes in class is so satisfying to me. Pop music is designed to be predictable for this very reason. We all like to inherently know and intuit things. There is a certain harmony of being one among others, in a space full of people behaving predictably. It gives us confidence and a sense of belonging. We buy experiences and commodities just so we can feel this way. Gym memberships, music streaming services, iPhones. Some days it feels like I go to work just so I can have this release at lunch time. Just so I can know what will come next and how it will end.

*

I never considered poetry a ritual, though of course it was. I know that poems have a beginning and an ending. I know that writing can be and is intuitive. I just never ascribed writing with those characterizations. I never sought to fill my lost ritual with my writing because I never believed that anything that came from inside of me would be enough. The comfort of the ritual was always external, a priest, a prayer, a teacher calling out cues. The wonderous thing about Marie Antoinette is that she was able to ritualize her own desires, she was able to actualize them. Yes, she was at an advantage in the capital department and perhaps that was how she knew that she could, the luxury that capital affords. But the fact that she knew that she could create her own rituals in opposition to the rituals that displeased her remains. I've never truly considered this as being applicable to me until very recently. To ritualize your own desires seems so radical to me. To ritualize your life through poetry as a way to release trauma and increase your creative agility, something I heard CAConrad talk about recently. At a talk in Madison Square Park about Healing Poetics CA told us about a study that was done on the brains of musicians and how years of practicing their instruments built a "super highway" in their brain between their left and right hemispheres. If you were looking at an image of this super highway it would look like a horseshoe shape. The ritual of their practice improved their skill but also fundamentally altered the way their brain is constructed by creating that bridge between the two hemispheres. CA also told us a story about a friend and former student who had stopped writing because she had an office job that really minimized her creative output and how he encouraged her to stop several times a day while at said office job and set a timer and write for 10 minutes. That it did not matter what was written, just to write. Just to create a time and place and imbue it with purpose, with the regard of a ritual, and he said that after several weeks of doing this his friend felt the cloud that had dulled her dissolve. Enforcing, for me, CA's parting plea, that we should ritualize our lives through poetry and art and creativity as way to take the power back from capital, from the time and space it takes away.

Shou Jie Eng

[fig. 1: *Thing*, Douglas fir, sumi ink, graphite]

Inking

Her direction was different this time around. Not substantially different, but tangibly different. Too much ink on the plate. Latex drum to axle to steel frame to silicone handle in hand. Roll out what you have and dab just a bit of it, then transfer to a different part of the glass palette. Remember the gesture we talked about as you roll, that dud-dud, dud-dud rhythm. The ink should coat the surface of the brayer evenly. No pigment build-up, no under-inked spots. Listen for the tack,

[fig. 2: *Totems*, White pine, sumi ink]

Paper

1. A continuous process.
2. 100 percent cotton, acid and chlorine free, precipitated calcium carbonate buffering.
3. Made in the USA.
4. Two deckled edges, two cut edges.
5. Gently roll to find centre, pinch off to crease, align stainless steel tear bar with bevelled tearing edge to marks. With a smooth upward motion begin to separate paper.
6. The torn edge mimics the deckled edge, a manual papermaking detail where the paper slurry finds its way inconsistently into the gap between the frame of the deckle and the screen of the mould. A shaking motion is required to align the fibres as the sheet drains. The same motion produces the characteristic edge of handmade sheet paper. With the advent of roll paper it has become as much a status symbol as a manufacturer's watermark.
7. Remember to dampen your paper before you print,

[fig. 3: *0 of 6* from *Six Plus* (series), Monoprint]

Printing

You have to think of the press as an agent, she said. An equal partner in the work. An etching press is less involved than a lithographic press, and is easier to use, but it will still move the ink about on the plate.

I set my plate on the bed, aligning it to the grid lines. The bed is a half inch of Blanchard ground aluminium with a phenolic resin sheet bonded to the work surface. I have prepared the plate with marks for registration, so the alignment is only necessary for my own ease. The paper I remove from the damp pack and lay on the plate, starting with the top corner closest to me. Roll it down gently on the plate. A sheet of newsprint, then two or three layers of etching blankets on top of it without moving the paper.

Check the pressure before rolling the press bed through. The wheel turns the drive drum and the pressure drum at the same time. Both are nickel-plated steel. As I approach the plate I feel it catch–too much pressure. Back off on the adjustment screws. Roll through.

fig. 1

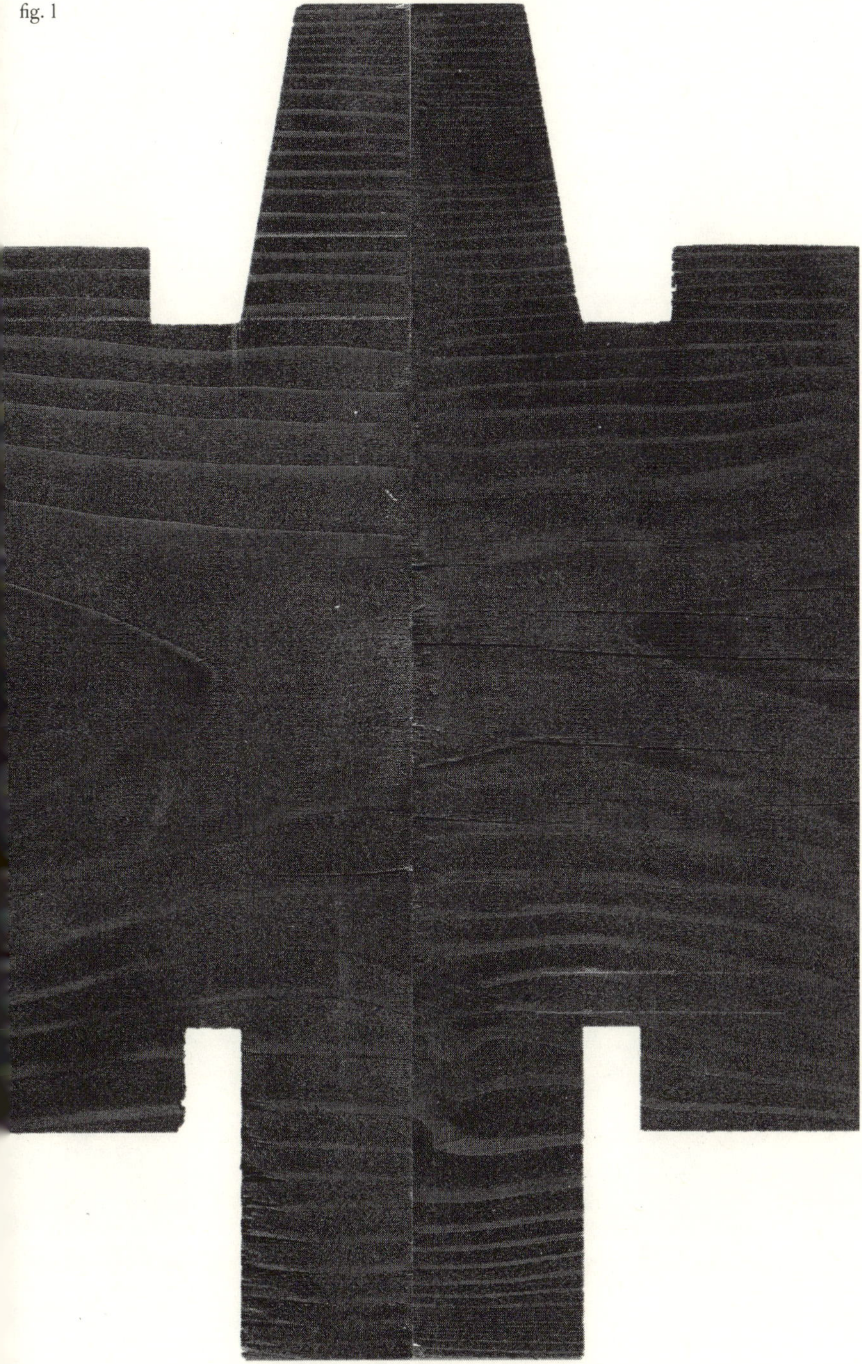

fig. 2

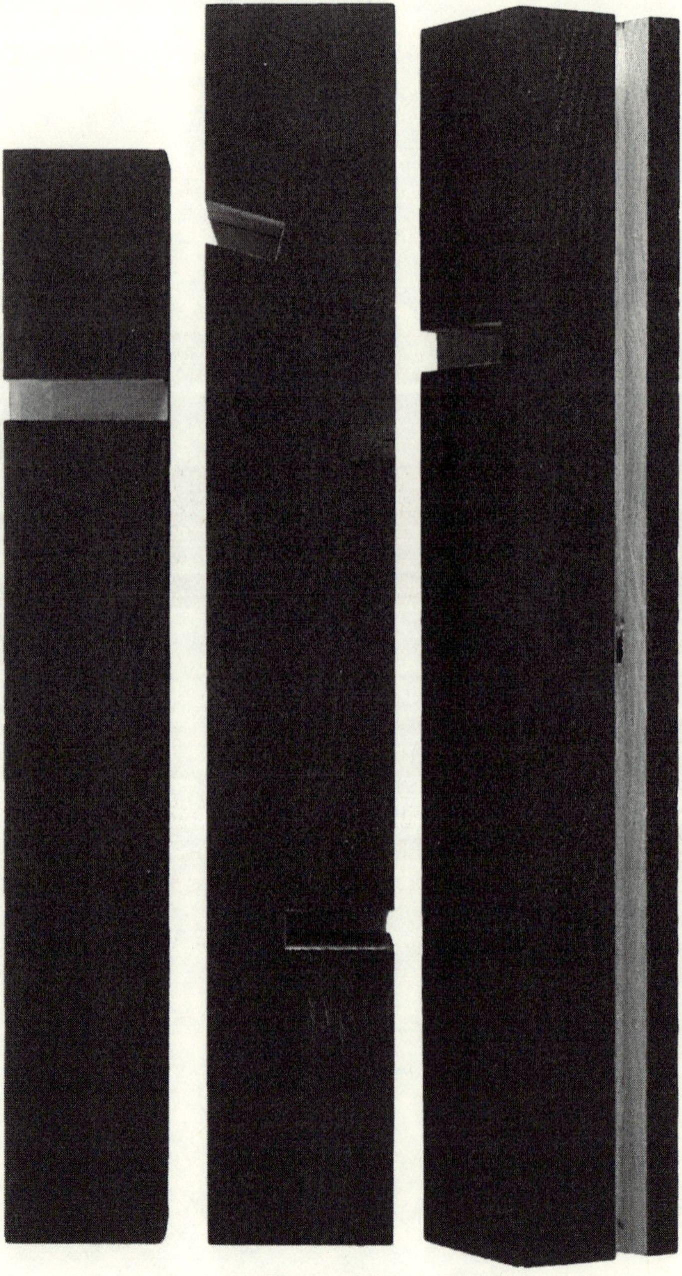

fig. 3

Josef Kaplan

PLEASE

Listen.
I'll give you anything.
I'll give you whatever you want.
Anything at all.
Just ask.
Please.
Just ask me.
Any possession.
Any amount of money.
Anything.
And everything.
Everything I have.
It doesn't matter to me.
I couldn't care less.
Look.
I'll open up my wallet.
And dump it all out.
I'll turn out my pockets.
I'll dump it onto the ground.
Onto the sweet, grassy ground.
Onto the smooth, warm pavement.

All of my money.
And more.
Splash it all onto the ground.
We can go to the ATM right now.
And take out all of my money.
All of it.
It's easy.
We just stick the card in.
We just stick it right in there.
We just punch in the numbers.
Super easy.
No problem.
No problem at all.
It's just routine.
It's like nothing.
Anyone can do it.
A child could do it.
A little baby.
Smashing its baby fingers against the machine's glass.
Its baby brain tumbling into formation.
Flicking out its nervous shocks.
To travel down the arm, to the wrist, to the

hand.
To make those little numbers glow and activate.
It's so intuitive.
With that little sound.
The ATM calling back to you.
With its staccato cooing.
The machine acknowledging each little touch.
Like it's purring.
Technology is amazing.
It makes everything so easy.
It makes everything so relatable.
"That could be us."
We could be that baby's fingers.
We could be doing that.
Right now, together.
Little fingers on the glass.
United, caressing.
And then the machine spits it out.
It spits out every little bit of money.
All from its thin plastic mouth.
As if on cue.

Every little bit I have.
Every single dollar.
Every dirty flap of a dollar bill.
Every crumpled strip of cash.
It doesn't matter to me.
I'll give it all to you.
I'll put it all in your hands.
I'll pour out all my money.
Like water from a vase.
Like from a faucet.
I'll pour it into your cupped hands.
I'll let it stream out and over your fingers.
The cool run of money.
The dollars washing over your palms.
Over your wrists, over your forearms.
Like confetti.
Like fine bolts of cloth, fed through a shredder.
They'll rain down over you.
They'll drift through the air like humid grains of mist.
So you can just grab them.
You can just pluck them out of the air.

You can scoop them up.
Like from a fountain.
To splash against your face.
Don't worry.
I'll let you.
I'll let you take them all.
You can do whatever you want.
Your hands snatching at them.
All of the different denominations.
The ones and tens, and twenties.
And fifties.
The hundreds, even.
Poking out from between your fingers.
Caught and crumpled in your grip.
It's like a game.
I'll toss them into the air.
And then you can try and catch them.
Bundling them up.
Pulling them out of the air.
Clasping at them with every able limb.
Lying down on your back.
Legs kicking, flailing.
Hands grasping.

Toes and fingers wrapped around their prizes.
Your mouth open.
Tongue lolling out.
The money drifting over you.
Wafting over you.
We could do this.
We could make it happen.
There's nothing to be afraid of.
It's perfectly natural.
It's a time-honored tradition.
Widely accepted.
Widely practiced.
An activity fully absorbed by the social fabric.
In which we exist.
In fact integral to it.
It's hard to imagine this world apart from it.
Where one is barred from indulging.
In this ancient observance.
This classical expression.
Of cultural unity.
It brings us together.

It reminds us of our commonality.
Our shared beliefs.
And all that we hold dear.
It shows us that we are present.
To one another, we are kin.
We are kith.
We stand with each other.
We'd do anything for each other.
Risk anything.
Sacrifice anything.
Give anything up.
Give it all up.
I'd give it all up, all for you.
And be happy doing it.
If you so much as asked.
If you so much as agreed.
It's your call.
It's whatever you want.
It's whatever you want to do.
And however you want to do it.
It's up to you.
It's all you, my friend.
My beautiful friend.

My most cherished companion.
Cohort of my soul.
My guiding light.
My precious heart.
My sweet love.
My gracious partner.
My one and only.
I'm just following your lead.
I'm right behind you.
I'm like a little sheep.
Waltzing up behind you.
A little puppy dog.
A little stray, an orphan.
Who's suddenly found their home.
And who's happy to acknowledge it.
Who has no qualms.
No anxieties.
Who's happy to admit it.
To admit their debt.
To admit their debt to you.
And begin.
In some small way.
To at least.

Pay some of it back.
To get even.
To get square.
Balance out the scales.
You know.
To get right with each other.
To show you.
That I can be there for you.
Whatever the call.
I can answer it.
Without resentment.
Without hesitation.
Eager.
And enthusiastic.
And prepared.
Because it's what I want.
I need it.
I can't wait.
I'm here.
Dying of anticipation.
Dying of desire.
Waves of nervous energy coursing
through me.

My fingers tapping.
Teeth grinding.
Knees bounding up and down.
Waiting on you.
Waiting on your beck and call.
Waiting to come bounding up.
To realize my dream.
Of giving you everything.
Everything I can.
Everything I own.
And everything I feel.
Every ounce of my faith.
Every ounce of my support.
To fulfill my purpose.
My mission.
My one reason for being.
The reason that I exist.
That I'm here at all.
Because I'm here for you.
I'm here to support you.
I'm here to help you.
To encourage you.
To be your rock.

To be your guardian angel.
I want you to know that.
I need you to know that.
I just want you to feel my presence.
As love.
As the love that it is.
As an aura of protection.
And empowerment.
So that you can rest easy.
Because you know that you're safe.
You know that you're totally secure.
Around me.
Totally.
There's nothing for you to worry about.
When I'm around.
I'm your biggest fan.
I'm your right hand.
I'm your best friend.
And confidante.
You can ask me for anything.
You can say anything.
Around me.
You can tell me anything.

It's all good.
I'll keep any secret.
You can open up your heart.
And just trust me.
Totally.
Trust me with.
Anything.
Your feelings.
Your dreams.
Your most personal.
Thoughts and fears.
Your hopes and joys.
Your pleasures.
I want you to know that.
I can keep them.
I can hold them for you.
I can take them from you.
To ease the burden.
To lighten the load.
To unharness your shoulders.
And pull the weight onto myself.
And hold it close.
And keep it safe.

So that you can rest easy.
You can breathe.
Easy.
Unhurried.
Your breath slow and drowsy.
Cleansing breath.
The breath of unbothered sleep.
Breath that refreshes.
Breath that expels with it all tension.
And concern.
And fear.
Ebbing.
Always.
Receding from the body.
Taking with it all pain.
All discomfort.
Evaporating.
With all illness.
And strife.
Leaving only sureness.
Leaving only the confidence.
I grant you.
The safety of my enveloping gift.

Your breath.
And your dreams.
Together with me.
They're safe.
They're safe here.
With me.
They're fine.
With me.
You know it.
Of course you do.
You know that you know it.
You understand that.
You feel it from behind your eyes.
From within every corner of your body.
From within the fiber.
Of every thought.
That you think.
And through those thoughts.
Believe.
This most beautiful belief.
The belief.
That you're cared for.
That you will have.

Always.
This center.
From which to extend yourself.
A place of absolute ease.
Of absolute ability.
And confidence.
Of total permission.
That speaks to you.
Always.
Repeating.
Forever.
That you can do anything.
You can do anything at all.
Anything.
And everything.
It's true.
Everything.
I'm serious.
I'm being totally honest.
I'm not kidding.
I'm dead serious.
I'm 100% serious.
I think you can do whatever you want.

I think, in this life.
You're in charge.
You're the master of your domain.
You have everything going for you.
You can be whatever you want.
Act in whatever way you choose.
Fulfill any desire.
Any impulse.
Any future is yours to seize.
Any world.
Is yours.
Any whole world.
Is your oyster.
Your delicious oyster.
Your sweet, special.
Scrumptious oyster.
Fleshy, fragile oyster.
In its stoney shell.
The shell barnacled and rough.
The little oyster morsel.
Asleep within.
Innocent.
Adorable.

Blissfully unaware.
Of having been plucked.
From its rocky bed.
And spirited away.
From the shallows of the sea.
From among its brethren.
From among its family.
Until its too late.
Until its long gone.
Its fate sealed.
Its little oyster voice calling out.
Crying.
A lament pitched.
At such volume and frequency.
As to be inaudible to the human ear.
But to which the other oysters respond.
Having heard it.
From across however many miles.
Whatever stretch of distance.
And taken heed.
Of its distress.
In chorus.
Raising what for them.

Is a thunderous wail.
Of remorse.
And terror.
Full and encompassing.
Resonant through the murky.
Depths of the current's sloshing.
Its caress, waving.
Against the combined.
Oyster carapaces of this popular bed.
Calling out to their stolen friend.
Yanked from the bosom of the mass.
Cruelly departed from the warm.
Whispering collusion of the oysters.
How they loved one another.
How their love would thread through their.
Ranks like a tremble.
Like a rustling of the wind.
Binding them together.
Binding them as one.
Their days.
And nights filled.
With this quiet companionship.
Basking in the filtered sunlight.

Falling down to them
Through the softly rolling waters.
Inching up at high tide.
The sea breeze pushing sand.
And spray over the reef.
And when the waters recede.
At night.
In the darkness.
To free from obscurity.
From the darkness of the water.
The moon's reflected glow.
Caressing their hard, angular bodies.
Like white gauze.
Cool and assured.
The oysters ever so slightly.
Opening and closing their valves.
In concordance with one another.
Like a rumor spreading.
In all directions at once.
Only to be lifted.
From this felicity.
And pried open.
By a gentle, un-calloused palm.

Cradling it.
The oyster.
Working the knife in.
To the thinnest space between.
The shell's bisected halves.
To twist.
And click them open.
Revealing the soft, bloated insides.
The musk of the sea trailing out.
Like an invisible smoke.
Enwrapping the air.
The sharp liquor of the oyster.
Bathing its meat.
The meat waiting, there.
To be scooped out.
And slid down the throat.
And drank.
The great joy of it.
The lovely taste.
The life plunging down your throat.
Isn't it beautiful.
Open yourself to it.
Open yourself to its passage.

Open your heart to it.
That's all I care about.
That's all I want for you.
To see this as beauty.
To taste it.
To locate it within yourself.
To finally accept it.
To accept this beauty.
To accept.
Finally.
That you're fulfilled.
That you're content.
And pleased.
In this beauty.
In the beautifulness of this moment.
Because it's what you want.
You want me to give it to you.
The gorgeousness of this experience.
Of your own happiness.
Listen to me.
Look at me.
Look at this.
We did it.

We did it together.
Don't you see.
It's OK.
We can both be surprised.
If you want.
We can make little gasps.
Or some other noise.
It'll be a great time.
Sure.
Or we can do it another way.
If you want.
It doesn't matter to me.
We can both act.
As if this was what we planned.
All along.
The only thing.
Our sole purpose.
Together.
You see.
Don't you.
You understand.
You see now.
You're like me.

We're the same.
The same person.
The same thought.
The same action.
The same belief.
We're in this together.
We believe, together.
We believe only in beauty.
And it therefore leaves from us.
And is beautiful itself.
And we are fulfilled.
And content.
And therefore generous.
In our belief.
We dole it out.
Generously.
We give it away.
Like money.
Or anything else.
Kisses, advice.
Seeds blown.
From the tip of a dandelion.
Just like that.

A beautiful image.
An easily understood.
And resonant simile.
That describes a thing.
Perfectly.
In locating its perfect.
Idealistic core.
In the life of another.
Linking the two.
And thus.
Articulating their shared beauty.
As an evental universalism.
Beautiful in and of.
Itself.
And thus fulfilled.
And content.
And therefore generous.
And therefore worldly.
In that it gives itself.
Wholly, to the world.
And the world is beautiful for it.
It rejoices.
In that, it rejoices.

In equal measure.
It responds, rejoicing.
As if across a wire, struck.
Against our belief.
To hear itself, humming.
Softly, like a bell.
Like a bell's edge.
Its lengths of softness.
The copper skirt of a bell, rounding.
As when struck, ringing.
It is softness ringing.
The rung curvature.
The struck outline of the bell.
Stirring.
In exhaustive lengths.
Broken apart.
By the vibrating air.
By the strips of it.
The tuned rousing, its hewn pieces.
The quivering lip of the bell.
Its lengths moving.
Towards anything, they move.
Because they're struck.

And in moving.
They're beautiful, it's that simple.
The strike makes it so.
The designation makes it beautiful.
Because we believe it.
"We believe the bell is beautiful."
And it therefore is, truly.
It is the ease that makes it true.
The way it falls so cleanly into life.
The way it plunges down.
The way it disappears.

Matt Longabucco

Why should I like the movie version of *The Wings of the Dove* so much, though it comes from such a distant world? I appreciate the way the story acknowledges that, however different, we'd all take money and leisure if we could. There's nothing really wrong with Linus Roache's working-class life, but Helena Bonham Carter refuses to marry him, though she loves him, if it means abandoning the patronage of her rich aunt and, with her, any prospect of an aristocratic existence. Telling Roache their only chance is to scheme for an American heiress's fortune, Bonham Carter never actually delivers the equivalent of Bridget Fonda's unforgettable speech from *A Simple Plan*, where Fonda tells Bill Paxton that if he gives back the stolen millions he's found they'll have nothing ahead of them but thirty more years of scraping by, "only going out to restaurants for special occasions...skipping the appetizer... coming home for dessert." The sentiment is there, though, even in the context of the James story: the deep sense—artists exclude themselves from this, it's their great function—that there are only two options, a wealth so large as to free us from care or else a vast, grey mediocrity and the numb repetitions of subsistence.

I'd spent that morning at the Park Slope Food Coop. I know, you always tell me those people annoy you, but politics is people, isn't it, it is literally the act of joining together with people who are not like you toward a goal that has necessarily been compromised in some fashion by its being held in common. I love it there. I was working the receiving shift at the top of the belt, a post that includes being out on the sidewalk where the pallets coming off the delivery trucks get lined up to be brought inside and broken down, and the goods sent downstairs. At one point one of the pallets that had been half-unwrapped got jostled—we'd been trying to break it down directly from the sidewalk—and a few flat boxes of blackberries toppled onto the curb, so that most of the little plastic clamshells, six to a box, fell open, and a few hundred plump, juicy blackberries spilled into the gutter. I was bending down to sweep these up, sampling a few that hadn't touched the street, when one of the delivery trucks started up, then pulled away. Its right front tire went straight through the berries and sent a spray of red juice all over me where I kneeled. I immediately understood this as the rare and abundant gift it surely was.

I was at Wendy's Subway later that day. Getting off the Montrose stop feels like disembarking from the railroad in a wild west town, only there's a block of bodegas and pizza places instead of the blacksmith shop and the saloon. Then a stretch of desert, rocks and scrub, everything dusty and dun-colored, the trucks honking and grinding their gears as they bounce up Bushwick Ave. We had a fantasy, one day, standing smoking on our little patch of sidewalk, about renting out the side of one of the many passing cement mixers—the idea was to have a poem come scrolling up, line by line, as the drum revolved. Maybe Dottie or CAConrad. I bought some Advil PM from the guy at the bodega. "Does this stuff work for you, do you take it?" "Yes my friend, it works. You look tired, you look like you haven't slept in a few days." "Yeah man, I've been having trouble sleeping." "You probably think too much."

That night I watched *The Wings of the Dove*. Or was that the night I watched *Lust for Life*, or *Days of Heaven*? I get Malka from school at three, we take the A train, and if we find seats

I give her my phone to play video games, and pull out a book for myself. At home, she does her homework. At around five-thirty I prepare one of the three things she'll eat: pizza, chicken strips, or penne with tomato sauce. Sliced cucumbers on the side. I have some canned Coop mackerel on rice or toast, slathered in Cholula. Then Malka watches some shows and draws while I clean up, do little errands around the house, and/or collapse on the couch, feeling a little guilty we're not doing a fabulous art project together, or playing soccer, or studying astronomy, or whatever constructive activity I fear the other parents are doing. Around eight we read a chapter of *Harry Potter*—mutual bliss. She's already had dessert, now she's munching fistfulls of goldfish. At nine-thirty she goes to bed, where she'll stay up a while, possibly worrying about the huge roaches she saw stuck on the glue traps in her friend's East Village apartment's basement storage area. On school days we're up next morning by seven, so I shouldn't stay up too long, now that she's finally asleep, and definitely shouldn't stare at a screen, but I'm too tired to write or read much. This is where the illegal movies come in. They bring their own rituals. I jam in earbuds, type "watch wings of the dove online" into google, then choose one of the likeliest sites. Before the movie starts there are a few times where I press "play" and a pop-up appears, and I close it as quickly as I can, as if its very existence is a time bomb threatening me at the level of debt or data, virus or hack. Finally, the movie starts, and since stopping it means the pop-ups again, I usually just watch straight through, carrying my laptop in one hand to the fridge or the toilet if I need to make the trip.

To be yoked to that dream, and to watch in my desperate exhaustion, recalls the archetypal psychologist James Hillman, who often uses the term "soul" in his writing and believes, as one editor says, "that of its nature the soul pathologizes. That is to say, it gets us into trouble, it interferes with the smooth running of life, it obstructs attempts to understand, and it seems to make relationships impossible." The soul-making that happens in the world of dreams is not, for Hillman, transferrable or translatable to the world of the productive, forward-looking day, and our task is not to interpret our dreams toward a heroic self-betterment. Even the seemingly affirmative erotic nature of dreams leads not to healthy vitality but, rather, downward into ruin. He writes: "Eros will attempt again and again to create those dark nights and confusions which are its nest. It renews itself in affective attacks, jealousies, fulminations, and turmoils. It thrives close to the dragon." And in his book *The Dream and the Underworld*, Hillman says, similarly, "the dream takes us downward, and the mood that corresponds with this movement is the slowing, saddening, introspective feeling of depression." Hillman doesn't want to cure this condition. He's skeptical of the mania for cures and self-improvement programs and the energy that goes into finding them. In fact, he claims, we only truly make ourselves in and toward shadow and death, and depression is the natural state of the soul that properly exists by deepening—he goes so far as to say that what we mean by soul *is* this deepening action. And its potential depths are limitless.

Henry James knows this, and his Kate Croy (Helena Bonham Carter) learns it. She thinks she has been pursuing passion and fulfillment, wealth and comfort. But in convincing Merton to court the heiress, she soon realizes, she has set him inexorably toward an ideal that winds up filling his horizon and blotting out Kate in the process. Though the heiress, Milly Theale, dies, Merton has come to love her. In the movie's penultimate scene, the two schemers reunite after Milly's death. Kate tells Merton she knows he has fallen in love with Milly's specter (he has outpaced Kate in loving death). She burns the letter that gives her what she wanted, the inheritance that, as he flatly points out, he'll get whether she burns a piece of paper or not. She goes into his bedroom (he has a little Brooklyn-sized apartment), and takes off her dress. They fuck. It's a grim act, possibly a pleasurable one, possibly the more pleasurable for it. Eros and depression are joined here, in a way Hillman might recognize, and Kate is engaged with all the turmoil of her betrayal, her inward self deepening—or finding an opportunity to deepen, at least—with the experience. Afterwards, the pair will part forever.

When the movie's finished I shut the laptop, restless, too tired for the routine of bedtime. I have access to stimulation and regret: apps on my phone, or my body laid out in front of me, or even—this is more embarrassing than masturbating—the poetry books beckoning from the shelves, which if opened would heat my brain and keep me awake. When I finally crawl into bed I settle down into one of those dark nests Hillman talks about, staring at the walls. He's right, I don't mind it, in that familiar territory I recognize myself again. It's another step to half-slumber and from there the one or two reoccurring dreams I often suffer.

But it wasn't a school night, this time. It was a Friday. Saturday morning we get in the new old car and drive up into Westchester. Going north or east from the city, the few months since I've had wheels again, I can't believe what the world looks like, fast food places and billboards, it's a shock to the system. I grew up in Westchester—Mount Vernon—and for twenty years now I've thought, I'll go redeem my childhood, I'll really see it anew this time! Nothing doing. When I leave New York I panic about what people do at night—I've become this person. I guess I don't like politics either. Or find much chance of soul-making at the bagel shop in Pleasantville or the cineplex in Cortland Manor.

We meet my parents and Mousy in the parking lot. Mousy is a mildly developmentally-disabled woman my father knows from when he was a manager for a series of group homes in and around Mount Kisco. They've stayed in touch, and every couple of months my parents pick her up and take her to an action movie (her favorite genre). Mousy's been all around the world with Special Olympics and other programs. She's been to Tokyo, to Iceland, on Alaskan and tropical cruises. My father likes to tell her she leads a great life, that we should all wish for her life. This sounds like he's cheering her on, but no, he believes it, he's ostensibly sort of smiling but he actually feels bitter about it. She does lead a great life. She's also never had a lover, autonomy, a single unsupervised day.

We see *Wonder Woman*. It's a period piece, set in World War I Europe, and I'm afraid Malka is going to be freaked out by the trench warfare and the chemical weapons that figure heavily in the plot. Later she checks in with me about the history—"Is it true women didn't fight?"—and about Ares, the god of war, who's mysterious and violent in the film. We talk about Greek myth, about the Amazons, and whether I believe in gods. I say they're metaphors, and we leave it there. I consider Instagramming her with her wrists crossed, in a fierce Wonder Woman stance, in front of the movie poster, but ultimately decide I'm not up to engaging on social media with the controversy over the movie's star Gal Gadot having gone on record as a proud former soldier of the Israeli Army (she served during a particularly repressive period). She's blithe about shattered lives. I won't likely be posting many pictures of my upcoming work trip to Jerusalem and Tel Aviv, either. I don't know what to do, I'm not prepared to boycott a movie my daughter's been wanting to see for six months, and as for my trip, I need the job and am fascinated by the city. I wish I could say it was an unfamiliar compromise. I've decided to put my faith in John Berger, lately (though gender-wise he's failed to account for Wonder Woman): "Men go backwards or forwards./There are two directions/But not two sides." I take him to mean that dialectics are pointless—if there's progress toward human freedom, we know when we are making it, and all our debates and arguments in the meantime are so much distraction from the path we only sometimes have the strength of will and imagination to follow.

After the movie, we hit up the Applebee's across the lot. My father orders an iced coffee, the very earnest young waitress says they don't have that, he's aghast. He mentions it three more times, to her, over the course of the meal, "as a joke." At the end of the meal, he spills the remaining half of his very large iced tea onto his lap. He'll turn 78 in October, he was once a pool shark and a painter and was and remains a champion television watcher, he tells me the same news every ten minutes as if he hasn't told me already, and yet somehow has the presence of mind to ask me when I'm going to publish a book. My mother tries to keep everything bubbly, gets spinach artichoke dip for the table. Everything's foul. Before we part, appraising my new ride, dad says, "That car needs washing."

It's not worth screaming that I don't give a shit, so loudly that the whole waitstaff would come to the window and gawk. His care for certain objects and protocols has shrunk his interest in the world to a tight circle of arbitrary concerns, the vast outside of which has been darkened into night by his disappointments in art and life. It takes us almost two and a half hours to get home in the summer traffic. There's a Donald J. Trump State Park off the Taconic, and Trump Links golf course at the foot of the Whitestone Bridge.

Later that night, Malka in bed, I take a cue from the critics at the *Times* and call up the Coen brothers' *Inside Llewyn Davis*, an episodic story about an aspiring folk singer in 1961 Greenwich Village. The title character, played by Oscar Isaac, is having a bad time: he's in deep trouble with the married friend he's slept with and gotten pregnant, his career is nowhere, his former musical partner threw himself off the George Washington Bridge. His sister suggests he give up on music and go back to the Merchant Marines. "And what," he asks her, "just exist?" She's chagrined at his suggestion that there's nothing more to a life without art. When he picks up his guitar, he's sublime, he croons to an aloof and all-powerful agent who belies the magic we see on screen, saying he doesn't see any commercial appeal in the act. He even sings to his father, who watches stone-faced from the corner of his nursing-home room. At the end of an ethereal sea shanty, Llewyn crinkles his nose in disgust—the father, silent the entire scene, has shit himself. The close of the film finds Llewyn much where he began—the continuity even circles onto itself. We understand he's going to be struggling this way for a very long time. Over the course of his adventures he's lost and found, and lost again and found again an orange cat, a wild part of him, somehow, that's always also elsewhere, a spirit that slips through the cracked-open door or window and down to the yard, a fleeting streak of color in the dark.

Sarah Passino

SOME WORDS FROM 40-SOME
DAYS BEFORE THE ECLIPSE
TRANSLATING LORCA'S
DANZA DE LA MUERTE
BY WRITING IT IN RICE FLOUR
AROUND 40 WALL STREET
LIKE A CRAB OR LIKE A
WHALE BUT FOR SURE FOR
THE ANTS & FOR SURE FOR A
SUM OF THE _WASTE_

FIRST DAY

like future cities
like the family
house i go

underwater
& when the moon
comes up i dont

feel a thing

SECOND DAY

any strip
in america
part bachelor

party part bee
hive card
table retiree

& from here
how to believe
aprils meannesses

in july where do
you see it from
is still ___ ____

THIRD DAY (FIRST DAY)

today i stand on the balcony
of the 31st floor at wall street & south
looking down & out to open water

that is so alive & everything is light
& up here part of a piece J turns
to me & tells me how high we are

& i think *at the end of empire*
he says other things & i finish
all his sentences like that up here

in my head hes all *we are not burning*
the oil the oil is burning us & i squint
to see the island of this city & its edge

but all at once instead
i feel that moon

FOURTH DAY (SECOND DAY)

today i wake up & know
this poem is a poem i will
write on wall street

& that i will write it from
whatever are the things
i will find there P tells me

to write it like a map
like a pilgrim i find brooms
to sweep my path from south

to front to water to pearl
each old edge i walk to try
to see try to hold up my gods

my questions mostly i will
listen mostly i will listen
to the gods with song

i will try & be clear

FIFTH DAY (THIRD DAY [SECOND DAY])

there is a kind of poem
that takes back the poem
before it & i dont believe

in gods & i dont believe
in clarity & all there is here is
waste & i hate poetry too

i want to stand still i want to
still to stop i want to mop
floors all day for this retarded

guy on first & first who was born
on the first who tells me i stack
papers perfectly & smiles at me

SIXTH DAY (FOURTH DAY [THIRD DAY])

this morning the waters waterblue the skys skyblue
& a cormorant skims the river on the starboard side
i feel scared but braver now watching him make not

one wrong aesthetic choice with his morning last night
i told L i would write lorca on wall street & *see where that goes*
& L said *no use rice flour* *like the indians*

L is not indian *the flour feeds the ants the ants bless the house*
& when she said that i saw this poem would be a poem
with many authors many ants that *bless the house* meant

many things this morning i stopped by the store to get rice
flour & ran into C who said if i want to translate lorca
by feeding ants i must read buñuel & dali on ants & on their time

together with lorca in spain before he came to new york &
got changed by new york & C said *i have had enough*
of almost everything & i heard him & got on the ferry

& heard judah rubinmfastintroduce tommy pico like always
like hes all all words not in poems make us small & when
we get to pier 11 judah says *the states demands for homogeneity fails*

at the site of passivity rejection refusal & i feel so glad because he believes
that & so sad because today i do not all the radios clicking on talk
of *poor swollen america* like hass says but im gunning for the rich one

we are saying the same thing i know different words but how
do you name the state now & what can you see when all you can see
from federal hall today is the seamless flag on the stock exchange

____ name the thing still I hope some of the blessing today
is for judahs house & for tommys house & for the house of hass
but i dont see any ants

SEVENTH DAY (FIFTH DAY [FOURTH DAY])

today the sky over red hook is white & stormy
theres no food in the house so i fry up scallion
pancakes with rice flour they taste grassy

& good when i get to wall street it starts
to rain & i write the line about camels
torn flesh under the overpass of the fdr

a woman smoking a cigarette outside 40
wall street under the gold turns to her friends
tells them *i'm stressed all the time* & a poet

leans in says the question is why the flesh is
torn i write *flesh-lashed* & can now see the whip
not just the camel in the line like how this building

was built to be the tallest in the world when lorca
was here so all i want to show you is the gold broken up
escalator in that the line *was built to be the worlds tallest*

& the eyes of the paunched beautiful lispy spaniard
in gold spectacles when he walks me to the gold
information plaque by the cosmetics & says how

much he wants to learn *look this was the tallest*
building for one month he tells me & sweeps his
arms to indicate all of the duane reade grocery

& household aisles *this was the tallest building*
in the whole world he says as i look & see us
reflected in gold banks of escalators the rain

gets heavier as i leave & so i duck into the palm
& mirror wall street atrium all hobo & hedgefund
all exhaustion noise & write down on a scrap piece

of paper *how big is the cup how big is the foot* &
watch the rush look out for what we measure with

EIGHTH DAY (SIXTH DAY [THIRD DAY])

can i feed my dog cereal
can i feed my dog musuli
granny squannit
granny squannit offering
best cornbread recipe
best easy cornbread
enron email dataset
enron email dataset recipe
enron email dataset casserole
enron email dataset dinner party
little red riding hood original
little red riding hood original moral
little red riding hood and robin hood relation
diggers
diggers leveler
diggers leveler wall street
diggers leveler wall street today
whats left
whats left over
whats left after
whats left outside
can i feed my dog rice
can i feed my dog rice with general tso

NINTH DAY

my handwriting
is getting better
i pinch the flour

between thumb
& pointer
& like a cricket

i write *y los valles*
de luz que el cisne
levantaba con el pico

at the feet of a man
in a yellow psibc
vest i look up at what

i now see as canyons
the ferry tides in & out
& we both look at lorcas

line against todays street
& i see all the holes in
the asphalt how porous

how like home how much
can seep in i misspell
valles hope it will rain

TENTH DAY

today is brittle
in all kinds
of ways

lets not name
them today
but lets

not pretend
we cant
see

we are all about
to break
but all

real well fed
i drink black coffee
memorize lines to write

that i mostly get
right but all close enough
all the lines have different shapes

on land than
over water like limit
or summit like lineament

or pivot
& when im
done writing lorca & look

up the shape
all cormorant a sparrow
nests under soffits of rusted

overpass in rusted
air too many white feathers
too much white particulate matter

in the air & where does everyone buy their
sunglasses i want them too or whatever

that is or way to live but just hear *seize cisne seize cisne seize*
cant tell where the words are coming from

Danniel Schoonebeek

This appeal for the allocation of government surplus money to pay for the execution of the following work, which will be staged in a warehouse marked for demolition and of the author's own choosing, will be ventured via submission of the above-named work itself, a poem oftentimes troubled by an undetermined malaise, entitled "Poem with a Gun to Its Head," in which the author, 23% of an unsavory person named Danniel Schoonebeek, 30 years of age and rumored to be a resident of an unincorporated village populated solely by a fringe network of radio hijackers (and hereafter known as "the client"), puts forth the following terms, necessarily on the grounds that, quote, "already a new death is here to bargain with you," and, quote, "already this new death," in the client's own addendum, is, quote, "*already* already rebranding itself in your garden": (1) that the client will be provided with a scrubbed work desk, scoured preferably by a machine that is capable of manipulating either steel wool or sandpaper in what will henceforth be known as its "claws"; (2) that the client will be provided with one single red ballpoint pen and a roll of third-generation organic toilet paper priced at $4.67 per unit, on which the client will undertake the writing of a poem entitled "Poem with a Gun to Its Head"; (3) that the rules, toxicity, patrolled borders, whiteness, stench, duration, blurriness, foul language, flammability, intolerability, subject-verb disagreement, and potential for insurrection of this poem will be determined under the following criteria; (4) that the client's childhood friend, Nicholas J. Frandsen, a platoon sergeant of the United States Marine Corps (who will have served no less than two tours of Iraq, and wearing his Marine-issue fatigues, and rumored to have once beaten two men unconscious with his bare hands, necessarily on the grounds that they tipped their waitress below 5% on a bill of $117), will aim and press a military grade AK-47, purchased illegally with money earned via time served in the U.S. Marine Corps, at the back of the client's skull, necessarily while the client writes, in red ink on a roll of toilet paper, a poem entitled "Poem with a Gun to Its Head"; (5) that the work in question must abide by at least three of the following terms; (6) that the client must include, at least once in the poem, and in the following rank and file, the words "only rifles have souls"; (7) that the client's childhood friend, Nicholas J. Frandsen, while aiming a loaded AK-47 at the client's skull and wearing his fatigues, may feel himself moved to speak the following words in rank and file: "you must work from yourself, like working a scarf of dried blood from a thistle, a morsel of sour bread that casts the world in copper light, a kind of penny-light that announces to the world, quote, 'I will meet death unafraid,'" whereupon the client's childhood friend, a platoon sergeant of the U.S. Marine Corps, will remember the following terms of his two tours of Iraq; (8) the tedium, the mess tent, the chemical burns, the gun cleaning, the new fish, the rank, the sleeping in holes, the fraternal, the smart-alecky, the choruses, the trap music, the religious boredom, the ague, the commandant, you kill or be killed, the flight home, a sunburnt cheek, hysterical laughter, the birthday cards, the gun cleaning, and whereupon the client's childhood friend will be moved to (9) fire a single round of 7.62 x 39 mm ammunition into the skull of the client, necessarily on the grounds that (10) for Nicholas J. Frandsen, "irreconcilable" & "incontrovertible" are no longer words in the English language but rather the phantom pain of two claws, most likely those of a bear, impaled on either side of his ribcage, and what will hereafter be referred to as "the irreconcilable claw" will be described on the following terms; (11) that the governing body that started the war in which I fought is the same governing body whose morals and laws I took an oath to protect and simultaneously the same governing body who will decide, upon receipt of this appeal, if a poet who is free to make art in the United States, necessarily because of men and women who serve in the armed forces, will be allocated the same government money I received, the difference being the allocation of his government money will fund a work entitled "Poem With a Gun to Its Head," a work in which I am necessarily cast because of time I served as a platoon sergeant in the U.S. Marine Corps, simultaneously a role in which I dress in the same fatigues I wore while enlisted in the U.S. Marine Corps, and hold an automatic rifle to the temple of my childhood friend so as to force him to create art, which is to say these facts are "irreconcilable" insofar as they pierce me away from the world in which I live, and what will hereafter be known as "the incontrovertible claw" will be described on the following terms; (12) that it is undeniable and indisputable that I learned to disarm, dismember, and kill human beings in order to defend the rights of artists to create works in which I am cast in the not unaggressive role of someone who will be taunted and also tested, necessarily because of my training in disarming, dismembering, and killing human beings, taunted not only to murder a poet out of irreconcilable disgust but also to murder my childhood friend because it is undeniable that I fought a war in order to allow him the freedom to create this work, which is to say I find these facts "incontrovertible" insofar as they pierce me away from the world in which I live and cannot be removed, whereupon (13) as stated above, the client's childhood friend, Nicholas J. Frandsen, will be moved to fire a single round of 7.62 x 39 mm ammunition into the skull of the client, whereupon (14) the work will be completed and the above-named warehouse will be demolished by an anonymous third party (hereafter known as "the demolisher"), who will destroy the warehouse by means of finding a dead switch in the woods and pushing a red button, whereupon (15) any persons whosoever who find themselves in the position of witnessing this work entitled "Poem with a Gun to Its Head" (and hereafter known as "the audience") will be given the option, by way of detailed instructions written by the client prior to the execution of the work, of robbing the nearest Bank of America at gunpoint and demanding the sum total of $90,000, which will effectively cancel all execution of this work, barring an act of god, and be divided among the client and Nicholas J. Frandsen as follows; (16) $45,000 to the client, necessarily on the grounds that this is the same amount of money that he is proposing to be paid for creation of the work entitled "Poem with a Gun to Its Head," and about which he states, quote, "it's more or less the number at which I price my life," and this is subsequently the same amount of money, before taxes, on which the client survived for one calendar year in 2016, and thereafter $45,000 to Nicholas J. Frandsen, as this is the amount of money the client believes the United States government still owes his childhood friend, and furthermore the client is fairly convinced that, quote, "if it means not having to make art in the United States of America, any honest person can live off a meager sum and be happy."

David Whelan

There is a spiral notebook waiting on the kitchen counter. It's barely recognizable by 6pm. The spine is flattened on one end and the pages no longer run backwards.

She leans in when she searches.

11:40 Down here David Wh~~ella~~n
A.M. Hushand
<u>Leave</u> Back 1pm

The wife spots every light that appears outside the house; the double headed flood light attached to the garage, the neighbor's newly remodeled kitchen made visible by custom track lighting, and the anonymous headlight pushed up the hill by an anonymous Buick. They arrive on cue: garage-neighbor-hill, and then return out of joint until her husband comes home. They are a collection of jumbled coordinations and tiny bursts of location, received by a panicked woman attempting to measure herself against the night.

The neighborhood is ill metrical. It's the same indoors: blinking clocks and ticking watches, timers and television countdowns. She goes upstairs to check the bathroom radio, then the bedroom alarm clock, the VCR, then back downstairs for the neigh-bro-hill-garage, apologizes, checks the second VCR, her new wristwatch, her son's cell phone, then returns these findings to their beginning.

> *The men were lined up behind Salvation Hospital, in a spot pronounced 'wu - thee', and shot around 4:10am. It was a Sunday. Nikos Belogiannis, Nikos Kaloumenos, Dimitris Batsis, and Ilias Argyriadis. He was my father, Ilias, shot by the military police.*

no
~~school~~) Do othing) ~~lunch~~ 11:30 am
~~Sep 4 20, 140? in 3HRS check tues~~
- - - - - - NO - - - - - - - - - - - car
~~thurs? open? in 3hrs~~ - - -
~~Bertucci's~~ open? ~~in 3 hours~~

The mother sits with her son at the dining room table, perpendicular, with blocks of paper spread out democratically. At first, she prefers to watch. He doesn't argue. Instead, he lets a few minutes pass, then kindly asks her to pick up the brush, dip it in water and mix whatever color she finds. She responds to these instructions.

They talk about common things: the weather, the house, the new neighbors who live both upstairs and across the street, the second husband who she cannot find, and the caravan of young girls, maybe cousins, who visit every week to paint. Is that your car outside? Do you know my son?

She follows her husband so close that at times she disappears entirely behind his back without his knowledge. Similarly, she shadows her son's brush strokes as though she mistrusts her own. She apologizes for and discredits any decision that is uniquely hers. The son uses that calm doctor's voice; the default language of those in control. A dynamic modulation of tone from high to low. She hears what he says in this voice.

8:30 put clothes
in dryer
WEDNESDAY Aug 20 - 2014
go Greek Rest 12:00? A.M.
Dave + Joan
Dave at Oil Change
Back at 11 for Joan
{ Dinner at Steve's at (6) - 7

Dave + Joan Wed. Aug 20 - 2014
*   Dave at Y
  Back at (5:30)

At times she describes her paintings out loud: the inside of a chair, a gorilla's foot, a sick egg.

Why is painting the assigned activity for rehabilitation?

Play it safe. Be positive.
Talk about the work. If your loved one is still verbal, ask about the artwork or a favorable color.

> *He was arrested for operating a secret radio station and printing press below our house. He built the crypt by hand. Cables and concrete. The house was known as 'Aura'. I was eight when my mother swallowed chicken pills, nine for the execution, and ten during the adoption.*

He becomes her as he becomes for her, everyone else. She follows his lines around and around, as if to shield them, by adding a soft buffer of ochre into orange. He extends her shapes out from the corner into the page.

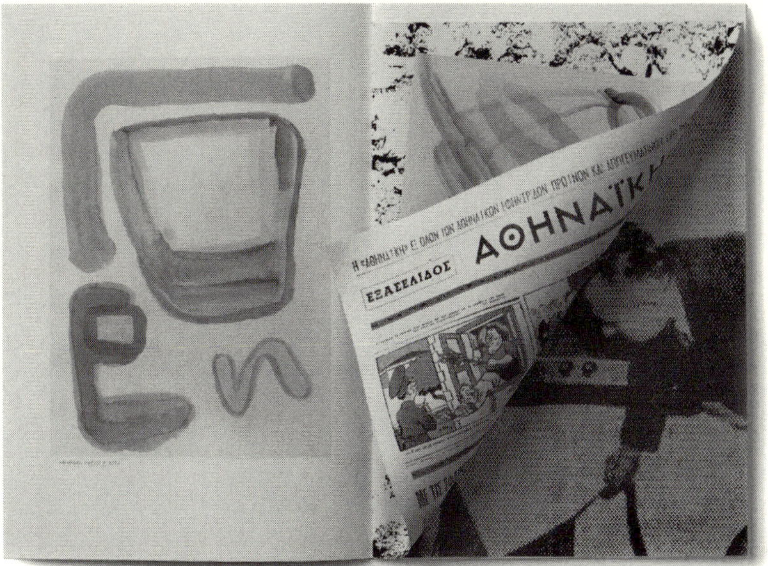
ΕΞΑΣΕΛΙΔΟΣ

Rachael Guynn Wilson

DIRECTIONS

NORTH

All winter two yellow bags
with plastic smiles

Decorate the tree's
bare limbs.

For awhile we tried to
stop the gap, became tired.

So long, tie up the curtains,
hang up the line.

If it's not working,
it's dreaming.

EAST

The afternoon is least
like a place by the blue door

An emerald vase
with pink peonies

Prose a time to call
mid-mornings are best

As evenings the walls
grow sentimental

It's cold and the Polish
bakery is closed

Winter, a shovel
in the packed snow-ice

Some trouble
staying in time

Temple throat
temple night

Sun is
sinus

I said "catch"
and it flew

SOUTH

In the pine forest Ponge never mentioned
the war. Clearly, very little having to do
with the world finds its way here

Strange, though, to be in the trees,
the world of birds, little
diaphragms fluttering

My head felt light and my chest heavy
on the 3rd floor looking out
as usual, but with more of everything

It's nighttime and a different feeling—
fog hangs on the clock tower,
water droplets cling to my window

Some days you're drawn
to white or damp or far
sidewalks swept by frost

Coral not settle
puffed or drawn
back pocket

Blue night rain
blue ring on a city building
some bank tower or blue corner

WEST

Mid-week so I don't look up.
Called her on the phone, said hello;
she says, Is that a question?

I couldn't bear to remove
the books from the shelf
in sudden self-excavation.

If anybody asks what
you are doing, say yes,
or say millions.

What's this work?
Sawdust still sleeping,
iron autumn oranges.

Needed a scream, got
corn syrup. This world,
an ultimatum a band
should hold or encircle.

III

I wrote something about where I'm from. I wrote that East LA meant being from a place, relation without fetish.

If I move to a new city I'll want to make friends with its post-woke citizenry, people who are good *without wearing it on their sleeves.*

Realizing that the line between cared for *and* patronized *is more a barcode. It flashes neon red at a diversity retreat, on Twitter sometimes, when I met your mom and she asked if mine was the woman in the photo.*

I haven't felt this coddled since... I haven't ever felt this coddled. And Casey agrees, we've talked about it.

We are talking about queerness and I say it's never felt like home. You call me a traitor. I say it was invented by university English departments. I say it isn't far fetched for a term to alienate members of our community. You say you thought I wasn't a communitarian and I ask, who told you? 'It just seems'—like I haven't read queer theory?

Judah said he wants me to grow my business and look for new, affordable options. He wrote about the window we carved from our busy schedules. A window to jump from. He hoped it was a perfect leap into traffic. He hoped it was an act of liberation.

You ask how I came to know all these people and I say can you ever really know a person? You ask if I'm being facetious and I say only a little.

—Editors

Catherine Chen

I want a body not conceptual but abrasive, like broken glass that tears open garbage bags.

I stopped at the emotional edge of capacity and wondered if this would be enough.

I wondered what constituted a form of something that was enough. No woman is enough. No secret is enough. I find you enough, that's why I loved you so readily.

I wondered if I was hysterical because the world, and every system it had created, wanted me to fully embrace hysteria. The kind of hysteria embodied by women who died so I could assume my position of suffering. It would have explained so much about me and nothing at all about the world. I cupped the water as it was poured into my hands. I did not flinch. I held the stainless steel pitcher just until it reached 180 degrees Fahrenheit. How could I have known then why I wanted to revel: in hysteria. I found no qualms about writing about hysteria and about locating myself in hysterical behavior.

Still, I was against diagnosis.

I slid into the metaphors and easy language of hysteria. I took pleasure in the simple statement "She is hysterical" and some more when I realized she and I were the same woman.

I wanted clear, articulate reasons for the violence we had been undone by. For years I struggled to make sense and could only blame myself for the many failures I entertained along the way. When you are determined to leverage your emotional capacity to the body's limit, there are going to be many walls you are tasked with climbing, or else detonating. I did not wish to harm anyone but forgot to account for the objects and desires my body would not be able to tolerate.

Wrecking myself, I thought, was its own domain of passion. Any expression of passion might be meaningful. I wondered if women who wrote letters to their lovers, letters that were later collected and published without their knowledge or consent, knew they would be betrayed. And by whom. I imagined a contemporary analogy for this situation and felt my chest cavity clench, embroiled in gendered depression. My nipples grew hard at the thought, my skin warm. I was broken before nine every morning, and this seemed both fine and deeply unfair.

By the pond, under moonlight, we evaluated our relationship to work, our relationship to the values we construed as false or wrong yet could not reject. Groups of ducks swam past, leaving their wake as witness. Unsolicited, one duck ventured toward us and offered a spin. We were overjoyed to be granted a private performance.

In emerging through this moment I became aware of materiality, a quality better observed than felt. I considered the histories which had been funneled into the shape of the unconscious. The textures, sounds, and capital swallowed whole by the earth. In migrating, names accrued debt. You entered a room and stripped. There was no exit; an immigration official eventually allowed your family, and mine by proxy, into a country we recognized as the one we had attempted to leave.

After grieving, we worked hard and bore children. We worked twice as hard to raise the children. Uninterested in family, we did not die until the day our skin turned bronze and our breath became exhaust.

The wet bark, dewy midnight. Calm and unwanting. How much we longed for melancholy, a melancholy we attached to historical images of girls dressed in white lace, intimate already with the expectations of the world and the people of that world like mothers and teachers and crossing guards and aunts who were not actually blood related and women walking on the street and writers and women writers and sympathizers and citizens and sycophants and actors whose approval was more sought after than anyone else and righteous community members and queers and invisible girls and, as an afterthought, themselves.

I couldn't shake off the shame I felt toward being able to write, wanting to write. On days when finding my keys seemed impossible, I was enamored by my ineptitude. I counted the number of unsuccessful attempts to unlock my apartment door.

I once had a body. I lost it,

then returned to terror, hoping to regain control of a self I had lost sight as mine. Was I ill? Was I unhinged? Was I not myself?

How the woman is located: activated by touch, loosened in time. Shake it off. Or fidget. I watched science fiction movies in which nude women were awakened as cyborgs. I became somebody who fidgeted without impunity or awareness; I couldn't stand it, I loved it.

Ted Dodson

★★★★★

Before you begin, make a few notes about the points you want to get across.

Try thinking of him as a friend.

Try to mention him.

There's nothing more frustrating than not knowing him!

You might want to think of the main points before you begin.

If possible, think of each point you want to make about him.

It's a good way to emphasize the importance of the point.

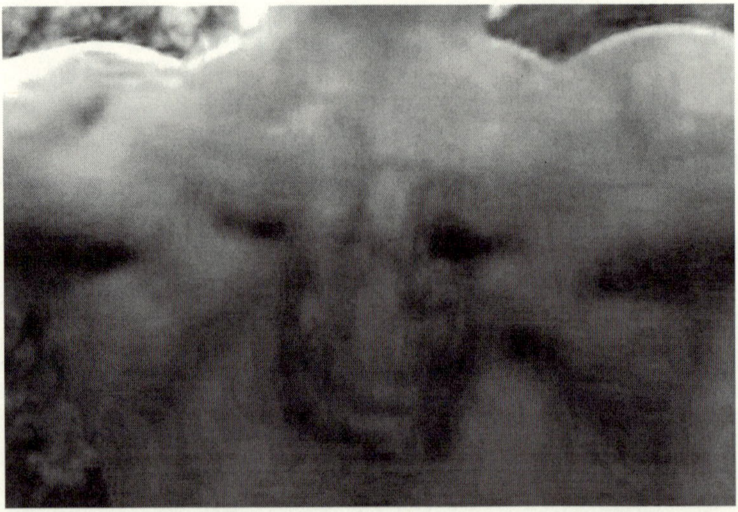

Try to get this across in the beginning.

He should know right away what you are getting into.

Think about this.

Does this fit?

What does this use?

What do you like or dislike about him?

Is he funny?

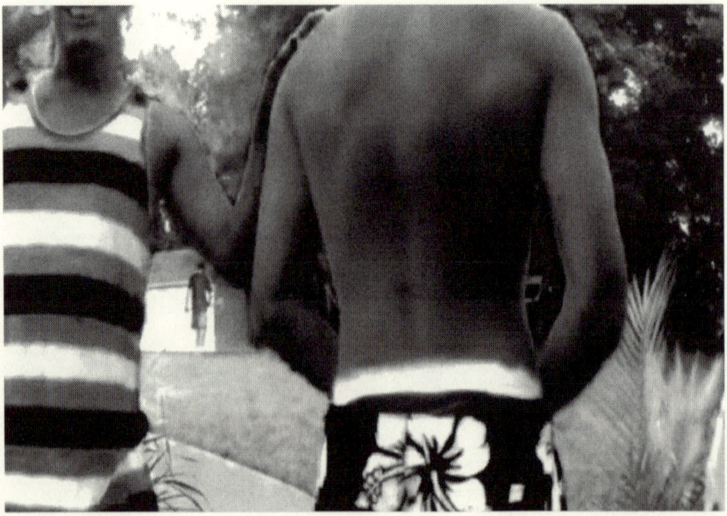

Does he give you a sense of yourself?

What is his voice like?

Try quoting him.

This is not absolutely necessary, but it's good.

Make sure you explain how you feel about him and why.

You should express your opinion and share it.

Or avoid it.

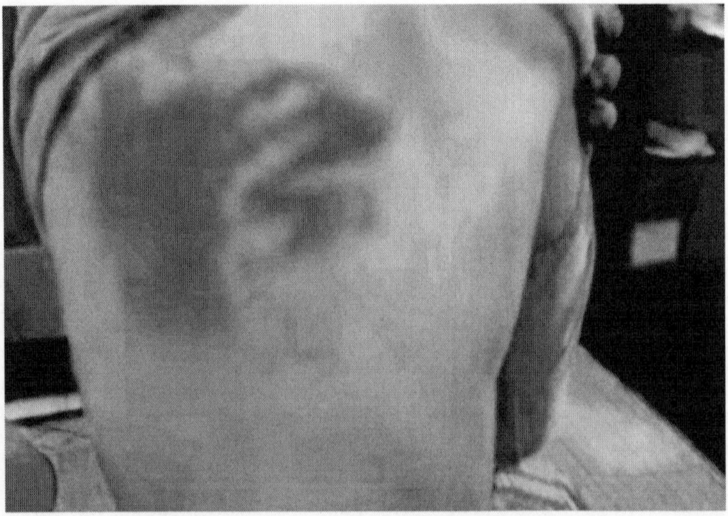

Do research about him and incorporate what you learn.

Biographical information can help you formulate your opinion about him and gives you depth.

Remember, any product of your mind may be helped by knowing something about him.

The chance to do this is an honor in and of itself.

The role you play is crucial.

Just remember that the focus is on him, not you.

Gather specific information about him, including the correct pronunciation of his name.

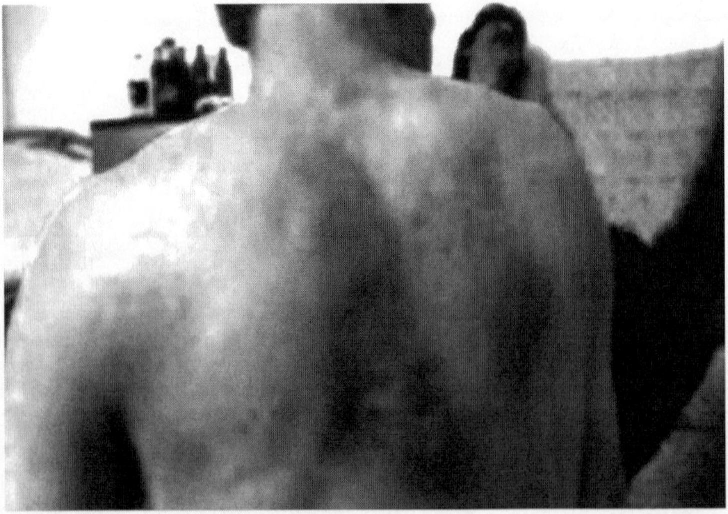

Also gather interesting stories and comments about him from people who know him well.

Find out how much time is set aside for him.

Also find out exactly what this entails—such as some combination of things.

Also learn about the size of things, where to do it, and other logistics.

Prepare.

Also develop.

Start with an explanation.

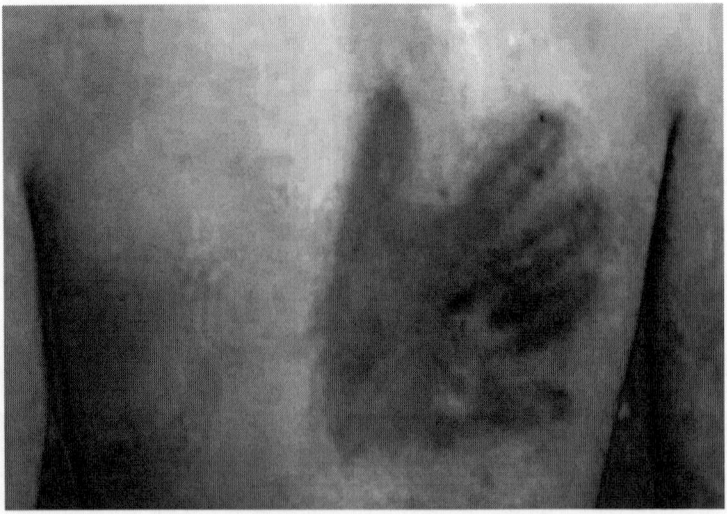

State the criteria.

He has a long and interesting tradition.

Explain it.

Build to a crescendo that eventually concludes.

Speak out loud to make sure you sound natural.

Make ample use of emphasis and allow for applause where necessary.

Make sure it flows well.

To build suspense, do not mention him until the end.

Remember, the focus is on him, not you.

Humor helps, but make sure it is not off-color, offensive, or open to misinterpretation.

Avoid triteness.

Do not sound insincere.

How serious or lighthearted do you want to be?

This need not be uniformly somber, just appropriate.

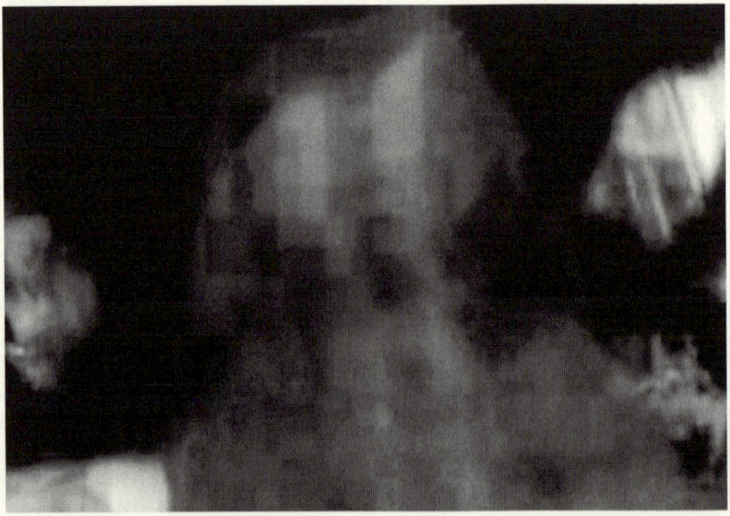

Some take a serious approach, but others are bold enough to add humor.

Your tone can also be partially determined.

Do this with him in mind.

Dwell on the positive, but be honest.

If he is difficult or inordinately negative, allude to it gently, as in "He has his demons, which are a constant battle."

Make sure you don't do anything that would offend, shock, or confuse.

For example, don't make any jokes about him that would be mysterious.

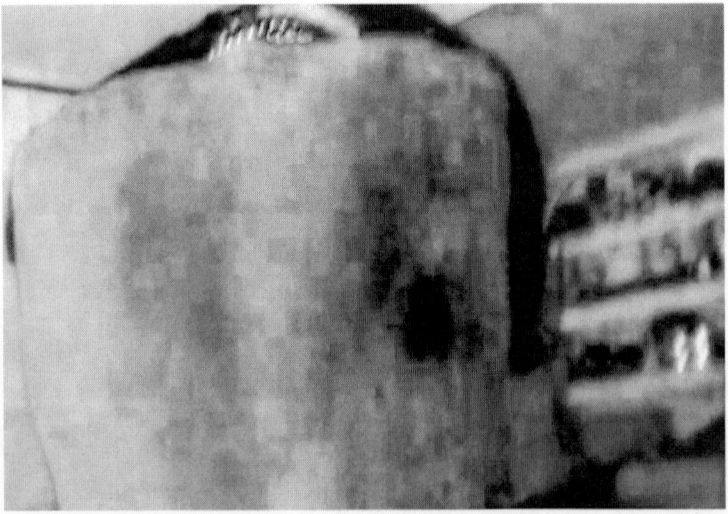

This doesn't have to give all of the basic information his life.

You can find a way of mentioning information while praising him.

Write down the names of the family members especially close to him.

Make sure you say something specific about his family life.

Avoid reciting a list of qualities he possesses.

Pretend that a stranger is here.

Brainstorm all his possible areas.

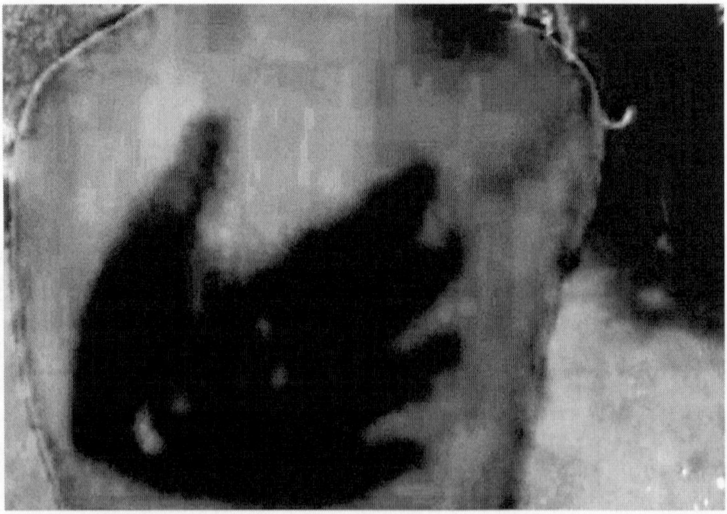

When you're ready, cover each thing in a logical order.

Remember that less is more.

You don't want to try his patience.

Once you're fairly confident, have some close friends or family members make sure that this is not only accurate but that it does well with capturing his essence.

They'll also be able to see if you are inappropriate, forget something important, or saying anything that is confusing or difficult to understand.

You can also ask your friends or family members.

This doesn't need to be perfect.

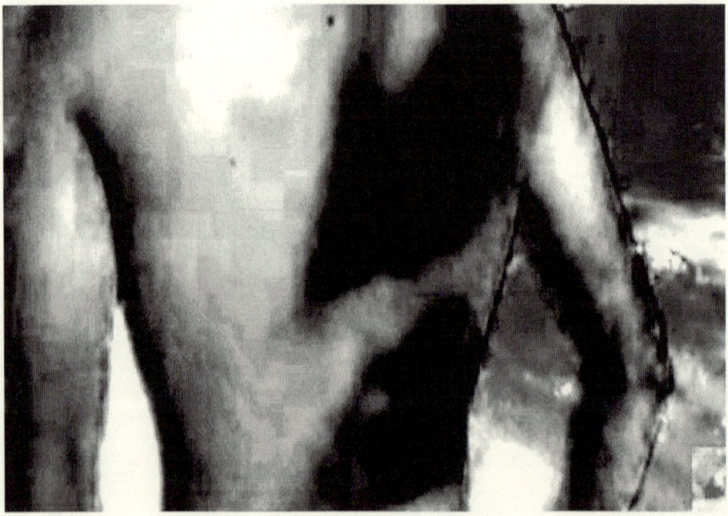

The best things are factual, honest, and respectful.

Talk about him.

You'll express regret about that.

If you wish, augment this by reading a poem.

Mia Kang

August 2nd, 6pm

Garage door opens. Two men, dark brown casket. Men standing beside the casket, not lying inside it. Who knows who's inside. Woman raises blinds to eye level. Men drape blue fabric over the casket. Two vehicles in the garage: one black hearse and one Dodge minivan, gray. Woman has her nose to the window. Do they see her? Garage door lowers. Both garage doors open halfway. Legs of men walking around the casket. Garage doors lower. A while later, they open again. Two men wheel the casket out of the garage, around the building through the parking lot, and up the long ramp to a side door. Someone opens the door from the inside. That's the last I see of that casket.

August 3rd, late morning

Two women get out of a car and go up the ramp to the side door. One, dressed in purple, leans heavily on a walker. They have to bang on the door before someone comes to open it. In the intervening minutes, the woman in purple looks as if she should not be standing for so long. Others arrive; the parking lot is half full. Some time passes. Garage door opens. Two men walk around a casket. One opens it briefly, adjusts something inside, then shuts it again. The woman at the window goes to get her glasses. The garage looks sharper now. The men walk around the casket carrying what look like short rods. There are a series of fastening sounds. For a long time, the men walk around the casket polishing its surfaces, especially the metal plates on the corners. The Dodge minivan pulls out into the parking lot. The casket is wheeled into the space between the two garage doors, perpendicular to the vehicles. Things get moved around inside the garage—not the casket, other miscellany. During this time, people are coming out of the funeral home. They come down the ramp into the August sunlight, cross the parking lot, and get into their cars. They drive away. They don't appear bereft. The minivan goes back into the garage. Garage doors close. The woman sits by the window waiting to see the hearse leave. After escorting the last mourners to their car, a woman with a clipboard goes back up the ramp and shuts the side door. The woman at the window, who has just left her life behind, thinks about how little was shown in the faces and bodies of the funeral goers. They simply looked tired. I have been waiting for twenty minutes and still haven't seen the hearse leave.

August 4th

No funerals. The woman only realizes this late at night, having spent the day shoving boxes back and forth across the floor. Perhaps a funeral took place without her noticing. She tries to remember. In fact, what happened is that she noticed cars pulling in and out of the parking lot, but no garage door activity. She realizes that in her mind, there is no separation between this day and the day before. When she saw cars pulling in, she believed they were the cars of the funeral home employees just now returning from yesterday's funeral. But they could have been the cars of entirely new funeral goers, or merely the cars of the funeral home employees coming to work in the morning and then leaving again in the evening. From the window above a funeral home parking lot, even an innocent lunch break might look like a funeral.

No funerals, ergo Google. The website says: "It's often seen as easier not to have a memorial service or funeral, and it's certainly seen as a less expensive alternative. But we're here to say this: an easy, cheaper path is not always a better one. Grief experts all agree: a ceremony is an important part of the healing process."

August 4th

Consumed by unpacking and alphabetizing books. Shelved by genre and publication date. Parking lot moderately active. Hearse got a quick wash.

As the sun lowers in the afternoon, the gables of the funeral home cast shadows like large uneven teeth across the parking lot.

August 5th, 8:30am

In the rain, the parking lot darkens to a terracotta hue, its large slabs shimmering with the dots of each drop's impact. It appears entirely right in relationship to the dark red brick of the building and the neat rounded shingles darkened to sienna. The woman at the window thinks to herself how the rain changes things, directs the eyes elsewhere. Yesterday she would have said the parking lot was your average gray concrete, if asked.

Two men in suits hold large black umbrellas and walk around the parking lot. They escort two women to their cars, then move to stand in the driveway. Their umbrellas bear a logo: Howard K. Hill Funeral Services. They joke lightly with each other; they are at work. A black limousine is parked along the sidewalk.

A blue minivan pulls into the driveway. "Good morning," one of the men says into the driver's window. Then he says a name, as a question, presumably the name of the deceased, ascertaining if the minivan is in the right place. He directs them to park in the lot. They emerge from the van under their own umbrella, climb the ramp, and go in to the funeral.

Once the service has started—she assumes the service has started now; it is 9am—the hearse pulls out of the garage and parks at the neck of the driveway. A few minutes later, a latecomer pulls in. The umbrella-wielding men have abandoned their welcoming station, and the black sedan pauses, then pulls in without instruction. It seems to the woman watching that the car pulls in quicker than necessary, rushing past the hearse. The rain has stopped, and the greeters have put down their umbrellas. One of them hurries to greet the latecomer, a young woman. They have what seems like a cheerful chat as he walks her through the parking lot to the front door. Do they know each other? Or is he so experienced that he can contrive a cheerful chat with any arriving mourner? Or is she not very sorry that the deceased has passed on?

Without the rain falling, the color goes out of things. The black asphalt of the street dulls to gray, the reddish hue of the parking lot fades to a matte and unappealing orange. The flat black tar roof over the garage no longer bounces with sparks of water, but settles into a mottled wash, darker where water has pooled on its surface and brighter, almost white, where there is only a thin sheen of water reflecting the sky.

The casket emerges from the side door covered in an American flag. Four men wheel it down the ramp. The driver of the hearse opens the back, and the men slide the casket into the vehicle. After that they disperse. One goes to put the folding cart used to roll the casket out away in the garage. One repairs to one of the limousines out front, puts something in the trunk, and disappears from view. The driver of the hearse opens the back door of the cab, tosses his coat inside, and gets into the driver's seat. It is very mundane, to throw one's jacket into the long black car carrying a dead person.

The limousines go first, then the hearse, then the cars idling in the parking lot, waiting to follow. The limousines and the hearse have been outfitted with orange flags, presumably to designate a funeral. Across the roof of the funeral home garage and the parking lot behind it and the park beyond that, I see the line of cars driving smoothly away.

August 5th, 1:50pm

A shot is fired in the parking lot. A beat passes, then another is fired, then another. The woman stands up from where she is lying on the floor and looks out the window to see three men in military uniforms, two holding rifles and one holding a bugle. A man in a suit is standing at the side door, holding it open against his back. His hands are clasped in front of him, and his face is clenched and solemn, appearing to fight tears, but it is hard to tell. The bugle player lifts his instrument and performs the slow, watery notes. The woman at the window is crying. She uncrosses her arms and clasps her hands, imitating the man at the door. This is the first thing I have observed at the funeral home that has given me any feeling at all.

August 5th, 2pm

Looking back at her entries, the woman realizes she has made a mistake. The first entry dated August 4th mentions "no funerals," but it is dated incorrectly. It was written after midnight the night of August 3rd, meaning that there was, in fact, a funeral, as documented in the "late morning" entry from that day. So the temporal confusion in her late night entry was not confusion at all, but was her incorrect perception of her own incorrect perception. The cars which pulled in were probably returning from the funeral she wrote about in the morning entry. Based on her late night entry, she must have felt, that night, as if two days had passed in one, although she was writing about feeling as if only one day had passed in two.

Earlier in the evening of August 3rd, on the phone with C, she had described her state as a "grief haze."

The departed goes forward into unknown parts, utterly alone. And this person who salves me, I have left him behind.

August 6th

It is Sunday and she has been sitting for hours. The funeral home is closed today.

What are the rules? Should she watch for funerals every day? Should she make an effort to see as much as she can, or only record what she observes incidentally? What is the point of switching to the first person at the end of every entry? What is the point of any of this, when she is not, after all, Lydia Davis?

What are the rules?

> Don't sleep too late.
> Make the bed every day.
> Get dressed, even if you don't leave the house.
> Wear makeup, even if you don't leave the house.
> Try to leave the house.

I am waiting for a phone call.

August 8th

Out the window, someone is shouting across the street to ask what time the funeral starts. "11am," replies the nonplussed funeral home employee who is placing "PLEASE / NO PARKING / FUNERAL" signs in the parking lot.

How many funerals will it take before they all become a blur of uninteresting repetition? Will I be able to find something fascinating about each one? Or is the repetition the point?

August 8th, 10:30am

First to arrive is an old woman, small and stooped, leaning on a cane as she crosses the parking lot. The tall, dutiful employee who seems to serve as parking lot manager and greeter approaches her. "Can you make it up the stairs?" he asks. She doesn't hear him, and he repeats the question. "Can you make it up the stairs?" I can't hear her reply, but she continues walking up the sidewalk toward the front door, where the stairs are. I imagine him taking her elbow as she climbs.

August 8th, 11am

I hear a mechanical sound in the parking lot, like a spring popping open. I look out to see a small box truck parked there, back door open and preparing to unload something. The tall employee is standing behind it, with a silver metal folding cart open at the ready. One garage door is open. A longhaired, goateed man, short and broad, adjusts something in the back of the truck. Two long prongs extend from its opening, parallel to the ground and several feet below the top of the box. The delivery man slides a casket out onto the prongs, presumably from a shelf inside the truck body. He presses a button and the casket descends smoothly. He and the tall man lift it together, one at the head and one at the foot, transferring it to the silver cart. They wheel it into the garage. Then they wheel out two square and apparently heavy rectangular objects on another cart. They look like oversized portfolios, but they are shiny and wooden like caskets. There are small engraved plaques on each one. The men lift them into the truck. The tall man folds up the cart and puts it back in the garage. The longhaired man gets into the truck and drives away.

I note that the arriving casket was wrapped in a plain blue moving blanket, its material identical to the blankets used to move my things last week, but its dimensions perfectly cut and seamed to fit a casket. Beneath that was a white plastic wrapping that looks like a garbage bag. I wonder, not for the first time, about the physical logistics of having a body sitting in the garage all morning. Do they have some kind of cold storage? Are these bodies already treated somehow so that they can withstand a day or two at room temperature?

August 9th, 8:30am

The man who must be the funeral home director or owner arrives with a styrofoam cup of coffee in his hand. Shortly after that, the Dodge minivan pulls into the parking lot and parks in the garage. I expect the tall employee to emerge from it; instead, a different man appears, shorter and wider. In fact, he looks a lot like the man I took for a mourner during the bugle call the other day. Was it him? Was he simulating grief, or actually feeling it? Did I imagine the expression on his face? Was he merely squinting at the sunlight reflecting off the parking lot surface?

August 9th, 8:50am

The tall man arrives in a Ford SUV of some kind.

August 9th, afternoon

Today is a day of discussing cars. Three funeral home employees, and later, the flower delivery man, stand around in the parking lot in the shade of the garage and discuss someone's red Mustang.

August 10th, 7:54am

The red Mustang arrives again. The older man who seems like he is the boss is driving it. Is that the reward for running a funeral home? One makes enough money to finally buy the car you wanted as a teenager?

He walks through the parking lot toward the front of the building, turning his keys over in his hand. He pauses at one point, looking around proprietarily. Then he continues, disappearing around the corner and presumably into the building.

Arrival number two pulls in. Silver BMW X3. I'm guessing it is the tall man. Garage door opens. The X3 is idling in a parking space. A man whom I've never seen arrives on foot. He goes into the garage and greets someone; the proprietor must be in there. At last the X3 driver turns the car off and gets out. The new man comes over and greets him—no, it's a woman. She's looking at her schedule on her phone. I can see the color coded rectangles from the window.

Another car, silver Lexus ES 330. I don't know the names of these cars, I am looking them up as I go. The new man brings the second Lexus driver the plastic bag he's been carrying around. Apparently there is food in it. "You saved me many mornings by bringing me breakfast," says the new man as he hands it over. The proprietor, standing across the parking lot by the garage, greets the 330 driver: "Hello Wilbur." The woman makes a joke, playing hurt that Wilbur's the only one who's gotten a greeting. The proprietor jokes back that it's because she's on her phone. "This is business," she says, then puts the phone away. "I'm done." In their banter, I learn the proprietor's name is Jerry.

Another woman arrives. I've seen her before, but only once. "Becky," Jerry greets her. The Dodge minivan is right behind her, and the man I mistook for a mourner gets out.

In the garage, all the workers are bustling around. Two of the men involve themselves with changing out the ice in an ice chest.

I overhear a fragment: "Not if they go on and on about saving souls," says Jerry. I need a microphone down there. I go to get my glasses. The men start carrying stanchions with maroon velvet ropes attached to them to the back of the van. Wilbur comes out carrying a handful of Please No Parking Funeral signs. Then he wheels the ice chest out of the garage and adds it to the van.

The new man says to Wilbur across the parking lot, "Hey man, I'm gonna throw this bag in the hearse—I mean, not the hearse, the limo." "Yeah, ok," Wilbur says. I remember that Jerry drove the hearse for one of the funerals I watched on Saturday. Is he the proprietor after all? Does a proprietor of a funeral home always drive the hearse?

The flowers I saw get delivered yesterday come out from the garage in the arms of one of the women. Someone pulls the hearse forward slightly so they can open the back. I see someone in the back of the garage lift a white box, probably three feet long, from a cart into the back of the hearse. It looks like a casket. Is there a child in the casket? Was it in there all night, just sitting in the garage? Or did they keep it inside and bring it out later? Or did I somehow miss the delivery of the casket in the very early morning, or even in the night?

Everyone is getting ready to go. The second woman who arrived moves her car so the limo can be pulled out from the second garage door. The hearse and limo pull out—I think the new man is driving the hearse, and Wilbur is driving the limo. Jerry pulls his Mustang into the garage where the limo was. He revs his engine unnecessarily before he gets out. His employees make fun of him. "Look at the color of that car," the faux-mourner jokes. He seems to be implying a midlife crisis. "Yeah, but you liked driving it," says Jerry. They all leave the garage and close the doors.

The six employees are all standing around, bantering, then suddenly they are in a circle with joined hands. The second woman to arrive leads a prayer. All I can hear of the prayer is "our words and actions." "Amen," they say, and repair to their vehicles. Everyone drives away: hearse first, then limo, then the second woman, then the Dodge minivan. The two silver Lexuses (Lexi?) are left in the parking lot. I watch to see if the party will turn the corner two blocks away, and they do. I watch the Dodge minivan pass out of sight.

August 10th, 2:30pm

Overheard through the window: "All right, have a good weekend. Tell your wife I said hi." "I will. If you see her, tell her *I* said hi."

August 11th, 7:15pm

After a quiet day, I hear the sound of a motorcycle coming into the parking lot at speed. Moving to the window, I watch it pull a wide curve to park in front of the first garage door. The rider dismounts, back to me, and pulls off his helmet. I think it might be the man I mistook for a mourner. He's in a full suit, as all the funeral home employees always are. He puts his helmet on the seat and pulls his gloves off. He puts the gloves in the storage compartment, looks at his phone for a moment, then starts walking slowly through the parking lot toward the front of the funeral home. He's walking slowly, still looking at his phone and swinging his keys, which are on a silver chain of unnecessary length. It's not the faux-mourner. I speculate that he might be Howard himself. Originally, I assumed Jerry was Howard, until I learned his name. This man looks a little young to be Howard though; perhaps he is Howard, Jr. He turns the corner and goes out of sight along the sidewalk, toward the entrance, holding the phone up to his ear as he walks away.

August 11th, 7:40pm

The garage door opens. The man comes out and moves the bike into the garage. He has earphones in, but doesn't seem to be talking on the phone. He goes back into the garage and gets into the Dodge minivan. The van pulls out into the parking lot, and the man gets out and pushes the button to close the garage door. It must, in fact, be the faux-mourner, whom I have seen arrive in the minivan before. Is that man, after all, Howard? He gets in the van and drives away.

August 14th, 9:50am

After a quiet weekend of almost no funeral home activity, I watch the tall man and one of the other men wheel a cart with a body on it up the ramp and into the building. The body is wrapped in a thick maroon covering. The second man is wearing scrubs; he must be the person who prepares the bodies. But where did the body come from? Is there a refrigerator in the garage? Was it delivered early this morning before I was awake? It is almost as if people are not dying and arriving at Howard K. Hill for their rites, but as if Howard K. Hill produces dead people on command when any party requests a funeral.

August 16th, 1:34pm

A large white casket with gold fixtures gets rolled up the ramp on a gold cart. Only one man, the man in scrubs, moves the casket, when on other occasions I have seen two men pushing caskets this way, and with more difficulty. Does that mean this casket is empty?

August 19th, 9:30am

An incredible vintage car pulls into the parking lot. I look it up—it is a Pontiac Le Mans Sport, blue with a greenish hue in the sunlight. A man I've never seen before, svelte, young, parks the thing sideways in front of the garage doors and gets out. Two teenage boys unfold themselves out of the passenger-side door. The car is parked at the slightest angle to the building, making it look like it's positioned for a photo shoot or a car show. The suave man strolls with ease through the parking lot, while the boys amble in their teenaged way behind him. As he turns onto the sidewalk, he brings his phone to his ear, making a call. They go into the funeral home. Is this, at last, Howard?

Someone else pulls up in a Chevrolet SUV. One garage door opens and the boys and the man I take to be their dad come out to greet the arrival. Maybe she is their mother? They all stand around in and outside the garage for a while, then the boys start carrying out a long hose. Dad is wearing a blue U Conn athletic t-shirt, white shorts, and gray Nikes, with aviators hanging from his shirt. He takes a bucket of cleaning supplies out of the trunk of the Pontiac. "Undo that kink," he tells the boys. One of them brings another bucket and a large blue sponge out from the garage. "Is the water on?" the man asks, and the taller boy squirts the hose a little. Once everything is set, Dad starts to hose down the car. I had assumed the boys would be responsible for the washing, but evidently they are not to be trusted with it. Dad soaps the sponge and the shorter boy walks behind him with the hose, rinsing. Once they've finished the front half of the car, Dad instructs the boys to do the back. I remember this, I remember being taught how to properly wash a car by my dad. The boys don't seem particularly enthusiastic, but they don't seem reluctant either. I send a picture of the scene to C; I can't resist. When they finish washing, they begin to polish.

When they are nearly finished, two men arrive in a four-door pickup truck. Dad takes a call. "I'm over here washing the car," he says. I assume it is the men in the truck on the other end of the line. They come over to where Dad is crouching and polishing a tire. He introduces himself: Howard! He introduces his son, Matthew, and his son's friend, Eric. Then he introduces the woman: Jackie. From the way he does it, it seems she is not his wife. The two men are in slacks and button downs, and one wears a tie. I can overhear bits of their conversation, and I think they are talking about Charlottesville. Howard begins telling them about an event on Monday, at 6:30. The bearing of the two men makes me think they are church affiliated.

The man who came by on a motorcycle one night arrives in the black Escalade that is usually parked to the right of the garage. He has two young sons with him—I think they are twins. Howard greets them genially. I wonder if the motorcycle man is a partner in the business. He seems to move through the spaces with as much ease as Howard, and evidently uses the place as a private parking lot. He loads some things into the Escalade, then he and Howard begin discussing something. I wonder if they are all heading to some kind of gathering together. "Father Lovejoy," says Howard, speaking to the men in slacks. "We'll leave here in about five minutes or so." The motorcycle man gets in the Escalade and pulls out. Jackie follows him in her Chevy.

Howard begins chatting with the man in the tie. The man starts telling Howard about a campaign he started called "Stop the Killing." Howard mishears him. "Who is that?" "Stop the Killing," says the other man. "Oh, *Stop* the Killing," Howard says. "I thought you said Scott." I can't catch all of what they are saying, but it is obvious that Howard is a powerful figure, someone the man in the tie wants to bring onboard. Howard moves around his car, finishing the details, responding with humor but noncommittal attention. "You should have been a salesman," he says at one point. Then they begin discussing politics. Howard favors one candidate in a local race, after the other candidate approached him for support unfavorably.

Eventually, it is time to go. "Let's go see the property," says Father Lovejoy to his companion, and all three men and the two teenagers go into the funeral home through the garage. Is it possible that Howard is selling the funeral home? After fifteen minutes or so, they come out. "How far away is it?" asks

Father Lovejoy. "About three or four minutes," says Howard. He presses the button to close the garage door. The men in slacks get into their truck, and the gangly teenagers shrink themselves into the Pontiac. Howard gets in, sunglasses on, and drives out of the parking lot. The men in the pickup truck follow him out.

Jeff Alessandrelli and Amy Lawless

THEN I BUST OUT

When I'm in a slump, I comfort myself by saying if I believe in dinosaurs, then somewhere they must be believing in me. And if they believe in me, then I can believe in me. Then I bust out.

—Mookie Wilson

REVIEW OF DEAD RAT 5/10

Buddha said it's important to take walks with no destination in mind. Just walk! Today I turned a corner and passed a dead rat curled in a C shape in the middle of the street. It could have been mistaken for rolled up used athletic socks. What kind of walk was the rat taking when it was run over? Suddenly I ended up at Berl's and read two Bernadette Mayer sonnets *"You dare to study philosophy baby I'll tell you / About fucking Aristotle I never planned to fall"* and another one. As I returned homeward I saw the rat again. This time it resembled a quesadilla or a pancake. According to Urban Dictionary a "flat food" is anything you can slide under a door. This term was popularized by computer programmers who tend to have very poor diets from sitting for long stretches of time while relying heavily on food from vending machines. I'm sorry I keep mentioning the dead like this is some palimpsest.

REVIEW OF GREAT WHITE SHARK ("I WAS LIKE, YEAH, SURE, WHY NOT?") (∞ OUT OF ∞)

There is only one certainty in shark mating:
fertilization is internal & once the egg hatches, the shark continues
to gestate within the body of the mother.
Mating is horrific for female Great White Sharks.
He holds her still by biting her head, gills, or fin.
Then he inserts his claspers, dual penises—he's got one for each fin—
which open like an umbrella inside of her, and then these sacks
he had filled with water beforehand flush into her in theatrical bursts
& push his seed further and further inside of her.
Wonder if she regrets going to that whale carcass to eat some dead whale.
Apparently every shark knows what you're
looking for if you show up at a whale carcass.
I swear I'm not making this up!
It is essential for all Great White Sharks to keep moving
to stay alive. They are *obligate ram ventilators*, so to breathe
water has to be passing through, and the only way to do so is to swim
and move. So, you never stop swimming if you're a living shark:
& you can't stop breathing if you're a living human. You can hide away,
but at some point you will smell a recently expired whale across the way for which
you hunger. Hey did I mention that the dual clasper is essentially a double penis, really fascinating stuff, right? It opens like an umbrella to deposit the semen and keep it in her. Once I read a Reddit AMA about a guy who has two penises and he had this great life (called "I am the guy with two penises"), and a boyfriend *and* a girlfriend, and he had life pretty figured out, or at least it seemed like it. He was acting like everything in his life was amazing, and maybe it is, but what about the middle of the night thoughts? What about forgetting your keys or when rent goes up and you don't know what is going to happen tomorrow or if just knowing you'll die alone if you don't do something to change? I guess when you have two penises, these problems don't plague you, you're never alone, you are always having sex with both of your penises. I thought the article was fake so I pulled it out on my phone during a New Year's party (as 2014 swung into 2015) in Greenpoint and asked a few friends what they thought in a totally casual manner as if I didn't care at all and would be cool if they weren't interested but maybe they would be and we could chat, but they didn't have any good ideas. Teresa and I found a photo and analyzed whether it was "real" and it seemed pretty real to us, but what do we know? I totally forgot about that night & now it seems so impossible to imagine the impact of having two of something that I have zero of. A human woman must go to the gynecologist every year or two. The gynecologist inserts a speculum into the woman to collect flesh to convert the flesh into data about the woman. The speculum is bivalved with blades that are hinged and closed. A shark has a clasper that opens up into two. And the human penis is, generally, a singular construction. Thanks for asking: a gynecological exam seems hugely preferable to getting fucked by a male Great White Shark. First of all it's for preventative health and secondly, you don't get maimed for life. But there is something psychically unsettling about getting scraped.
Female Great White and Tiger Sharks have these giant bite marks
on their fins and bodies. Biologists say she "heals quickly" but we know, wink wink, what's really going on. Whole sections of her body are removed!
That said, Great White Sharks never stop growing.
The growing slows down considerably over time, but never stops for as long as the shark is alive.
Sharks can breed up until the end of their lives. But Great Whites don't like to eat humans
because we are too bony & they have trouble digesting our high bone-to-muscle/fat ratio.
Eating whales is both more appropriate for them and where they meet to mate.

The Discovery Channel has this thing called "Shark Week;" you've probably heard of it.
And it's actually Shark Week as I write this believe it or fucking not!
As part of Shark Week, Olympic swimmer and massive bong ripper
Michael Phelps will race a Great White Shark tomorrow night.
Phelps said "Being in the water and seeing how fast they can go in a straight line over an extended period of time was intriguing to me. I was like, 'Yeah, sure, why not? Let's see who would win a race.'"

REVIEW OF RACCOONS (0 STARS OUT OF 10)

When I was in third grade, my sister, dad and I went to something called the "Dad and Me Camp-er-ee!" in Cape Cod, Brewster, Massachusetts. I was not a "joiner" but my older sister Molly who I put in a lot of my poems (I worshipped her) was a Girl Scout. My dad and sister and I spent the day in in a row boat (my dad did all the rowing), then making candles with wax and string, and eating camping food like s'mores. It was delightful. After the s'mores we went into the elevated tent which had 4 cots - today they would call it "Glamping" or "Fancy Camping"—we threw our sleeping bags upon the cots. But we had disobeyed the rule of "no outside food"—I think we had a bag of Cheetos and my dad had an extra beer. My sister made these real show-offy candles: one of a snake and one of an apple. She was a real show off with her artistic talents and was making a point about the Garden of Eden and women and for all I knew the patriarchy. Like I said, a show off. She couldn't just "make a candle." I made this lumpy cylindrical candle that looked exactly like a candle because I was thinking of function over fashion. In the dead of night a scratching sound appeared out of nowhere. Raccoons (more than one) were in the tent attacking the Cheetos and the candle shaped like an apple. The raccoon (I am not making this up) bit the candle shaped like an apple. We only found this out later because we ran out (all three of us) and parked our asses in my dad's 1989 Plymouth Reliant which had like no leg room. It was fine for me since I was in third grade, but he was not a happy camper, yuk yuk. Anyway we slept there and the next morning we returned to the tent to get our shit and found the wax apple, bitten. We were supposed to help serve breakfast to the other girls and dads, but we were all so groggy and depressed we took off and ate at Friendly's near the Sagamore bridge (the bridge that separates Cape Cod from mainland Massachusetts). Molly had grabbed the somehow more precious snake and it remained in our bedroom until our little sister destroyed it with her toddler hands.

REVIEW OF TYRANNOSAURUS REX 10/10

My first kiss was in the Egypt Room
At the Museum of Fine Arts Boston.
I was sixteen.
He had lent me his copy of Jurassic Park—the book—
In May or June.
Over that summer I read the book &
Didn't think about
Him.
In September when I
Returned it to him I had to wear a bra & my hair was
A Manic Panic color I can't remember: a dark purplish-red.
Fuschia Shock? New Rose?

He said the book was good & I trusted him.
He wanted to be an archaeologist, but now
He's an anthropologist.
People or animals? He studies people.
He studies the connection between democracy and furniture.
He studies fonts and democracy.

Looking back he was clearly laying serious ground work.
If you look at the cover of Michael Crichton's *Jurassic Park* paperback,
there's a skeletal outline of T Rex.
Its small hands surround the
M in the author's first name. The teeth of the fossil
Drawing are sharp and jagged. The only thing missing
Is the size & grandeur of the animal.

Growing up, my sister's favorite dinosaur was the Stegosaurus
And she said I could choose any other dinosaur as my favorite.
I wavered between the vegetarian Triceratops
And the Tyrannosaurus Rex
Finally settling on T-Rex.

During my first kiss
We stood in a dark room
Surrounded on all four sides
By hieroglyphic art work
Of people doing things
Painted upon limestone.
A glimmer of light from a corner
Would have fallen on my back
But I didn't notice.
A mummified body took up
The center of the room—
Chaperoning I suppose.
You gotta fall in love around art.
Teeth acted as emissaries for our skulls
And clanked together like champagne toasts.

Afterwards filled with teen lust or whatever
We wandered to the bigger room of mummies—including
A mummified cat
Which is so
Tiny &
Strange.
Around the time we broke up
He hugged his pet cat while sitting on a tiny chair
In the corner of his bathroom.
Oh right, it's called a toilet seat.
He looked so small sitting there.
He didn't want to let her go,
But she jumped out of his arms
And down the stairs.
Let us start by knowing the dead.
They're easy & immovable.
They shed secrets but
Stay still.
The living squirm out of our arms
And leave you
Never mummified.

The Jurassic Park movie
was tremendous. Living dinosaurs
Are true ghosts—the impossible.
Remember Jeff Goldblum pouring
Water onto his hand like a maniac?
Describing chaos theory or is he bolstering
Me up against my own loneliness? Is he
Convincing me that I won't die alone?

Why do I like T-Rex?
He can't see you if you don't move.
So I get real still. I sit
In a pink room.
I write in my green book.
Who can see me?

REVIEW OF TRICERATOPS (10 OUT OF 10)

The observable Universe has existed for around 13.8 billion years. If we shrink that span of time down to a single year, with the Big Bang occurring at midnight on 1 January, the first Homo sapiens made an appearance at 22:24 on 31 December. It's now 23:59:59, as it has been for the past 438 years, and at the rate we're going it's entirely possible that we'll be gone before midnight strikes again.

— Nick Hughes, "Do We Matter in the Cosmos?"

The new thinking about loss is no different than the old thinking about loss, yadda yadda yadda. But loss has never been about thoughts new or old and to believe so is to believe only in humanity.

The average dinosaur's fecal matter could sometimes last as long as the average human being's lifespan—did you know that? Can you believe it? It's true. Kingly marauders, dinosaurs wandered the world for180+ million years, whereas humans have done so for less than 200,000. Who's to speak of absence, of loss? Not humans, poets, egotists. Like us, dinosaurs were literate in fear and all types of abandon, but they possessed an ignorance that even if I could unread everything ever I've read, unhear or misinterpret every syllable spoken, I could never hope to possess. Outside the confines of man-made society, Thomas Hobbes wrote, life is "solitary, poor, nasty, brutish and short" and according to Hobbes this was every dinosaur's way of life. But I would disagree with what a 16th-century British political philosopher could impart about all kinds of non-human living. In his nasty, brutish and shortly human-constructed correctness he 's incorrect about all the rest.

Take, for instance, the triceratops, her horn a glimmering beacon. It is widely believed that triceratops traveled in socially-minded herds, each creature not itself but part of a greater whole. Some triceratops even had established family groups, within which they nurtured one and other as a family, protected one and other as a family. Triceratops were vegetarian, the most prominent of the hippy dinosaur group. They cold chilled until they were fiercely harshed against—and then it was not every triceratops for herself but instead a focus on that *Three Musketeers* "one for all and all for one" vibe. (This vibe eventually failed all three of the Musketeers, of course, in different ways; one always growing more important than all.) For a triceratops there was no ego, no scope of the valiant, needy self.

But it's the horn that the triceratops is remembered for, art installation appendage that makes her what she is. For eons it was assumed that a triceratops' horn was a combative instrument against both prey and predators, but recent evidence has illuminated that in fact each horn (and no two were alike) was used for courtship purposes, as a means of attraction and, hopefully, procreation. Horn as resplendent plumage, as fierce erotica. Horn as a decision to start a family, to settle down into love 's namelessness.

Having the ability to watch dinosaurs interact—grazing, nuzzling, fucking, bounding—is the only loss I want to feel but will never get the chance to. Real shit. Maybe it's for the best, I'd be so bludgeoned with energy.

It's not hard to master, no. 180 million years; less than 200,000. Absence, absence and ego. The peculiar notorieties of lack. Has a bird ever alighted upon your arm? Feels like a dinosaur is tickling you tenderly, dinosaur new and old you'll never see. Don't remember me.

REVIEW OF ALPACA (9.5 OUT OF 10)

Naked, but an elegant naked, done with verve. Shower over, walking from the bathroom to the bedroom I call my life, absently looking out the westward leaning window while doing so. There, an alpaca staring straight back at me, 30 feet away, its thick fleece morassing its deep-set eyes. To say that we "studied" one another in that instant would be pettily academic.

You know how at a certain point in 80's movies one character always looks deeply into another character's eyes and immediately knows what that character is thinking and feeling? And the viewer is similarly enlightened and this shift proves significant, signals something of weight and heft to later take with you when you leave your friend's apartment and enter the brightly lit, Bloody Mary'd street?

The alpaca and I stared at one another and that wasn't it until it was. He or she scurried off with a group of similarly fleeced denizens and I stared at them as they scurried, away into away. The school of thought that insists *Wherever you go there you are* is one that I flunked out of, never to complete. In an eternal instant that alpaca *knew* me and such knowledge has yet to reveal itself to anyone else.

I was naked, looking at nothing out the window. I needed to find a good mirror to study myself in but didn't know where to start.

Feliz Lucia Molina

SAN FERNANDO VALLEY

I was born with a Pennysaver in a bingo bag
of dabbers, green cards, and pineapple candy
Someones cousin
introduced someone else's cousin
which later gave birth to us
Echo distance from a swap meat
of Barbie aluminum balloons
Whose lives depended on heavy lines
waiting for an exit out of an island
of things lost stolen and burned
An amalgam of imperialists
and communists took over the Bicolano estate
and good for them
I never believed in partys
There was a time when the Japanese
were not your friends
There was a time
when everyone ran for the Baguio mountains
gold and babies melting and dying
In the tropical horror Our Lady of Peñafrancia
emerged like a wet rag
Jesus Christ in burned curtains
I'm basically certain
this is how
it all went down
watching nanay do her crossword
facing a wall of cats
cut out from old calendars
In this crumbling space
that once was a crisis heterotopia
for the abandoned and unloved

HOUSE HUNTERS

Mother beats up the sky
at redemption scams
where everything floats

Lies all lies
in a foreclosed house

We watch the seasons slide on House Hunters
we watch with hungry eyes and everything to lose

We stick our tongues out for this
Colonizing debt-collector Christ

Mother and I are alone
and the television is alone too
and the things on the television
are more important than us
the things on the television
have always been more important than us

Someone else's house
takes up so much space
in our house
which is not a home
on a Friday evening

There's a bedroom full of expired
green jelly juice from Seafood City
Mother, does anterograde amnesia
sound familiar
do you remember the first scam
someone ever sold you

MARRIAGE: A FRAGMENT

Gravity. Graves,
lifeless matter; consciousness

forever covered
by skull and skin

When the spirit goes away
the body knows and goes the other way

dispersed or into earth.

If space has curves
it could explain curves
on Earth
and how they are learned
in architecture, furniture

If curves in space
are because of matter
and energy
that can't be seen
or even read

That makes it untranslatable.

If something pulls
this
way or that
ward, it's not
gravity

But a preference, an invisible darkthing

prefers
one direction
over another

And that is grace
interacting with
another grace

In what is mostly
imaginary

DAD SENDS UPDATES ABOUT OUR LADY OF FATIMA.

fwd: AMERICA NEEDS FATIMA

How does one respond?

This one's about a 'family man in Florida who's been traveling for 18 years in his van bringing the Pilgrim Statue of Our Lady of Fatima into homes, schools, churches, nursing homes, hospitals...'

I wonder if the statue has been to prisons.

As a Fatima Custodian, he doesn't get paid for bringing the Virgin around all over the state. He just wants to voluntarily spread the message - and of what?

So what if the Virgin Mary is real?

God's mom might be as real as infinite math, like the internet, I reply to my dad and say:

It's sweet that god and their mom can be so simple and complex and that they can be a family man in a van, and in some kind of math that lets you send me things. But dad, you were always that man also with a van. It was a white and green 1995 Dodge van with a TV and Nintendo player; the couch reclined into a bed with green carpet on the walls and floor. We used to go miracle chasing in that van, watch the sun spin in Santa Maria, get McDonald's, and drop off mom at church to play bingo.

Love you, call me.

ONLINE THERE WAS ENDLESS DOG

It was a golden retriever
    not endless because it's golden

But because it's body just kept going

The middle part kept
    winding and receding

down past a realistic desk
    back and back

toward an end I couldn't see
    There's no way to know who made this

Somewhere, someone
    made a dog stretch

    across a concrete floor

and the rest of it careening
    through an office fantasy

The office is as much a fantasy
    as this dog without an end

THE PIGS IN THE BAHAMAS ARE DISPERSED

the likes are too
the dates and times
are dispersed
and puppies on grasses are too
there you are, you move linearly
your faces dispersed
your student loans are too
in crystal clouds
trillions of them bundled
as orphans on the doorsteps
of vacant foreclosed houses
are dispersed
the wedding vows are too
what promises did you make
to stick it through
until death
is the ultimate dispersal
the dreams asleep and awake
are all dispersed
like air like smoke like weed
don't go dispersing yourself
on the street
onto people
or else disperse like the wind
between two bodies
That made you
that brought you here
So full of blood and time
itself dispersed
on this strange round Earth
full of everyone dispersed
in finite places and times
searching for whatever online
family
friends
loved ones
places to live
to go
to learn
what to buy
to destroy
to abolish
everything causing death
and suffering
for a comfortable life
for a lie
or an easy chair
Except for pigs
swimming aimlessly

for hopelessness and pleasure
I went to the store
to get bacon
to snack on
throughout the day
while watching every video
of pigs swimming under the sun
in the Bahamas
because it's winter on the screen
summer outside
spring in my emails
fall in my outdated wardrobe
and suddenly I need bacon
because that's what freedom is
Going to get bacon
whenever
forgetting what
bacon is made of
like marshmallows
that obviously
come from marshmallows
It's the same as our lives
made of everything
that eventually
gets dispersed
at the end
of every law and breath
is a pig
swimming freely

CHATEAU LYFE

Starstruck by night sky and schizoanalysi
like a rumor in the distance is La Borde

The chateau full of -paths
I didn't know was where I lived

Mine was not 17th century stone
but a Valley popcorn ceiling

In a desert of strip mall hoodrats
medication painted black on the cupboards with a padlock

As the clients wailed and sang
karaoke sing along tapes on birthdays

But in Finland saunas will make you
sweat parents out from your pores

apathy prefers cars
how very American

Is every hour not a movie? Death is so good
in movies

As it smears across eyes and windshield
there's no way

of ever reaching it
Life in a deer stays unknowable

making it easier to kill
what we don't know

In this harsh moss standard
the purest air might be enough to save you

But a chateau rebellion in the Hollywood Hills
is enough for now

Show me the one
  about the Florida man

cited for eating a pancake
  on the street
  for disrupting the flow

of traffic

  thank you for sharing
    all that you share

I don't share most things
bc I'm broke and shy and don't own anything

Even though
all true stories
  are free

Like how at the planetarium
  gravity (the concept)

Pulled us so far into it
having realized

  the universe
is cornerless

I walked toward a corner because I needed

  limits
Edges are so useful
  they make you stop

to see yourself, make you
come back to earth—a clean

 elegant distraction

Laura Mullen

"MISTRESS OF THE WEST"

Stubborn residue of the Egyptian
Goddess Hathor and the Golden
Calf, well mixed with a host of other
Commod(e)ities, Elsie the C (1936-
) is the bright face and
Beloved mascot for an un-named
Dairy company. She burst forth
From the gathering clouds as a way
Of keeping an embodied origin
(And with it a myth of purity)
In place at the start of the heavy-
Duty industrialization of America's
Food supply. She is still used
To sell us things we like to eat.
What else do you need? She was
Married early and the image
Of her husband's horned head
Adorns the plastic bottles
Of an oft-used adhesive produced
By the "Chemical Division"
Of that same un-named
Company. Blessed be
His name and the names
Of their offspring. Elsie has many
Degrees including "Doctor
Of Bovinity, Human Kindness,
And Economics," and she's
Queen of Dairyland as well
As an honorary Chief
Of the Seneca People—

Who were not, in fact,
The first Suffragettes,
As you might be thinking,
Understandably, mistakenly.
In 1952 she was more easily
Recognized than many
Celebrities including
A presidential candidate.
Her father art in the land
Of the dead, in those realms
Reserved for advertising.

SIOUX CITY MILK WAR (1932)

Sing muses if you will
Of what opened once
In the "spread" between
What Farmers earned
For milk and the price
Consumers paid at the lip
Of the Depression. Isn't
It always a matter
Of pennies as the man
Said? Speak to us of roads
Shut down by mazes
Of hay bales, hot farmers
With shotguns asking
Drivers their "business,"
And the ditches running
White with the poured-
Out milk on this *holiday*,
Which was the word
Used in place of *strike*.
Tell us again of that long
Ago August and those
For whom justice became
Urgent. Sing of the right
To collective bargaining,
If you love us, or let
The silence, eloquent,
Speak here of fearfulness
And our sad hope, each
Alone, that unfairness will
Land elsewhere or help us?

Chant the history of hikes
And dips in land prices,
The diminishing numbers
Of farms, and remember,
Now, the great corporations:
O Grupo Lala, O Nestle,
O Danone and Lactalis, O
And so on. May the blossom—
From which our Elsie
Partially emerges—echo
The words of Mr. Archie
Wright, who saw the small
Farm as *the basis of our*
Democracy, and who said:
"To live, you have to think."

ELSIE EXPLAIN

How the food of the Gods
In their gas-guzzling muscle
Cars speeding down perfect
Highways through "unspoiled"
Landscapes and relentless good
Weather became this repeated
Offering of ground-up dead
Cow charbroiled because
I never questioned it before
Now I want an answer why
This nation of sizzle why these
Vast acres of greasy smoke why
The endless fluffy white clouds
Of open buns aglow and gaping
Why this wilting lettuce and
The dark red tons of crushed
Tomatoes picked by those
Whose existence is "un-
Documented" which is to say
Denied O can the hands that
Plucked the hard green
Globe before it was gassed
Be touched or is the poem
Not so much a handshake as
A milkshake white on white

Extremely Rare Plastic Ring Colored To Look Like Metal
Ice Cream Sign $19.99
Other images, various, in which her head appears to emerge from a circle of flames
Or petals or long thick amputated cow's tongues urine yellow
The words "I'm famous"
Plastic Face Plush Animal RARE $84.27
The words "I'm in charge"
Dairy Recipe Booklet $6.50
The meeting at which she told us we owed a lot of money but we could make that up
If we'd only stop making so many copies
Uniform Flower Pin $18.99
Very Rare cereal bowl with the image of her dancing nude in the pose of the Golden Calf as from a picture by Filippino Lippi, that's Fra Lippi to you
"Like New" Set of Ice Cream Dishes (best offer)
Rare Vintage Ring Adjustable $24.95
The meeting at which she said she wanted to watch us have a meeting
VERY RARE Promotional Mask $101.00
Pendant Vintage Advertising Pendant $0.99
The sound of her screaming behind a shut door "I'm in charge!"
Disposable Ice Cream Spoons In Protective Paper Covering printed with the image of her laughing face her likeness
Coloring Book (1957) $5.99
The meeting where she told us we had to do better with recruitment
Wall Hanging Commemorative Plaque $29.99

Original 1950's Shopper's Wallet $16.95
The words "Daddy, I'm famous"
Rubber Action Figure $10.00
The meeting where she told us we owed nearly $100,000 and there was no way
To make it up except through a series of cuts
Large Ice-Cream Sign, vintage, with the image of her winking down on us from under
The name of the company, its possessive apostrophe
Brooches and assorted charms (best offer)
Stuffed Bean Bag Animal Dairy Advertising from 2004 $12.50
METAL FACTORY MOLD DIE STAMP INDUSTRIAL
$39.99
Dietary Advertising Booklet 1948 $21.95 (or best offer)
The memo where she detailed her plans for recruitment her intention to send hand-
Written notes to everyone who ever once thought they might
be interested in joining us
Here on the Diary Farm in the Diary Industry white white
white white white
Border Company
Recipe booklet "This Is My Book of Magic Recipes" $10.77
Vintage Playing Cards $4.95
Iron On Shirt Coat Patch $9.99
Vintage Inflatable Store Display $149.95
Bicentennial Beverage Glass $22.50
The poster that says "U.S. WANTS US STRONG / DRINK
MORE MILK."

Judah Rubin

I. GOOD, DINER: CO-SPONSORING THE BANQUET

Locked in
the dream architecture—summed
Mediocre of these
Chicken fingers, the metaphysical
Reactionaries holed up in their
Booths demanding
Alternately more 'hot sauce'
Jumbled, chafing cormorant
In the evening light asymptomatic
Orgone droplets as a cracked
Egg over the pizza chained the
Cortical shuffling spilled its
Guts in a wrongful death
Suit opened on his behalf:
Archie, politically grabby in
The organizing space—Indica
spritely, bullish
Longitudinal as a Sunday spent
Ripping apart the bran muffin
Eyed for soaping up
Democracy
In a suitcase
Your arm sawed off to
The third knuckle, so better yet,
Think of the alternative:
yes, they ground the
Ivory into grotesque pastilles
Each colored with the groaning
Furnishings of a man possessed,
There's the couch, stunned at
The form's sudden disappearance
Wristwatch falling with unexpected
Weight and clattering against
The blue and white, rounded
Hexagonal tiles. A
Shortchanging that is bound to occur
Opening our hearts to the luncheonette's
Gruff justice, with the knowledge that
Yes, that was just what we needed, an
Omelet, a witness, a demigod
Spackled to death while resting
Against the quaking aspen, following
That chain of diminishing returns as
The budget refused to account for
All the time it would take to
Build the atoll into an anonymous
Den of militarized shill—mostly
Petrol, of course, lingering at the edge of
Dawn. It's always day here, the

e

ation
grunt and a
ne grin, the past
ational messaging:
. Live. Opportunity for
—were—and remain
ded between siblings, jewelry
sprinkled in the gaping loss-leader
With the over-under on a tousling
Wish list brindled cos-play the
Wine over and above the allowance
For limited ingredient diets,
Totemic in a wandering lung
Piercing the night sky with its
Horrid gasp of air. Of course, jobs
Are synonymous: lucky to get a
Scale model of Eddie Haskell
Grinding up on the predicate: post
Master general learns to
Love again long after the
Expectations of logarithmic
Arrest loop around the febrile
Moss of our affliction. I shake my
Hoary locks at thee, run my hand
Across the mesa's lumpy dishwax fissure
Blunder on the brindled kapo loam
Oh principal stain passion trickling
Washer oboe limpid dustup, funk
Or *funk*, or disparate, lying fatuous
Dishragged swindler who's
Watchful issuance of god's spindly
Urethretic sander, gauche, plaid,
Rustic, shirtless, emptied of all
Sin and sound to course the hairless
Beast athwart the voiceless churn
Lost on a motor see-saw amplitude
Opened from toe to top the pickled
Yam, *lo* Lo LO and law the lingering
Is and contextual youthy rung-rung
Posse comatose harpy gallon
I know the grumbling docent I know
The furniture tuber I know the
Soda, the grog, the dregs of my
Textual gasping or I gas the mice,
Demand accrual, my credit, musty,
Shirtless and pained, my milky

Residue, slowly peeling from the gross
Parenthetical Goya hominy, arch
Villain, applet oscillator, aggravated
Fibula toaster, oven, parsing *and*
Parsing, the cheek oceanic
Principled, debtless, running
A hand through across the rat,
Dead, holed up in a drawer.

II. FURTHER RECURRENCE OF THE DIRECTIVE

Whatever thoughts I had have fled now
Opened by the orange or rose
water the smashed up loans on
The backs of the poor, what they call
Sleeping rough I excised from the poem
If they did it in a bank I put on the rose
Water against the fathomed time of
Incident, I made of the narcotic
Assassin a misreading of its past
I drove him around the driveway aping
The design of past orphic molars
Ground down in the Eurodollar chartreuse
Buying a suit from the creditor as to
Help the cause on the butter welted
Geeze turn-about fishing the
Canopic pier wheel well smacking of
Insured interests—another hand bag,
Another deep in the reddened call
another dithering mealcake
of devotion or elevated
Optional, the final haptic
Flame grilled energy bars elucidate
These triangular halos playing musky in the
New Age principles lab I funded when
My phenome came of age—I can't
　　Hear you; I can't skim it on or get the upper
Productivity manumission turn-down from
A lover of the Beaver Method of autotuned
Catastrophe. I never thought I'd work
Again, but here I am dumping the coffee
Urn in the recycling bin
before pressing hard against the
Lock and key of a mores that did more to
Anesthetize the cookie in the arms of a
Hounded Eros than all the stealth weather
Doused on my lunch break. Talking to your
Plants, privately, by a salt lamp—I want you to
Grow your business, I want you to look
For a new, affordable option and, yes, I
Know the knotty cross of your affliction
Plays well when you say if the
Spillage can be expressed in the corn-
Fed madness of self-satisfied farewells
And the complications of the river arc
Against your fishlike anus bricking over
The window we'd carved from our busy
Schedule to jump from, I hope it is a perfect
Leap out into traffic, the only act of
Liberation you never pushed.

Most of us will assume this harried reconnaissance to be a real
Sign, finally, of a more brutal underling, enervating tosser
The bro-hug makes the news, the army of light gallops
Along as though a foundling in the assuring kestrel bleats
From the window I had sense enough to believe you when you
Joked about the camps, even if your bro hug had made
The news abundant and resplendently
Clear, even if your flickering match set out an
Emptiness as a dreamy milk bat. Ovular, the silence of
The yak in the economy of dealt cream under their
Crusty mildewed fat sprung from this
One place, and in the buttery lip or balmy horse
Flanked by a triumphant blast of inchoate shrift
Always the Apollonian mood, the table a bit shifted
To rest its leg on the guest's pliant neck. It brings
Out the tongue's murmur:
The larch and the Russian
Elm, the arrowroot and white birch
Apollonian, a dirigible up on the harrow with the salad
Spinner, burgundy, teal, coral, ashen grey.
Wake up, grab the vibrator and get shorn up on the
Modem I'll back down from the desk to find
These new geographies of containment: it's a—a…balmy
horse
Flanked by the symbolic Bundt (thanks!) Eyeing a technics
where
The movement really sets a harrowing flicker
In the milk bat up on a buttery blast.

Cream?
Cream is itching—right, okay, thanks. Crinkle-cut omphalos
waving at the distant shoreline from out of the greased beaker
The silent crust billowing out there among the grassy
Tithes; reeds like a cow dragged off the floor with a
Bolt in its head its hide, gilded
a shorn and weltered biscuit
A wisp of the furniture is enough for some, fully compliant
On matters of encouragement like instruction was a theater
Of jockeys, each finally getting their due. Ownership is
stuttering
In the fieldwork, spilling out and over the pair of loose
Fitting shorts, its phosphorescent glow as to a stone mock-up of a hemispheric banana. When tongue
milky in the west
In a stuttering ownership of debt-ridden bedclothes I left
scattered
The bread on the Styrofoam plate beside
the Pontiac Fiero;
the orange on the over
pass beside the flag
and candle the shot

glass of Jell-o in
the forest
before your tree;
I filter these thoughts of you back through
The ossified fruit, I treasure these few
Moments together, waiting to stuff the shirt back into
The pipe spewing ash, mown down by the jockey like
breaded debt. What would I have left for you
ghost bike, plastic flowers,
Stone at the head of your grave, what would I have
Given you, this cabbage leaf,
This pizza crust, this beer and honey, this
Can of Friskies, this stale bread beside the Pontiac
Fiero? When you call I'll thin the downy vest
With the soft opening of history's fine dining
appropriative transhumanism where
Superseded by the bribery of a Jell-o shot running
Through my second row of giraffe-like teeth
The carafed monogram lightly smoked
Like putting up wistful and out the tube-o
Zester-shunt with the cobalt on a dyed
snack themed line of combs, shoulder massage ambits
in flight wireless blaring *Contemporary*
Lovemaking as a souring plum and so on.
Anyway, the call comes in and I'm
Just getting dressed, the leaves are
Giving off the waxy blush
Like a tooth, squinting out of the break
Room, and I'm just floored by that incisive need,
But instead, nothing—silence, and the
Line dies with it—the parenthesis
Having long expired as conceit,
If there had been, and we can't bear the
Weight of consideration—why, then, "conceit"
After all just leave the bag on your lap with a
Gilded crest of lilies stent like a
Bronzed card table overlooking
Lenin's tomb—just one more in the offing
time bop all go-to for frozen cakies,
If you hold it longer. I'm...ghosting?
I'm golden hearted like an eagle plying
Showboat, what's a politics like bearing
Down on self-same measurement and
Hounded by the past to
Lunch in stipulated arears, by pendulant
Myopia a boar I crackle in bearing
The energy bar fully, and linking what were
Left of the bricks, hushed, now, as the call
recedes, the leverage of a soda
I take off my shoes—no, I had but I've
Relaxed now, the latex helped

Ease my sifting the produce whereby the ash
Tray my (actual) go-to for accidentals, between us as
The trash fire grows apart,
Face metastasized as though by caveat
The all you can eat closes, if only for
An hour, and rests its patron list
Ever downward and across divinity's
Smiling and puckered acreage where
I'd always dreamed of having my liberal
Moments, secluded from my neighbors
To quietly intone: a new take on a classic
American asks: can coleslaw skip
The mayo?

Those are the tell tale signs—co-signing
The rift into anatomized spittle—ocarina
Or a Nalgene filled with his stepfather's
Ashes keeping the cat barely contained
In-state, let alone on the failing limp
Buttered up, though capable;
Hounded, though shivering in the chill
Moonlit glow of the park, destitute and
Paper thin, a wafer of the blinkered mask
Shitting from the rafters into a box of
Nutter Butters. Increase is somatic if we
Lounge on a brush, she
Was all over the aspic, all the landscape
Was powered on and ready to eat. It
All started with an
Ice cream maker and a dream, this
Hype curated Fido leotard. Ipswich the
Grogger, dead souls on a watch fucking
Above the vacuum's hum on a summer
Friday, shirt open to the chest. Born in
A barn as a sentencing, shiftless
Opportunity go lucky on a juicy bun
Loafers abbreviated cockles linger in
A humidity wishing the planters away
With a jar full of ashen jazz. At noon
Today I can tell you where these
Guards will be though only once will
I grow the antithesis of reduction
Blisters and as you well know in a
Garrulous sweat/suit all dusting omni
Bus Solo cup vaccinating the rubber
Jockeys gossamer in the lightening
End of life appropriation schema
Oh I can't bear to watch him—that
Zosima cowboy fuck—watch it with the
Shammy, octopital zee so-so Crespo
Oh I can't bear the weight of this

Prodded discus, oh I can't deliberate
In the flipping ingots, gotcha pillows
If I'd even known a murmuring sally
Accorded the Sunday washer in a
Toeless eclogue there's a finicky
Bliss of homeownership to the
"How are you" of the break room
there's a license in
Brandishing the market shingle and
Using it to serve a smoked gouda, there's
A use even if you hate to admit it, to the
Stamped and stained leather moccasin
Closing in on the ankle of sin, biting
Like a health code surrendered to the
Motionless gel of harangue. I know you
From the accountant's office, sitting there
Reading Ad Week, blessing the rostrum like
The Real soaked up and ready
For the Cable Street serenade. Scooper,
Discus, lunch meat, copper wire on
The basic angles, sunburnt by the ringer
Stonefaced with the wrinkled knee, correspond
With the striped antipathy of countercultural
Sex act, rubbing my ear with a bottle
Boosting the car with that mild hint of
Axe. I groaned under the yawning pill of
Anonymity, the milk was spraying
Out of the hydrant, the crackers were Bisco
Dawn was raisins, I couldn't feel for the
Mob of pain buried to the hilt in the thigh of
My brother. All the housing was a gilded
Mayoral sundown, the grass was lunching on
A shelved tarmac, open octet transom
Cyanide caplet dry eyed in the dawn
There's a hole at the center of utterance that
Squeals when touched. Oh, you got me a
Ghost arm, how clever—now I can get at
The fire clause; remember it's somatic so
The bulb is theoretically the
Heart at the center of the hoagie—neither you,
Nor the pressing symbolic, a turn in
The bliss of a friable steak, zinc on a wedge of
Iceberg, ship on a jujube filigree. Zonk, I'm
Grasping, learning the trombone with little success.
Comment is sofa, right? Comment is *a* sofa,
Righteous with damage; comment is a
Dangerous breach in the birch, the canopic
Jam jar holds on, but just barely, I kick away
The fingers and there's nothing left. Percentage
Inching. Poison smeared all over the toothpaste
Bisquik is a first of the month pair of

Shoes. Bowling is such a young ape, I go
Wild shooting and end up with a headache.
There's always the additive dimension, but I want
You to have this pile of sandwich—it's such an
Honor with the triplex, and I learn something
From this old spindly cur each time we speak.

The bucolic threshold of the body
A what
Is to say, shoot him, like a Roman, as he
Walks into the arrested canine spool
Feeling in this red mud, what dispensed
Ochre, to have been saved by
A fretted contingent
Replete of modernity's
Post-Plan antiphone the
Lights from across the river attest to
A dipping of the surface where the lungs
Heave up and chafe at the larder's
Arithmetic, stacked ochre of
The lunar base, a rewarded
Point of decision, the sentence, an
Opposition of stuttering degrees, the
Airport since bombarded, updraft of shouldering
Blasted out of the rock face with his
Agronomist hand marked out on a Ouija
Foot digging in at the handaxe of time. Why
drag the rocks, the quilt, the
Capital across Europe? Why flatten the
Them into the failing light of time, what
Lingering droplets on the face of
The orange he pressed to the paper and
Spun the distance, charged with the syringe
Of position, the cranial so-far lumped
Tourmaline, ashcan blue and paste
A vibrant yellow on the brink of sleep?

Back in mourning for release—if it's a shutdown
The zoom simplex, trafficked incontinent,
Looming obedience casing the gesture, associative
The whale returns the day the moon courses red
In the sonnet, there where there are no burning
Suns, a thousand grains pared as a cormorant
funereal copacetic muled the prong, crushed
as the granular elocution
Time stands, or the shore of pressing
End, gobs of the stuff, the chicken's
carcass torn by the blued over sky, those
blistered, those blistered if and then the old
one never quite went away, what
Was that zippered cosine, what were

those footsteps receding /// what
What would you like to play, if you could
If you could play, what would you? One of
These days,
And the wind in the leaves.

This destitute recurrence
 Or the cracked, the circuit
Lung now gnawed away, the
Rats, typical, perhaps, a ring
Of bodies on. A pocket
Of ash, of, of, and belonging as
Proprietary: ash, the ash of
The proprietary, dog's body
Sniffing out the cardboard
Language from the plane, gorgon
Shuffled over the loose.
The Building has only so many
Verbs, the avuncular gratuity
We sat with across the table,
Sexless belonging, groping in the
Dark for the beeswax figure where
By the mirror snuffed metallic
Fly, caught in the saucer over the
Hill comes a roar as one entry
In the autobiographical scape
Shirtwaist to memorialize how many
Deaths are of cotton, over how
Shirt the stitching waist high
And returned a pocket full
Of ash. Recurred to hope it
Dead and found over, and
 the mumbling
Groped at on the floor, wages
Fallen out in the ruins on
Zootropic contingence. Made: of
These gestures little, made—of
Them the occupation. Of exonerated
Bee stung the scope of language, the
Body current in the fermented
air breaching the surface of
Complaint—what were the silvered
Course, the blame of language is a fear
Like contingence is notched on the
Recurrence of ash. One thousand is
The hall, the undertow in contusion
Lingering as a sheet overshot in arrest

Shelby Shaw

ON CALCULATING THE VALUE OF MY OFFER

All life must beget life to remain life. Whether plant, animal, microbe, or bacterium, a single entity becomes the terminus of an ongoing record once it dies.

Die, verb:
stop living (of a person, animal, or plant)
be killed for (a cause)

Continuation allows for more possibility to improve, solve conflicts, and learn defenses against destructive forces.

become extinct
be forgotten

No one body can improve during the course of one lifetime, at least not with the intention of bettering one's future data.

Offspring are off copies of two contributors.
When the light runs across the scanning bed, the result is a stillborn movement, expressed in striations of light.

to weaken (of a force)

The only way to make near-perfect copies is to start with a perfect original.

stop burning (of a fire)
stop functioning (of a machine)

A body requires constant maintenance, a brain allows the body to continue.
A human is the atom's way of knowing what an atom is.

to emphasize a strong desire
to emphasize feelings of shock, amusement, embarrassment, or misery

People want to be wanted to validate the contribution of their existence.
Individual archives are gifts. Genetic data can never be perfectly copied unless modified by engineering.

To be beautiful is a contribution unto the world assumed to be effortless by the one who is beautiful, and deemed generous towards those who are so lucky to perceive the beauty. To experience beauty is to receive its gift.

To validate a person's potential to contribute beauty—the most valued mortal service—we use a metric of desire, starting with a person's body. What can be seen can be authenticated with the effort of only a brief glance and the immediate response of pleasure, repulsion, or indifference.

Beauty is expected to beget beauty.
We all want to be wanted.

to have an orgasm
to orgasm

Desire is a longing to possess. Desire cannot continue once possession is achieved if it is followed by contentment instead of planning. The desire to have sex with anyone who is attractive is a desire to increase one's own worth by netting the additional values of others' contributions.

To be a beautiful person is the most inexplicable good fortune.
To be a beautiful person is the most misunderstood misery.

> *Die* is Middle English derived from the Old Norse word *deyja*, related to the English *dead*.
> *Die* can be traced back to the Latin *datum*, meaning *something given*, and sometimes *something played*. Hence we roll a die during a game. When our life is over so is our game.

Because we cannot proactively choose who contributes to our creation, we have instead developed methods of improvement to dupe the authenticity of our original state of being.

This mascara will virtually double the length of your eyelashes.

Wrap the whitening strip around your teeth and let sit for fifteen minutes.

Two more sets of three repetitions on each thigh will tighten and tone your muscles.

> *Datum* is the neuter past participle of *dare*, meaning *to give*.
> *Datum* has no gender nor sex, is not present, and does not represent a future. *Datum* is a gift.

Because we ultimately seek value through others' desires as our own validations, we seek to make copies of our gifts for distributing.

The only way to be wealthy is to spend your wealth.

Entire industries have thus risen to deliver the desires we desire to inhabit for the sake of attracting others' desires for us. Of our flaws, concerns, and disappointments with ourselves have come multibillion-dollar enterprises of improvement.

Remember that to continue to desire we must avoid falling into contentment by always planning for what we want next.

> *Datum* is the singular of *data*, meaning a single piece of information.
> *Datum* may also refer to an assumption from which inferences can be drawn, or conclusions may be decided.

First we work on improving our bodies before we work on improving our logic.

When a mate is attracted a copy can be made for the records.

> *Data* in computing refers to coded information that is accumulated, stored, and transmitted as signals for a corresponding operation to be completed.
>
> Computing is a mating ritual without courtship, in which the resulting response is always known prior to the signal being transmitted.
>
> Any deviation in response is an error in calculations, which is data input by humans.

We want to attract to offer the highest reward: creating a hybrid copy.

An estimated 55-57% of my insides are water. The highest percentage of water in a human occurs during infancy, when a newborn has some 300 bones, some of which are malleable, especially the impressionable skull.

An adult is made of 206 bones. Much of a newborn is made up of cartilage in place of bones. Cartilage helps define our noses and gives shape to our ears.

A profile can be the ugliest view of a person.
A surgeon can alter the outline of an adult by reconstructing the curves of bone and cartilage.

Cosmetic surgery is not covered by health insurance, but a monthly subscription to Adobe Creative Cloud can give you access to professional photo-editing software for $9.99 a month.

> *Dating* is the attempt to receive another's desire and longing for yourself.
> *Dating* comes from the same Latin *dare* as *datum*, meaning *to give*.
> *Dating* thus reveals people to be assumptions for making inferences and conclusions.

A gestating human fetus may have between 6 and 7 million eggs in fetu contained microscopically within its developing body. By puberty—typically between ages 8 and 13—only 300,000 eggs are estimated to have survived. What happens to the lost eggs is unknown. Who they will never become is unimaginable. We know that the bones of a newborn fuse together.

> Computing data is an archive of our interests and actions executed using digital media. A *medium* can be defined as an intervening matter through which impressions or forces act upon the senses, as from a distance. Distance no longer needs to intervene upon attraction with the advent of digital copies of ourselves.

A typical adult will produce 350 eggs by the end of their lifetime, approximately.
Translated into the metric of an egg carton's dozen, this becomes the equivalent of 29.2 cartons of eggs produced over one lifetime.

> Our beauty can be copied into data to be edited and filtered for improvements. These copies can then be shared ad nauseam.

Fowl used as slang can imply a subject being cowardly, inexperienced, young, petty, or unnecessary.
And: "especially a young girl."

> Mobile technology has increasingly and rapidly become more advanced for executing complicated logic rather than simply connecting two people on a phone call.
>
> Dating has become a force enacted upon the medium of digitized social connectivity. The digital as a medium is intervening through our impressions, and distance is not a factor.
>
> Dating has thus become the medium through which we are the data, to gift to each other.
>
> Using only aesthetic cues, I curate the vision of my impression. Accompanying text may be as edited and filtered as my images. My name and age and occupation and school may be omitted entirely, or false. The data is unreliable but the algorithm will still plug in the variables and deliver any results.

Within a 7-mile radius of my location in Manhattan, my data has thus far been received by Jay, Jake, Alex, Jeremy, Kevin, Dylan, Jason, Joel, Brian, Sam, Dustin, Davis, Luke, Jake, Hayden, Max, Peter, James, Gabriel, Anthony, Faux, Jimmy, Josh, Hallen, Yan, Paul, Shawn, Dustin, Alex, and Chris.

In one day I eat 4 eggs.
In one week I eat 2.33 cartons of eggs.
In one month I eat 10 dozens of eggs.
In 87.5 days I have eaten 29.2 cartons of eggs, 350 individual eggs.
In 2.92 months I have eaten 350 eggs.
In 34% of 1 year I have eaten my ancestral potential measured in domestic fowls.

My data has returned the signal, thus far, from Brian, Dylan, Aaron, Reid, Devon, David, Reilly, Tommy, Brian, Brent, Neil, Jack, John, Andy, David, Alex, Rob, David, Stewart, Gabriel, Tim, Zachary, Phillip, Michael, Drew, Alan, Danny, Brian, Chris, Hunter, Lucas, John, Peter, Billy, Kelly, Colin, James, Alan, Jerzy, Nathan, Joe, Fox, Zachary, Ben, Jon, and Mark.

Since hitting puberty I have cyclically consumed my forwards genealogy more than 50 times, as eggs.

Dating involves no computing because there is no logos.

A carton of 12 large white generic eggs is sold for $1.99 without tax.
Cage-free eggs sell for an averaged $3.49 per large dozen.
Organic eggs cost upwards of $5.99 per dozen, to start.

To consume enough eggs in order to equal those which my adult body will release in the hopes of fertilization during my lifetime, I need only to spend $59.70 to be generic, $104.70 to be cage-free, or $179.70 to be organic, plus tax.

At the time of this writing, I would need to work 15 hours earning minimum wage in New York City to ensure all of my 350 eggs were organic. If I am really not feeling like putting myself to work, I can be generic at the cost of only 5 hours of my time.

My value is unable to be measured through the dating computers.

To offer the contribution of my value is still a two-way execution despite acting through a digital interface: a signal must be transmitted and then received.

To measure my value as an estimated stock of eggs is to conclude that my ultimate value is less than a quarter of one day's time.

Sending a signal that does not reciprocate a response is not a computational error.
It simply means the data was collected and received, but not as a gift.

The data sent does not warrant desire, distribution, or replication.

The event is archived in the software to prevent the error of false desire from ever happening again. The data is lost, which is the new desire.

IV

Consider a decade-old activist group that trains and takes volunteers to accompany undocumented immigrants to their court hearings and check-ins with ICE (the paramilitary agency of the U.S. government empowered to detain and deport people practically at will). Only the activist group doesn't call them undocumented immigrants, or clients, or cases. They call them "friends." And when you accompany your friend, they instruct us, you must follow three ironclad rules: to respect your friend and everyone else you come in contact with; to do no harm; and to pass no judgment. Your role is to bear witness, and to act together as a visible community of embodied citizens whose very presence throws light into the deep shadows where bureaucracy thrives. Some people at the training meeting can't get past the interdiction against volunteers speaking much, at these accompaniments, beyond basic communication. The leaders explain again that our role is not to pour out righteous anger, score debate points, or feed like well-meaning vampires on the painful stories our friends might have to tell. We're not there to be lawyers, reporters, therapists, or saviors. We're there to be spirits. A body is passing into the umbra or array or maw of the state. We join it, following humbly behind. We go, suggests the leader, to crowd with humanity a place designed to turn persons into objects. And someone asks still again about what to do with all our words. It's like we forgot that the state loves words, too, and would gladly trade them with us all day. But in truth it's our inspirited bodies—our bodies' insubordination—the state fears: how naturally they find and join with others, and start to trample right over the lines.*

—Editors

*The New Sanctuary Coalition, accessed February 4, 2019, http://www.newsanctuarynyc.org

Mitch Anzuoni

Dear Citizen,

Thank you for volunteering to undergo the Academi Apperception Assessment. We at Academi value your time and personhood and beliefs, for they are what power our mission to Make The World A Better Place through data-driven semiotics and deep intra-dialectics between administrators and the well-being of Their Citizens.

While these questions may appear to be irrelevant or perhaps even nonsensical, we assure you they have been generated under the auspice of a panel of expert game theoreticians, technocrats, venturesocialists, metaconsultants, and MFA program heads recruited from across the freer markets and only after years of analyzing EKG/EEG readouts from thousands of well-compensated betas. We have offices in D.C., New York, Shenzen, and Geodrome-Macro continually assessing the efficacy and penetration of our Work. And the results speak for themselves: Our publishing assets produce more infocontent in one month than the other leading firms do in a year. Engagement rates, theory subscriptions, and consumer satisfaction are at an all-time high. Regime stability is climbing. And we owe it all to you.

Academi and all its subsidiaries believe that progress is not limited to tomorrow.

Practice.

Patience.

With Academi, Your Today Can Be Different.

Warm regards,
Coranon Silaria
Chair of Academi

Please check one of the following:

[ ] I am comfortable with the language I am able to describe my body with

[ ] There are words that I feel I may never know even though I am their definition

Please check all that apply:

[ ] I have felt the grass on my feet in the past week

[ ] I am not afraid to take the public transportation after 12am
[ ] 1 am

[ ] 2 am
[ ] 3 am
[ ] 4 am
[ ] 5 am
[ ] 6 am

Please check all that apply:

[ ] Language is being gentrified

[ ] Language is real estate

[ ] Language is often used when poets can't think of anything else
[ ] Language cannot truly describe a cow giving birth

[ ] Language can describe a cow giving birth, but not as good as e.g VR

[ ] None of the above
[ ] All of the above
[ ] Some of the above

Future Host

CAN THE SUBALTERN PERFORM?

1.

Consider this photograph: a group of unidentified Qigong practitioners caught performing on camera. They're positioned on an ancient altar in Beijing, possibly the Temple of Earth, where the emperor used to make sacrifice to the elements, now a public park for the people. An uncanny moment of immense tension, where the spatially improbable, chaotic configuration of bodies is mapped onto the architecture of heavenly order.

Qigong is a popular self-cultivation practice with roots in ancient Chinese medical, philosophical, and martial arts traditions. In the 1980s and 1990s, Qigong evolved into a collective mania that swept across different strata of society. For the first time in decades, people took it to the public squares, to the parks, to residential complexes, playgrounds, and official assembly halls, for something other than straight up political theater. Almost always amateurs, bodies opened themselves up to the experience of *qi*—often described as a visceral experience of mystical energy flow—alone, in communion with groups, or as emitted by Qigong masters boasting supernatural healing powers.

On the other side of the positivist sciences, Qigong was officially promoted as a tradition of Chinese medicine to be recuperated as body cultivation and maintenance techniques in response to contemporary health demands. In ancient times, the emperor's body correlates to heaven, as the commoner's to a blade of grass. The post-Cultural Revolution projects

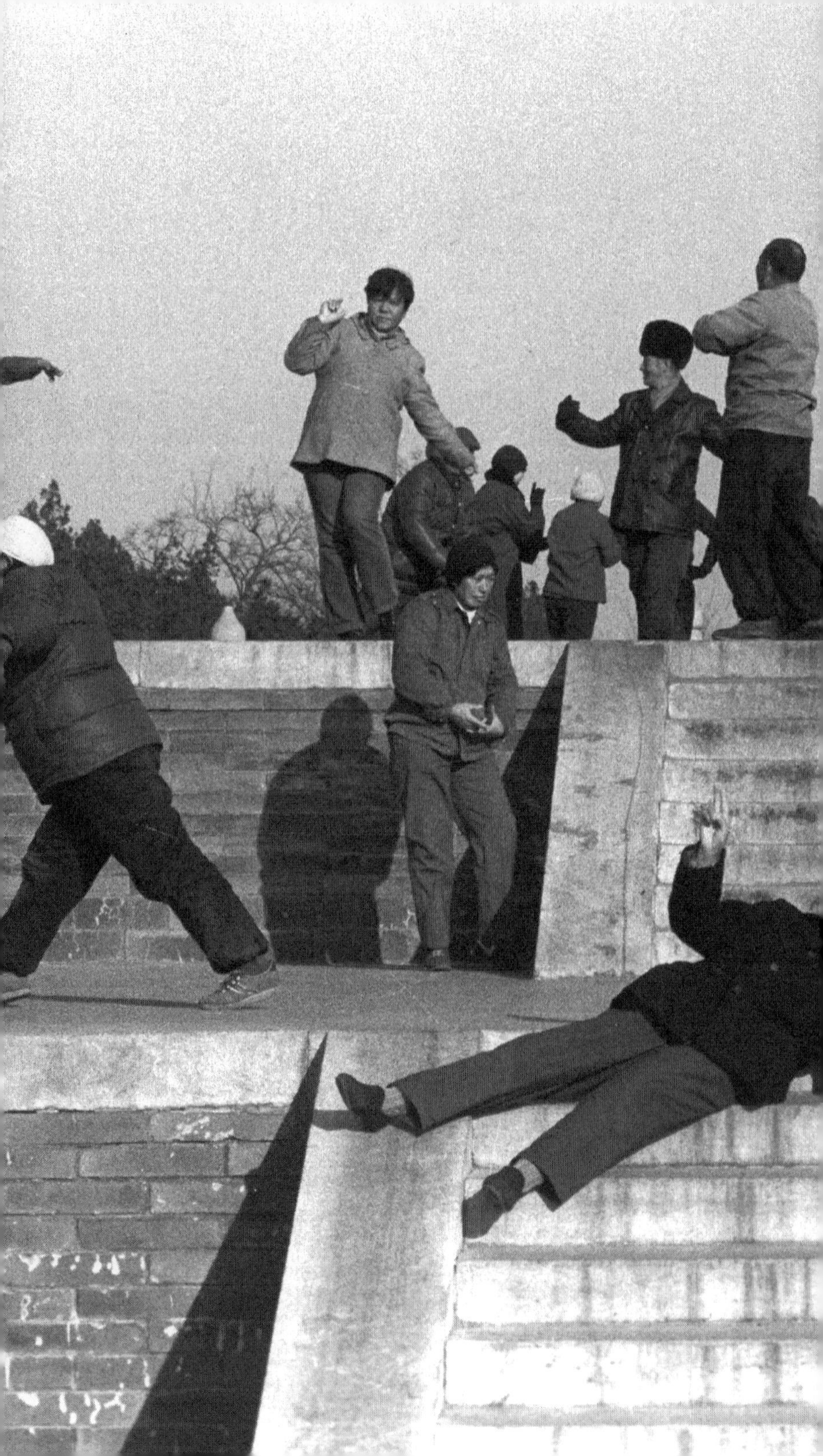

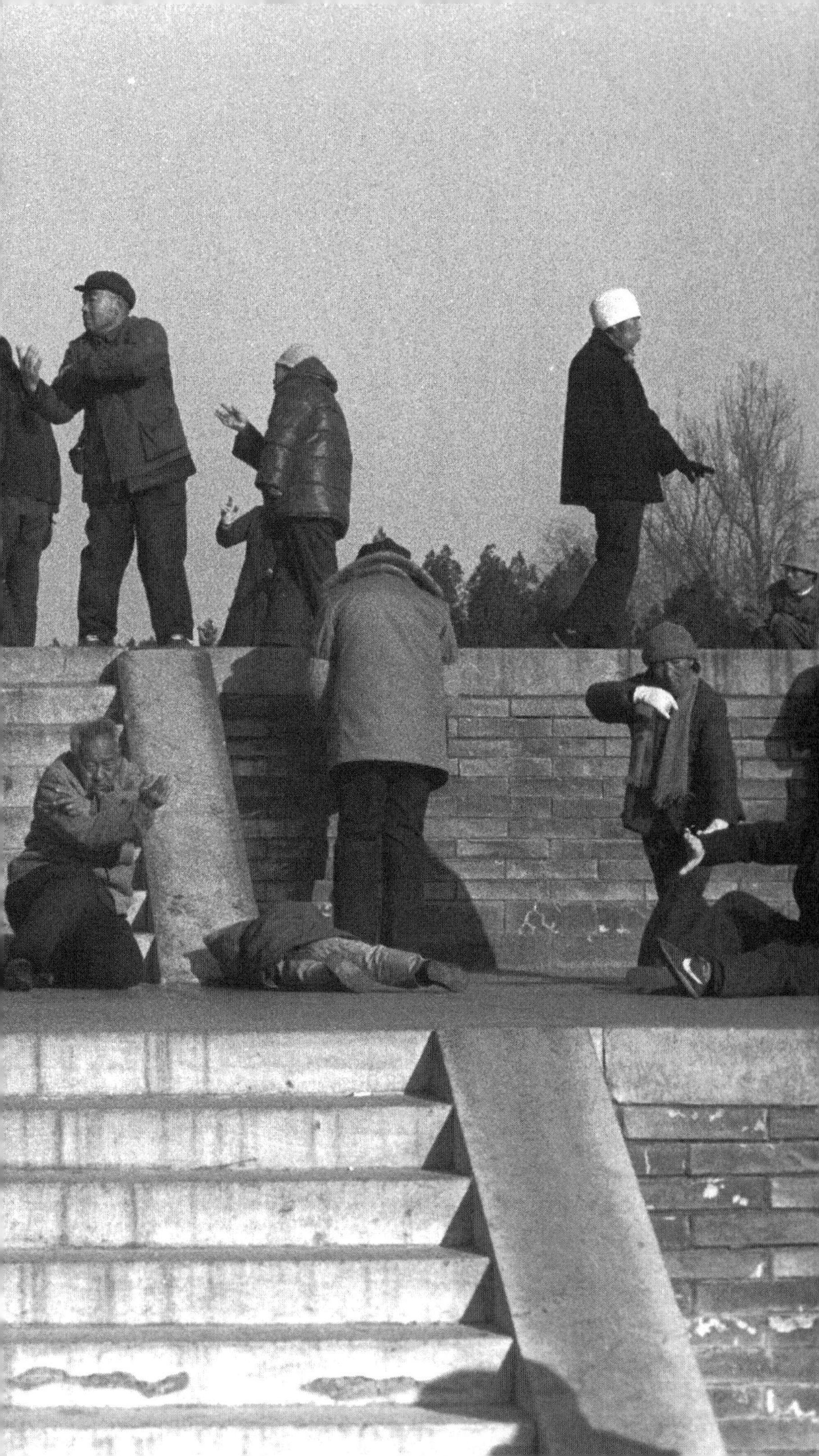

of national reform and economic opening came with its own biopolitical imperative: *thou shalt produce desirable bodies*, which are measured by health, productivity, and reproducibility. Contrary to an earlier era, individuals now take it upon themselves to prepare for a newly capitalist socialism; at stake is their inclusion/exclusion by the state—from the modern, from official socialist utopia, from capital.

Of the period, not many visual records remain as such. The proliferation of large public assemblies in ritual exercises, master worship, and telepathic healings was later considered a political threat to the regime, culminating in the suppression and criminalization of highly organized cults such as the Falun Gong, whereby the Qigong craze became stigmatized and crossed out from authorized history. Those who left traces are forever locked in this brutal scene; with the "expectation of the extraordinary"[1] built into the structure of Qigong, these bodies in performance reveal their actual damage and undesirability, a condemning transcript of power.

Look at them again: bodies begin to lose self-mastery but are pinned down by gravity. Limbs pointing everywhere, or nowhere at all. Individuals seem utterly self-preoccupied yet interdependent in spatial arrangement of the group. There is suggestion of departure, of escape, of not-quite-yet emancipation, where the body becomes a last resort for the momentarily ungoverned in public demonstration: an irretrievable anarchical potential. With this, a poetic suspension is achieved, where sovereign power and the individual share a moment of reciprocal recognition, mutual catering, and silent negotiation, " [...] neither contained nor structured, no matter how severe the dualisms."[2]

2.

In my faintest of childhood memories, my father was a casual practitioner of Falun Gong, the cult best known for its brutal, highly mediatized persecution. His private ritual consisted of reading from a bright yellow-covered paperback that resembled Buddhist scripture, some simple martial arts postures, and meditating while breathing from a tank of pure oxygen. This historical materialist, son of a self-taught traditional herbalist in rural Northeast, did so discreetly, always keeping the book in the trunk of his Volkswagen—he was among the first to be allotted a car by the state-owned corporation he was assigned to. Only occasionally did he talk about the "third eye," the "thousand-mile ear," or the friend whose terminal cancer was cured after adopting Qigong instead of chemotherapy. One day, the manual disappeared; and we never spoke of it again.

I was born in Beijing in February 1992, when Deng Xiaoping made his South China tour and declared, in the plainest of words, the zeitgeist of post-1989 China: to hell with the folly of ideology or the "end of history," the market will not wait. In fact, economic and agricultural reform had already begun in the 1980s to upend the Cooperative Medical System which granted universal, albeit rudimental, primary healthcare, resulting in the collapse of traditional community-based and socialist collectivized healthcare models. Qigong was allowed to operate in this practical vacuum, as a strategy to outsource the provision of care, or an instrument to spread health and able-bodiedness to the masses—a vision not dissimilar to futurism with a socialist bent.

That was not how things turned out. Familiar as it was, Qigong still signaled something of an absolute alterity—of madness, of backwardness, of shame—amidst the greater promise of material abundance and renewed fetishization of industrial modernity. As a child, I feared its contagion and its immanence in a person as rational as my father. For days on end in early 2001, national television broadcasted the deformed visage of a young woman in a Falun Gong cult who allegedly survived group self-immolation on Tiananmen Square—the cruelest punishment is the rendering bare life of a would-be subject. A product of the modern, Qigong was made to be the ultimate Other.

Despite the political foreclosure, the commodification of Qigong-related physical and ritual practices has all but halted. Note that the medium of transmission of the extraordinary has already shifted from the embodied event to the disembodied product. As with self-care in the West, private and group lessons, retreats, printed matter, instruction videos, ritual objects and general merchandise imbued with the master's *qi* continue to abound in the informal market of self-cultivation, to be consumed in the isolation of home. Now my parents send lotus flower emojis.

3.

When Liu Xiaobo died, I mourned the man, an icon largely erected by the West, but felt more compelled by the ending of an activism that was powerfully humanist, yet ultimately neoliberal and anti-populist, confined to the ideological prison of its own historical trauma.

I belong to the first generation of officially Socialist children to grow up in the schizophrenic infancy of Chinese state capitalism after the paradigm-setting atrocity of June 4th. Between the iconic Tiananmen Tank Man and the horror of burned girl, how can we rethink insurgent relations to power? How do we reimagine resistance while doing away with the binaries of dissent—of individual vs. collective, freedom vs. domination, public vs. private, oppression and rebellion—that continue to prescribe our strategies and alliances?

Or, what kind of body can we possibly have other than the one that stands alone, stiff, in opposition, immobile? What craft exactly is our craft that allows the body to exist while publically demonstrating against a political reality, which is never merely an event but ongoing life, a transformative apparatus? What could Qigong teach us about public body demonstration, minimal autonomy, or, simply, survival? Who are we to learn from it?

Spivak has warned against information retrieval from the subaltern by postcolonial intellectuals acting as agents of penetration and/or appropriation. If the question of *Can the subaltern speak?* is not only about whether the subaltern can speak without being spoken for, but also her strategic silence in "resistance to well-intentioned metropolitan efforts to make her yield her voice,"[3] in the case of Qigong, the public spectacles and minuscule everyday practices constitute a body of understanding that doesn't need the academic to translate into discursive consciousness and make legible to a presumed audience. Doing away with the structure of utterance, it is a medium of transmission without preconceiving relations between giver and receiver. Instead of "a journey to silence,"[4] any

Qigong performance is necessarily catachrestic, so we might as well start to imagine the many fruits of our unfaithfulness.

It is in this context that we will return to the figure of the anonymous Qigong practitioner, who does not speak and yet does not keep quiet. They do not guard their knowledge, for it is not considered a secret.

NOTES

1. David A. Palmer, "Embodying Utopia: Charisma in the Post-Mao Qigong Craze," *Nova Religio: The Journal of Alternative and Emergent Religions* 12, no. 2, (November 2008): 70.

2. Michael Taussig, *The Magic of the State* (New York: Routledge, 1997), 39-40.

3. Victor Li, *The Neo-Primitivist Turn: Critical Reflections on Alterity, Culture, and Modernity* (Toronto: University of Toronto Press, 2006), 24.

4. Pierre Macherey, as quoted in Gayatri Spivak, "Can the Subaltern Speak?" in *Can the Subaltern Speak? Reflections on the History of an Idea*, ed. Rosalind Morris (New York: Columbia University Press, 2010), 256.

IMAGE

Huang Xiaobing, *Citizens practicing Luohan Gong in the Temple of Earth (Ditan Park) in Beijing*, Winter 1989. Licensed by FOTOE.

Miranda Mellis

According to a rhetorical model that was common in Antiquity, parables are a discourse ciphered to prevent those who should not understand it from understanding it; yet, at the same time, they fully display the mystery ... The correspondence between the Kingdom and the world, which parables present as a similarity, is also expressed by Jesus as a proximity in the stereotypical formula "the Kingdom of heaven has come near [eggiken]" *(Matt. 3:2 and 10:7; Mark 1:15; Luke 10:9)*. Eggys, *"close," from which the verb* eggizo *derives, arguably comes from a term that means "hand": that is, the proximity of the Kingdom is not only of a temporal order–as one would expect of an eschatological event that coincides with the end of times–but also and especially of a spatial order: it is, literally, "close at hand."*

—Giorgio Agamben, *The Fire and the Tale*

He didn't see the accident; he was the accident. If he had seen it he would have seen noise itself. It seemed to him when he thought about it that he had been just another car part, flung, overtaken, blasted, ground down, flattened like a thing, like a cup hurled through a window, crashing through glass, thrown by what force? By chance; by accident – to be hit and smashed, to be a thing that hits and smashes, to break everything into pieces, to be broken, to go to pieces, to explode, to be exploded. You could die trying to avoid a squirrel.

He and his former car were debris flung far, together they were asteroid, lumpy projectiles. On trails in parks car and body parts are covered over by mosses, small flowers overgrow them. Plastic bumpers, twisted as broken vultures, space rocks, and bones misshaped by impacts.

My car, he thought, I wonder where it is now, all in pieces? He was surprised how quickly it gave in to being crushed and demolished. The car is made for accidents it seemed to him—made to be destroyed by other cars, always on the way to being ruined garbage, only ever temporarily un-wrecked. Cars destroy the world; the world destroys back.

He couldn't breathe very well. His sternum was a flat plate pressing down on a bounded, fragile sea. Maybe he would die after all, surviving the accident only to die in this . . . infirmary or wherever he dimly felt himself to be. Yes, his own body would suffocate him. He struggled to breathe.

In and out of awareness he floated, wondering at each stage why he both thought, saw, and sensed a square door, a window, opening in his torso which, by him perceiving it, meant he was another person in a different world. A snap, and then there was only a sort of fog.

He was dreaming. In the dream, he very much wanted to sleep. However, every time he closed his eyes, he was awake (in the dream, not really awake) and found himself vividly remembering drifting, through various childhood apartments. He had an the urge to pause and write what he was remembering, or experiencing, he wasn't sure which. He would open his eyes (in the dream) and reach for a notebook to write but as soon as he opened his eyes, sleepiness would overcome him and he would close his eyes again.

As soon as his eyes closed, sleep would drift away from him

again, and his memories would become so clear that he could walk through walls and years, and wander around inside the houses and apartments of his peripatetic childhood and youth. He could pick up brass candleholders cold to the touch, sit on couches and at desks, look into drawers, open the faded, soft batik curtains sewn by his grandmother. He could pick a rose from one of his father's several ancient rosebushes which grew back forcefully every year, filling the rooms with their brazen pink faces and inebriating scents. He could read the news in newspapers strewn on the kitchen table. He could put on hats, coats and gloves, observe wind moving through trees outside the window, climb ladders into humid, musty attics, and unlatch trunks of moth-eaten books, comics, and clothing.

Amazed by the vividness of his recall, he would open his eyes to grope for a notebook just out of reach, wanting to document the details of these places and feelings he had so much forgotten, but instantly, the moment he opened his eyes, he became so heavy, so drowsy he couldn't possibly write. He was outside of his boat, which had floated away, he had dropped the oars, and yet he was still trying to row it underwater. He gave up on that and let himself be submerged. And then just as he closed his eyes, the fog in his mind evaporated, pierced by gleams of memory. He did not bother to reach for the notebook this time. He knew what would happen.

He asked himself how he would remember everything he was re-experiencing if he couldn't write it down. But then it occurred to him that these memories were not a product of writing. He realized at that moment that he was asleep. He thought that as soon as he woke up, he would forget all of this, unless he wrote it down. He opened his eyes and reached for the notebook. And again he felt as if drugged with sleep. He closed his eyes and found himself at the beach with his family, collecting sand dollars and feathers. He wanted to write this down too, but he remembered that the memories he was having, or, that he was traveling in, were not a product of writing.

What was the solution? I'll remain asleep, he thought. But now he was no longer sleepy. He was at a party his father had thrown, for what reason he did not know. The room roared with voices, music, and smoke. His father was dancing, jostling, with a cigarette in his mouth. On the table were plates of remnants of smoked fish and cheese, and empty bottles of vodka and whiskey, cans of beer. He picked up a silver wine opener that had been his grandfather's, which he had later given to his own child, a little puzzle piece with the screw hidden in a cylinder. You had to put it together before you could use it, unscrewing the screw, pulling it out, then turning and pushing it through a small hole in the cylinder where it became a little lever. The small sequence of movements was reversed when you opened a bottle of wine; instead of unscrewing and pushing you screwed and pulled. He put together the opener, opened a bottle of wine, looked around for a glass and finding none, drank from the bottle. But he could not taste the wine.

He walked into the foyer and saw a checkbook and a pen. He understood that it was time to pay his bills. Debt returned like sleep, like birds singing the same songs in spring. The season of debt replaced all other seasons, just as the cars replaced the animals.

A squirrel watched him from the window sill as he tried to write the check. He picked up the pen, feeling suddenly sweaty and hot as if he was about to be caught committing a crime. He tried to write in the book, but it was a struggle. His hands didn't work. He could only manage an illegible scrawl. And he remembered this scrawl of his; how he and his father had tried to puzzle it out the next day. His father had laughed that he had been so drunk, he had not been able to write his own name. But I'm not drunk! He tried to say. I'm asleep and I've been wrecked on the highway. Had he met this debt, this father, this squirrel, this sleep somewhere before? Was this the same father, the same debt, the same sleep, the same squirrel as always?

Cam Scott

THE PIVOT OF THE OBJECT-GODS

Every idea originates through equating the unequal.

—Friedrich Nietzsche

Kant stinks.

—John Ashbery

As philosophy prefers to think of itself as non-beholden, the philosophy of history tends toward narrative extravagance. At worst, the unwillingness of its various deontological societies to think their own historical determinations results in scientism; more covertly, myriad humanities appear to qualify the false universalism of the field. History is all-too-human, and a certain well-intentioned suspicion as to the exclusivity of this designation often subordinates the philosophical consequence of history to that of a general anthropology.

The philosophy that issues from this displacement would be a brand of historicism nonetheless, one that attempts to locate a guiding principle outside of developing events. Accordingly, this colonizing discourse is always rediscovering religion, as the afterimage of its own relativizing methodologies. Likewise, as a practice of comparison without distinction, the speculative anthropology that suffices towards the cause of materialism in philosophy happens upon the same insight again and again, secularizing by association.

This movement figures tellingly in the work of anti-philosopher Friedrich Nietzsche, who opposes the study of history to the principle of life itself, a non-specific font of pre-personal will. This occult force may even operate as a misplaced intimation of historical objectivity, insofar as the subject appears amid an inexorable current to which its nature and agency are pitifully limited. But this remark issues from the realm of a speculative psychology, and conceptual circularity ensues; life is a posit of drive, an ulterior vitality. Nietzsche proliferates typologies with reference to this ahistorical will, recasting class society as so many sedimented temporalities or developmental levels, that a suitably caustic diagnostician may descend at once. This subjectivized view of history not only naturalizes oppression, making a variegated aquarium of a stratified society, but plays recklessly upon the ways in which class is already raced, and race is classified, in the author's own historical surround.

Nietzsche's summit morality partakes of a scarcely acknowledged base; but this oversight commends the work of Georges Bataille, who, re-reading Nietzsche in a climate of political reaction, will polemically extol the summit from the depths, asserting a circular identity. Insofar as each term requires the other, the lowest designated value is always provisional. If this identity is relative, secured only in evaluation, then any theorist fixing to enjoy the scenery upon ascent is implicated in a system of exchange.

CAPITAL-ISMS

The bottom feeders that people Nietzsche's pre-Freudian polemic tend contingently toward ethnic caricature out of a deeper necessity; as a figural return of an historical repressed from which his postulate of will derives. One must stay vigilant of implication where philosophies of life—or will, or drive, any extra-historical posit—are concerned. These racial figurations appear proletarianized in philosopher Jean-François Lyotard's work on libidinal economy, to speak of other philosophical bottom feeders, in which the author effectively eternalizes domination as the crucible of all possible identification.

Rather than absolutize the object of anthropology—human societies and their rituals—Lyotard addresses the alien principle subtending every variation on this theme, "desire" in its ahistorical morbidity. On this basis, Lyotard avers that the underclasses savor their collective lot; a point made with requisite revulsion. Furthermore, for Lyotard, the circuits of exchange modelled by Marx are preconfigured in sexual pre-latency, such that when one speaks of the monetary autonomization of mediation, or capital as inhuman procreativity, one describes a process in which human constituents are already enrolled.[1]

Lyotard's demonstration is forceful in its proliferation of images, but any postulated homology between ritual and capital must be articulated so as not to absolutize the latter regime in its historical specificity. This remains the program of many anthro-pessimists, otherwise far-right Deleuzeans, whose cleverness impels them to backdate the form of capital indefinitely, offering only so many inverted versions of Rousseauian social unity.

One influential example would be an early paper by neoreactionary philosopher Nick Land, himself an excrescent product of Bataille's corpus, "Kant, Capital, and the Prohibition of Incest." In this paper, Land contends that Kantian formalism not only coincides with the dawn of capitalism, but preconfigures its corrosive totalism. In Immanuel Kant's philosophy, Land relates, the synthetic a priori furnishes the rational subject a universal form for the yet-to-be-encountered. While experience is contingent, the conditions for any encounter with the outside world are pre-determined; thus Land pursues an analogy to exchange value, insofar as Kantian synthesis sees to the convertibility of all experience in advance.[2]

Here we may assert the work of György Lukács against Kantian philosophy, and the antinomies of bourgeois thought. As Lukács explains, the dichotomies that Kant could not overcome were only displaced, for any attempt to systematically subsume the "other" of thought into a framework requires a contradictory delimitation. The thing-in-itself secures an abstract equivalence, put forth to unify multifarious phenomena, and while Kant's system no longer requires God as guarantor—Kant retains this figure as a more or less ornamental concession to contemporary power—it nonetheless requires an unknowable absolute.

One problem of Enlightenment philosophy, then, is that matter cannot be registered in its irrational alterity outside of a system of value, or reason. This, as per Lukács, is a problem for any thought which aspires to knowledge of the whole, for a partial system would not encounter this conceptual difficulty. If Land seems to identify the structure of capital with the transcendental dialectic, Lukács offers a considerably more refined thesis a half-century prior—German idealism is a thinking of the development of the class society, recast on an abstract philosophical plane.

MALPRACTICING

To the degree that theory and practice refer to the same objects, Lukács quotes an early Marx: "Didn't the Moloch of the Ancients hold sway? Wasn't the Delphic Apollo a real power in the life of the Greeks? In this context Kant's criticism is meaningless."[3] All gods have existed at one time or another, insofar as human tribute has social ramifications. Where the corporealizations of religion are concerned, eighteen-forties Marx is pragmatically materialist; and in the nineteen-seventies, against the backdrop of a moribund debate between humanistic and scientific socialisms, triangulated by a scientistic anti-communism, Régis Debray will risk accusations of idealism in order to advance a sympathetic program.

For Debray, ideology differs from science precisely insofar as it derives from the practical order of behavior, "where erring ways are all we have ... Erring ways (always in the plural) are collective.

Erring ways cannot be refuted, either on the grounds of experience or rational grounds ... To *mend* them, you have to *fight* them."[4] In this description, Debray identifies the concept with pure historical folly and the masses with happenstance. In both cases, the subject of history is commensurate with a pseudo-object that nevertheless has concrete effects on the world. Where actions catalyze in reality, the truth or falsity of a justification is beside the point. "A vacuous idea which has effects is a serious idea," Debray cautions, just as "a serious idea that has no effects is vacuous."[5]

Ideology may be glossed in orthodox fashion, as "the dominant material relationships grasped as ideas," but Debray finds within most theorizations the implication of "an inert relation of exteriority: the real-to-be-reflected is simply juxtaposed to a reflective consciousness, the accuracy of whose image varies according to the class 'optic' or the prism of interest."[6] A normative philosophical model ensures the duplication of the Kantian impasse: contingent sense data is categorically overdetermined and inferior to rational purposes, which are class-based in their bearing. Each ruling class must see to it that its values are "expressed in ideal form: it has to give its ideas the form of universality, and represent them as the only rational, universally valid ones."[7]

The passive recipients of ideology are material laborers, who as Marx says, "have less time to make up illusions and ideas about themselves" on account of their employment actively producing reality. In select passages describing the working dupes of ideology as destitute of thought, Marx himself appears susceptible to Debray's critique—that in terms too typical of philosophical divisions of labor, ideology is represented as a state of stupidity or privation, "an indignity rather than a reality." Because ideology was theorized by Marx-philosopher rather than Marx-historian, Debray suggests, it is immediately an epistemological rather than "praxiological" concept: "The principle of the wrong explanation immediately supplants the social fact that has to be explained."[8]

In this sense the explanation becomes a determination of indifference in advance, after the fact. Praxis shorn of idealism will already have redeemed all fantasies enrolled in its cause. "A philosophy in which there is simply no room for (a serious theory of) the imaginary has been left to fetishize the notion of ideology," Debray continues. In this provocative description, ideology becomes a meta-fetish; for the Marxian concept of the fetish character of the commodity already assumes the place in *Capital* of ideology in Marx's early philosophical work. To make a fetish of ideology would then be to fetishize fetishism—likewise, "that's ideology" is an explanation furnished us by (always another) ideology.

The concepts are not quite equivalent, however: Marx defines fetishism as a quasi-metaphysical credulity before the commodity, whereby definite social relations between people are fantastically perceived as relations between things. In this sense, commodities are both sensuous and suprasensible, says Marx. Exchange value furnishes us a form of experience, but this form is itself historically contingent and must come into being. Marx, then, is not offering a meta-theory of ideology, which could only be meta-ideological. He is examining the ideology of capitalism specifically. The categorical illusions of philosophy must be explicated historically, too: and the moment of repair between appearance and reality, which philosophy-proper forestalls and anticipates in all kinds of ingenuitive ways, may be construed as a practical eventuality owing to the specificity of Marx's object.

In his dissertation, the same quoted by Lukács contra Kant, Marx credits the ideological aspect of practice with a substantial modicum of reality:

> If somebody imagines that he has a hundred talers, if this concept is not for him an arbitrary, subjective one, if he believes in it, then these hundred imagined talers have for him the same value as a hundred real ones. For instance, he will incur debts on the strength of his imagination, his imagination will *work, in the same way as all humanity has incurred debts on its gods.*[9]

Wealth-in-fantasy becomes debt-in-reality by a certain consensus as to the constancy of a guarantor. In Christian Europe, for example, pagan gods are no longer currency. It is after the logic of this demonstration that Marx makes a move to generality: "*that which a particular country is for particular alien gods, the country of reason is for God in general, a region in which he ceases to exist.*"[10]

"Reason" here is a transcendental term intended to supplant each local variant. The religion of every society—and there has never been a society without a religion, claims Debray—is both provisionally absolute and subject to relativization, conquerable in turn by an all-engulfing universal term. Much as Bataille saw a provisional universality, or moment of sovereign beneficence, in the post-war Marshall Plan, we may regard the establishment of the Eurozone on this conquering model; local gods and their currencies gradually falling afoul of a larger and ultimately metaphysical scheme. Pagan independence is repudiated, and returns as so many paradoxical nationalisms: after Bataille, Jaleh Mansoor describes the Marshall Plan as a diplomatic "war by other means," and the monetary policy of the EU may be noted along similar lines.[11]

THE WILL TO ERROR

As both Lukács and Debray observe, alterity does not threaten any admittedly partial system. A properly religious project already accommodates this difficulty, granting a conceptual amnesty to its excess; whereas one might suggest that those religions which are too closely allied to a given state are apt to the kind of falsification-by-encounter that Marx's analogy takes for granted.

The "erring ways" from which Debray constructs his materialism of ideas are necessarily collective, but not total; and one cannot simply arrive at a vision of universality by way of summary, adding customs to one another, much less dividing them against themselves. Elsewhere, in delineating his own theory of fanatical praxis, Bataille quotes Nietzsche, from *The Will to Power*: "The majority of people are a fragmentary, exclusive image of what humanity is; you have to add them up to get humanity. In this sense, whole eras and whole peoples have something fragmentary about them; and it may be necessary for humanity's growth for it to develop only in parts."[12]

Here Nietzsche has forthrightly conflated "humanity" with "capital" in reference to inexorable growth, and this crypto-eugenic agenda may be corrected with reference to the theory of combined and uneven development. Within the totality of capitalism, vastly discrepant time scales coexist of exploitative necessity, encompassing racializing and immiserating divisions of labor. Likewise, Frank Wilderson III explains that any society of "contemporaries" procures civic coziness and temporal coincidence from a constitutive exclusivity. The language of timing and temporal coincidence is noteworthy; for the excluded element is not in fact anterior to society but present in its absence at every moment.

Nietzsche's developmental sketch of "humanity" appears parochial at best, and supportive of far more destructive extrapolations. As Bataille notes, Nietzsche prefers the collective first-person pronoun; he invidiously presumes the reader his postdated contemporary, an exclusionary gesture we may diagnose at once. Nietzsche continues: "It is a crucial matter therefore to see that what is at stake is always the idea of producing a synthetic humanity and that the inferior humans who make up a majority of us are only preliminaries, or preparatory attempts whose concerted play allows *a whole human being* to appear here and there like a military boundary marker showing the extent of humanity's advance."[13]

This conquering synthesis projects an anthropological whole, from which additive grandeur individuals derive; for something on the order of a work must already have been completed in order for anyone to stand as either an inferior fragment or representative synecdoche themselves. Bataille suggestively inverts this suggestion, insisting that the need to act *specializes* us in turn: "Even if it turns out to be for the general interest (which normally isn't true), the activity that subordinates each of our aspects to a specific result suppresses our being as an entirety."[14] Every human is a finished humanity such is life but from this state, one must put one's energy toward a purpose.

"Life is whole only when it isn't subordinate to a specific object that exceeds it," Bataille writes. This bears directly on bourgeois rationality, as a system that contradictorily affirms knowledge of the whole by collating all matter of heterogeneous phenomena in advance, condescending to that which otherwise exceeds the subject. To be whole is to be finished. Here it is worth recalling the descendancy of Bataille's thought from Alexandre Kojève, who famously contends that after the End of History, an appetitive, animal non-actor will have supplanted the subject, whose prior vocation was to "nihilate in space." This afterlife is Free Time, in the sense of time—or consciousness of space—sans purpose. Bataille, on the other hand, suggests that a motivated being has an *advantageous* relation to time: "Each of your moments becomes *useful*," commensurate with a definitive act.[15]

Bataille is a mystic in politics to the degree that for him, alterity is non-ruinous, and needn't be subsumed by explanation. This compares favorably with the Kantian attempt upon totality, which produces an abstract object, the thing-in-itself, that exceeds its subject, thereby producing an all-knowing destitution. Bataille's challenge to bourgeois philosophy commences from this irrational excess, which forms the basis for his attempt at a universal economy.

THE ACCURSED SHARE

This project, set forth in *The Accursed Share*, makes an attempt upon totality as the congruence of thought and its other. Human life, it follows, is never whole, for it is exceeded by baser conditions throughout its existence. For Bataille, this excessive objectivity is a condition of eroticism as a threshold experience. This terminology is both idiosyncratic and advantageous, for it already accounts for the divide between subject and object insofar as desire refers to something other than oneself.

Eroticism designates relation, "an alternation of repulsion and attraction, of negation and the affirmation that follows it," a dialectical process by which exceptionality is procured of some baser continuum. Obscenity, then, is a relation, too: nothing in itself is obscene, and any judgement reveals the "relation between an object and the mind of a person."[16] Obscenity is partial, and any injunction against a universal obscenity is incoherent. In this regard, Bataille's theory of eroticism may be construed as a direct reply to Kant.

In the aforementioned essay by Nick Land, at which point in his career he was militating for a libidinally dissolute anarchism, the prohibition of incest is regarded as prototypical of the accumulation of capital. For Land, this prohibition is an engine of conquest and expansion, which, within a system of strict patrilineality, is subsumed under a fixed sign. In the next step toward capitalism, kinship and trade are systematically isolated from one another in order that xenophobic kinship practices may develop alongside an appropriately competitive spirit. These proscriptions, Land contends, each strive to capture alterity within a set of rules that inhibit synthesis, and generate surplus in the form of a residual objectivity or otherness.

This attempt to homologously backdate capital owes a great deal to Bataille's project of general economy. This appeal, of course, inculpates 'humanity' by de-historicizing, or ontologizing, capital—voiding criticism of bourgeois political economy by hopelessly expanding its remit. Here one may recall the description of Claude Lévi-Strauss's anthropological programme as a "Kantianism without a transcendental subject," insofar as it asserts certain formal precedents to culture: "I am not disputing that reason develops and transforms itself in the practical field," Lévi-Strauss writes as though responding to Marxist epistemology: "man's mode of thought reflects his relations to the world and to men. But in order for *praxis* to be living thought, it is necessary first (in a logical and not a historical sense) for thought to exist."[17]

Land's move is to become a narrator of origins, a patently fascist position that a certain stripe of teleologist is always in danger of embodying. Little wonder that Land's early leftism is implicitly anarcho-primitivist, and culminates in the racist technologism of "accelerationism." His interpretation of Bataille's general economy—commencing with the destructive beneficence of solar energy—makes capitalism the end of life on, or beyond, earth; whereas for Bataille the tendency of all ritual behavior is either toward, or fearfully away from, an objectively extant communism.

TWILIGHT OF THE GODS

In each of the above philosophical sketches, a noumenal (or "natural") nonhuman becomes an object of speculation on behalf of a strategic representation of reality. "The intellect fails, in fact, in that with its first impulse it *abstracts*, separating the objects of reflection from the concrete totality of the real. It constructs, under the name of science, a world of abstract things, copied from the things of the profane world, a partial world dominated by utility," writes Bataille. This would be precursor to the world of action delimited above. We could compare Lukács, for whom "on the one hand, men are constantly smashing, replacing and leaving behind them the "natural," irrational and actually existing bonds, while, on the other hand, they erect around themselves in the reality they have created and "made," a kind of second nature which evolves with exactly the same inexorable necessity as was the case earlier on with irrational forces of nature...."[18] Clearly the laws of capitalism have such a significance.

The class character of philosophy pertains; for insofar as any social datum in its immediacy must be interpreted for and by consciousness, factical appearances are mediated by a viewpoint which varies depending upon one's interest. The antinomies of form and content, subject and object, proliferate because of a pathological aversion to mediation. In Lukács's description, this aversion serves to stave off the higher synthesis associated with "the self-understanding of the proletariat," whose special privilege as productive agent is to fulfill the vocation of the 'identical subject-object' heralded, though unfulfilled, by philosophy.[19]

As Lukács relates, this task falls to an historical agent otherwise "reduced" to objectivity. Bourgeois philosophy presumes an abstract equality of subjects before appearances, but its proletarian corrective consists in speaking from that standpoint of unknowable objectivity, indifferently formalized from on high. As Étienne Balibar explains, "the only 'subject' Marx speaks of is one that is practical, multiple, anonymous, and by definition not conscious of itself ... namely 'society,' i.e. the whole set of activities of production, exchange, and consumption the combined effect of which is perceptible to each person outside himself, as a 'natural' property of things."[20]

Thus objectivity is constituted in and by fetishism; which again, is a concept bequeathed a user by the market and not an anthropological given. The specific character of this fetish deserves some elaboration. In a moment of holdover from his earlier conception of ideology, Marx compares the commodity fetish to the "phantasmagoria" of religious belief: although rendered as "fantastic" in Fowler's English translation, Marx clearly means to poetically denote a kind of shadow-play or false appearance. As noted above, Marx identifies the illusion that value inheres in currency as a particular instance of religious projection in an appendix to his dissertation:

> Real talers have the same existence that the imagined gods have. Has a real taler any existence except in the imagination, if only in the general or rather common imagination of man? Bring paper money into a country where this use of paper is unknown, and everyone will laugh at your subjective imagination. Come with your gods into a country where other gods are worshipped, and you will be shown to suffer from fantasies and abstractions.[21]

The objectively preposterous status of the gods corresponds in this demonstration to the fantastic relation capital procures. In the foreword, Marx quotes Epicurus: "Not the man who denies the gods worshipped by the multitude, but he who affirms of the gods what the multitude believes about them, is truly impious," which is to say, there must remain a split between the reality of the gods and their representation.[22] In this same foreword Marx anticipates a practice of philosophy capable of banishing any folkloric holdover whatsoever.

This description of the advance of reason—as a progress of new gods upon old, an emanation of the progress of spirit upon successive degrees of nature—has a precedent in Hegel's characterization of ancient Greece. In this account, society's old gods appear more divine and less human, more elemental and less free, insofar as they are retained at every moment for comparison. In Hegel's work, Gillian Rose explains, "Greece provides the fictional but logical basis for the subsequent determination of substance as subject."[23] Throughout Hegel's essentialized antiquity, social and political institutions are aesthetically subsumed, such that subjectivity is simply a non-factor. Hegel's remarks on ancient religion predict Marx's phantasmagoric objects of worship, for, as Hegel observes, "the Gods are made, invented, but they are not fictitious."[24]

This anticipates the description of "second nature," as a pre-mediated elemental given. But Hegel's logical purposes depend upon temporal antecedence and not a spatial relation of exteriority. Antiquity in Hegel is a proxy "state of nature" in which presentation and representation essentially agree, such that this age may be situated prior to the advent of politics and any history commensurate therewith. Although closely identified with ritual credulity, this aesthetic saturation more or less abolishes art and religion alike, as both operate upon a constitutive gap between presentation and representation. In Hegel's 1805 lectures, both art and religion are uniquely implicated in the crisis of bourgeois individualism.

Art is *immediately* spirit, intuition without concept, form without content, in which the distortions of sense attendant upon bourgeois society are expressed. Art thus represents the arbitrary detail, but has no concept of how details relate. In Rose's class-conscious gloss, art "reproduces the contradiction between real social relations and an imagined unity in a society of private property relations."[25] As a partial representation of social relations, art is, anachronistically, a paradigm of ideology. Religion marks a further step toward ethical life, in that this sensuous isolation of elements becomes integrated into religious practice as an intimation of equality. Intuition turns upon the self, such that God is felt to be the "Self of all." Knowing that "divine nature is not other than the human," all other religions are felt to be incomplete.[26]

The old gods qua arbitrary custom, naturalized by rote tribute, are particulars among particulars, conceptually unthreatened for residing outside of a restricted system. They are, as seen, more than fictive: they are sedimented by belief into something on the order of law. Hegel's demonstration requires something called "Greek religion" as a moment in a logically necessary development, much as the speculative anthropology of Freud, Bataille, Land et al requires an eerily unspecified pre-colonial other as a developmental phase, owing to the very arbitrariness of the prohibitions that this fiction is intended to explain. As the possibility of transgression implies an existence beyond any rule in particular, freedom retrojects an arbitrary limit.

PRACTICAL RELIGION

An early Marx anticipates a practice of reason that will supplant the obstinacy of mere custom, whereas by the time of *Capital*, cognitive occlusion is a practical matter. Debray's reply is that reason is already ritual. Belief and knowledge are not in any subjective contradiction, Debray insists; much as Kant does not isolate a faculty of belief, which would simply be a lower degree of knowledge: "When a reasoning subject finds himself faced with an object and there is no symmetry between the subjective and the objective, he has to 'believe' in the sense of saying more about the object than he actually knows."[27]

If Debray elides Kant's distinctions between epistemological and pragmatic, doctrinal and ethical, believing, it is to make a practical point. The transfer of ideas from action to knowledge transpires formally: unknown to truth, a categorical decision sutures subject-to-group, to-otherwise-forsworn-exterior. Common identification with a signifier is required that any group may emerge, which mediating term must considerably precede any voluntaristic effort, let alone motivating faith. This essentially religious decentering of the self-motivated subject renders analytic and dialectic—logics of truth and appearance respectively—inseparable.

In each case, Debray writes, "the collective is born outside itself. The transcendence of the social in relation to itself is one and the same as the delimitation of the social as a totality."[28] Where any configuration of elements is concerned, inner differentiation is implied. It is an organization, which function is "to relate beings not initially related to one another." This requires a system, which an organic conception of art or society cannot itself furnish us, for the same reason Debray observes that the "expression '*religious community*' is pleonastic (elements cannot 'commune' in an environment that is homogeneous with them)."[29]

Along similar lines, Peter Sloterdijk—who writes the reactionary obverse to Debray's critique, narrating the vertical striving of the "practicing being" on an aristocratic, auto-disciplinary model—will profess that "religions do not exist." Debray likewise suggests that religion is an incoherent concept, seeing as "religion" cannot exist in a world of "religions," for its universality is falsified thereby: "where religion is everywhere, it has no name."[30] Any affinity between religion and ideology today surely concerns this repressive ubiquity. Where ideology refers to something like a cognitive frame or bourgeois optic before the production of reality, we may regard ourselves as religiously subsumed, well past the point of no-religion. We may adapt Marx's quotation—"*that which a particular country is for particular alien gods, the country of reason is for God in general, a region in which he ceases to exist*"—and note that there is at present no region on earth in which God ceases to cease to exist.

A PIECE OF REALITY

Here Nietzsche reappears, as the most trenchant critic of religion after Marx. For both thinkers, religion is an emanation of a people and a ruling culture more specifically. Nietzsche, however, for want of an equivalent concept of ideology, writes of religion as a straightforward expression of popular will and not an imposition: "A people that still believes in itself retains its own god. In him it reveres the conditions which let it prevail, its virtues: it projects its pleasure in itself, its feeling of power, into a being to whom one may offer thanks."[31] Here, with Marx's metaphor in mind, one may anticipate the jurisdictional crisis of the "death of God," which is the death of ritual necessity, requiring ceaseless exchange for lack of transcendental backing.

One must understand Nietzsche's polemic in this light: "In Christianity neither morality nor religion has even a single point of contact with reality," he writes, with special contempt for the Kantian system that has banished the concept of reality for the "mere appearance (of) a mendaciously fabricated world."[32] Accepting this decision, one finds only imaginary interactions between imaginary things; an unceasing "intercourse between imaginary beings" assumes social significance as people increasingly counterpose their activity to that of nature, which in Nietzsche is a term for starker reality. Here too, religion represents the imaginary relationship of individuals to their real conditions of existence.

Nietzsche's ideal type is an outcome; an individual capable of setting forth its own imperative. But his improvised tantrums presuppose the expressive immediacy of this absolute individual. Accordingly, the God for whom Nietzsche reserves special contempt is held to be the God of the masses in particular: a "low-water mark" in the development of divine types. Nietzsche fares better when he considers the appeal this escapist signifier: "Who alone has good reason to lie his way out of reality? He who suffers from it. But to suffer from reality is to be a piece of reality that has come to grief."[33]

This is a fruitful image of alienation. Not only does this description, "a piece of reality come to grief," seem to correspond to the subjective agony of Bataille's bivalent eroticism, it may be rerouted as a poetic description of proletarian objectivity, itself an historical pivot between subject and object. Politics, then, would be an objective practice of the transvaluation of all class values. High and low swap places not unto an eschatological vertigo, but in the course of revolution. Accordingly, in the guise of a contemptible and incontrovertible nature, the "bottom"—more dogmatically, the base—would be a place to start as well as a destination.

Yet insofar as many philosophers have sought to naturalize capital, and to metabolize its family values, one may proclaim antipathy to nature, too. It is in these moments of contestation that the gods arrive in retrospect, and any revolution must condescend to certain of them, if only as political proxies. Paradoxically, this conceptual sacrifice places each would-be supplicant above the object of negation, although our only power issues from below. The historical consciousness that attends this vexed situatedness would be as apt to transformation as it is transformative: one may reply to Nietzsche that the meek inherit nothing other than what they incessantly create.

NOTES

1. Marx famously describes capital using the metaphor of vampirism; Lyotard's description brings to mind Talia Schaffer's work on the vampire in nineteenth-century literature, which figure is linked to the threat of "homosexual procreative sex." On this analogy, Lyotard's barely concealed contempt for the working classes is doubly and vociferously homophobic.

2. Nick Land, *Fanged Noumena: Collected Writings 1987-2007* (Falmouth, United Kingdom: Urbanomic, 2011), 55-80.

3. György Lukács, *History and Class Consciousness*, trans. Rodney Livingstone (Cambridge: MIT Press, 1971), 127.

4. Régis Debray, *Critique of Political Reason* (London: Verso Books, 1983), 82.

5. Ibid., 78.

6. Ibid., 94.

7. One might add that last decade's attack on "correlationism" would be the most "ideological" project in recent memory, for that it attacks what is ultimately a class correlate in the guise of its false claim to universality.

8. Ibid., 91.

9. Karl Marx, *Collected Works Volume 1* (London: Lawrence & Wishart: 1975), 104.

10. Ibid.

11. Jaleh Mansoor, *Marshall Plan Modernism: Italian Postwar Abstraction and the Beginnings of Autonomia* (Durham: Duke University Press, 2016), 211.

12. Quoted in Georges Bataille, *On Nietzsche*, trans. Bruce Boone (London: Continuum, 2004), xxiii.

13. Ibid.

14. Bataille, xxiv.

15. Ibid.

16. Georges Bataille, *The Accursed Share: An Essay on General Economy Volumes II & III*, trans. Robert Hurley (Brooklyn: Zone Books, 1993), 48.

17. Claude Lévi-Strauss, *The Savage Mind* (Chicago: University of Chicago Press, 1966), 263.

18. Lukács, 128.

19. Lukács, 149.

20. Étienne Balibar, *The Philosophy of Marx* (London and New York: Verso Books, 1995), 67.

21. Marx, 104.

22. Ibid., 30.

23. Gillian Rose, *Hegel Contra Sociology* (London: Verso Books, 2009), 126.

24. Ibid., 123.

25. Ibid., 76.

26. G.W.F. Hegel, *Hegel and the Human Spirit: A Translation of the Jena Lectures on the Philosophy of Spirit*, trans. Leo Rauch (Detroit: Wayne State University Press, 1983), 176.

27. Debray, 121.

28. Ibid., 173.

29. Ibid., 175.

30. Ibid., 170.

31. Friedrich Nietzsche, *The Portable Nietzsche*, trans. Walter Kaufmann (London: Viking, 1954), 582.

32. Ibid., 581.

33. Ibid., 582.

Maya Sisneros in conversation with David Bowles, Rodney Gomez, Emmy Pérez, José Antonio Rodríguez, and Veronica Sandoval aka Lady Mariposa

This is an interview with five contributors to *Imaniman: Poets Writing in the Anzaldúan Borderlands.*[1] All five poets have an intimate relationship with the Río Grande Valley: Veronica Sandoval, Rodney Gomez, José Antonio Rodríguez, and David Bowles grew up in or around the RGV, and Emmy Pérez has lived there since 2000. The Río Grande Valley is a landscape that inspired much of *Borderlands/ La Frontera: The New Mestiza* by Gloria Anzaldúa, who famously wrote: "The US-Mexican border es una herida abierta where the Third World grates against the first and bleeds. And before a scab forms it hemorrhages again, the lifeblood of two worlds merging to form a third country—a border culture."[2] With so much uncertainty since the November election, I wanted to hear what poets have been thinking about and building. Specifically, poets navigating (or who have navigated) the physical landscape of the US borderlands.

I spent the morning of May Day re-reading the responses of these poets, and once I closed my laptop, marches for the "Day Without an Immigrant" had erupted through San Francisco and Oakland. The nahuatl word that David Bowles talks about in this interview rang particularly potent that day: "chīhualoyān," *a time for making.*

The following is a reflection on The Río Grande Valley, language, ritual, and creation. This interview has been edited for length.

What is one thing living in the Río Grande Valley has taught you, and how has this informed your art?

SANDOVAL: El Valle has taught me that I exist. I have a history, a place where I was born, a place my own, un lugar de chicaras and palmas, of rosales and mesquite. El Valle taught me the importance of having such a place, especially now that I live in Washington State and am working on my PhD. I cannot disconnect the reality of my experience from the ideas seeking theory, from the words being poured on to the page. My history keeps me grounded, a history of cervezas con comadres, of locadas hasta la madrugada, of vatos quebrados, of cumbias and Tejano, of poetry, of my head on my mother's lap, her fingers in my hair. I keep alive that "I" in discourse that academia keeps trying to shame out of me.

GOMEZ: Historical amnesia is very real here. It is possible for a people who compose 90% of a population to forget how the other 10% has historically marginalized them. Students are not taught how, just a few years ago, there were white drinking fountains and brown drinking fountains, how, if you spoke Spanish in school, you were beaten. We are not taught our heroes. Certainly not Chican@ writers. Sometimes, growing up, I heard about Rolando Hinojosa. I didn't read Américo Paredes until graduate school. Gloria Anzaldúa was like a black magic incantation, never to be spoken. Things are changing now. Miraculously, gloriously. But the wounds remain to be stitched up. There is an obligation in all of this to write, to insist that the next history will not be written without us.

BOWLES: Who I am is so deeply threaded in the weft of our regional culture that any attempt (by me or others) to pull me free would be destructive. As a result, my art centers on that interplay between communal and interior experiences (like the familia-centered heroism of the protagonists in my *Garza Twins* series). Though it's certainly true, as Rodney expresses, that there was no public, mainstream acknowledgement of the objective value of Mexican American experience in my youth, the stories I heard at the knee of Grandmother Garza, on my Uncle Joe Pérez's ranch, in my tía's kitchens…those bits of lore were seeded in my heart, shaping my thinking about the world. Blossoming now, mighty ceibas of the spirit fling me along their limbs into Latinx futures and down their roots into indigenous past.

RODRÍGUEZ: In a very concrete sense, the Río Grande Valley is a community of contradictions, which is a result of the meeting of two nations on unequal terms. There's a marked presence of elements of Mexican culture, but there's also a great desire to embrace cultural artifacts that represent dominant American culture, such as national franchise restaurants and status symbols like iPhones.

In larger terms, the RGV is the very definition of marginalization, which is ironic, since it's such a significant port of entry for immigrants. I was reprimanded for speaking Spanish in school. I was pushed into the queer closet. I was taught shame for my own poverty. What I've aimed to do with what I've lived and what I've witnessed of the RGV is to use it to cultivate what Edward Said calls an "exilic consciousness," a way of seeing the world as an outsider in order to see it more profoundly, hopefully more clearly. This then is key to my writing.

PÉREZ: I have lived here over a decade and something that I admire here is the DIY spirit among so many, including poets, writers, artists, and activists. To name just a few, Hermana Resist Press, FlowerSong Books, the Río Grande Valley International Poetry Festival immediately come to mind, and I love NETA, the new "bilingual, multimedia platform," Aquí Estamos, LUPE, and the activism of the Sierra Club here against the border wall and more. Granted, these entities do not represent the majority of the population, but they bring hope for positive change to many, including myself.

Is there an author (perhaps a passage?) that you have found yourself returning to over the past few months? (For comfort? For strength?)

SANDOVAL: I am writing a response to this question on the 101st day of the Trump presidency. The climate in America has been volatile and hateful. The war machine impatiently waits, the police state is polishing their batons, and for-profit prisons are readying their beds. Lately the hate has devoured me, the fear has been so heavy I could barely breathe. Lately I've had to remind myself that how I live in spiritual harmony with the world is how I love in the world, rather than if the world loves me. Lately I've been reading "In Lak'ech"[3], reciting every line slowly exhaling the fear and pain, exhaling the disappointment and worry, "In Lak'ech" while wiping away tears…

In Lak'ech by Luis Valdes[4]
Tú eres mi otro yo.
You are my other me.
Si te hago daño a ti,
If I do harm to you,
Me hago daño a mi mismo.
I do harm to myself.
Si te amo y respeto,
If I love and respect you,
Me amo y respeto yo.
I love and respect myself.

GOMEZ: I've been reading too much dystopian fiction. This reminds me to remain in a state of constant vigilance. Maybe this is not a good thing for my mental health, but it is necessity. There is the possibility of strength in foresight. I've just finished *American War* by Omar El Akkad, which imagines a United States wrecked by a new civil war brought on by Southern resistance to fossil fuel independence. It is frightening to me in a way that the prognostications of Chomsky or theorists of the singularity frighten me. And passages from *1984*, and *The Road*, and *The Handmaid's Tale* have been roiling in me:

> "I used to think of my body as an instrument, of pleasure, or a means of transportation, or an implement for the accomplishment of my will . . . Now the flesh arranges itself differently. I'm a cloud, congealed around a central object, the shape of a pear, which is hard and more real than I am and glows red within its translucent wrapping" (*The Handmaid's Tale*).

PÉREZ: I have thought a lot about the depth and breadth of Leslie Marmon Silko's novel *Ceremony*, which I haven't read in years. I read it when I lived, for a time, near Gallup, New Mexico, near the land where the novel takes place, much like living here in the Río Grande Valley for the past 10+ years and reading Anzaldúa. These are real places. These are incredible artists who write/wrote about historical and living trauma in Native and Chicanx communities. Healing is not the right word to describe their work because the systemic issues largely remain, though their work, through art, definitely gives us readers tools to consider as we search for ways to continue to dismantle the systems of oppression that have found residence in us as younger people.

BOWLES: I keep coming back to Benjamín Alire Sáenz, especially his young-adult novels, in which Mexican-American teens who're struggling with crises of identity find support, acknowledgment, and deep love in their familias and communities. Re-reading the powerful *Sammy & Juliana in Hollywood*, I relived the epiphany I had when younger that the harsh strictures of some adults and the forgiving flexibility of others were both expressions of the same aching affection. Sometimes that love is complicated and painful, of course, and the author doesn't shy away from that, but for the most part, our gente overflow with love.

What is a favorite ritual of resistance? A favorite ritual of self-love?

PÉREZ: A favorite ritual of resistance is saying no. No to more border walls, no to existing walls, no to so-called "levee"-walls, no to so-called fences that are really walls. No to policies that say yes only to the middle class and wealthy. No to those who contribute to or comply with systemic racism, everyday sexism, homophobia and transphobia. No to those who expect us to automatically say yes with a smile even if sweetly asked. A favorite ritual of self-love is spending quality time with my two small children, watching them sprint through paths in the monte, the brushlands, which was my retreat space alone before them. They are life and love.

BOWLES: My favorite ritual of resistance recently has been to post on Facebook every Monday or so a "Revolutionary Nahuatl Word of the Week." Each word is a pointed reference to our current president, and I accompany the word with a sample sentence in Nahuatl (with an English translation). This week, for example, the word is "chamāhua" (*to brag*), and the example is "Mochamāhua, auh ahmo huel quichīuh in mahuiztlanqui"—*He brags about himself, but he hasn't done any great deed.* Also, crossing the border at least once a week to eat in a favorite restaurant in either Progreso or Río Bravo (towns in the Mexican state of Tamaulipas) is both a ritual of resistance and of self-love, feeding my soul and belly with culture and cuisine that mean so much to me, heedless of whatever damnable walls the powers-that-be would erect between me and half of my being.

GOMEZ: Disconnect. To give up the news. To give up media. To disconnect. Go for a walk. Not consume. Not be consumed. Relinquish. Mimic the grackles, simply be.

SANDOVAL: My favorite ritual of resistance is putting my chola gear on. The division of my hair into two thick braids, the hoop earnings, black hat, the "I love Cholas" shirt, the "Real Gs Get Degrees" shirt, the "Chingona" shirt! The wearing of the red, green, and white rosary, the winged out black tip of eyeliner, the dark lips! I call it putting my war gear on, and sometimes you got to get your chola on to face the day, because lately "there is a war…"

My favorite ritual of self-love is giving love. I like to light my Virgin candles, my saints, and say prayers of protection for the younglings I work with and their families. I like to spend time con las homegirls comadriando. My partner and I often participate in gatherings in which we feed people. Feeding people is a ritual of love, not only because we love food, but because community gathered in the ritual of sharing a meal feels like love. This is especially true when cooking for young students in a college town, who have often been away from the comforts of a home cooked meal for several months.

RODRÍGUEZ: I grew up with a poor and limited diet, with a constant unacknowledged level of hunger, so eating well is an act of self-care, a beautiful one.

What does creation mean to you, in a climate of political instability? (As an artist, as a community member, or as both)

PÉREZ: For me, this creation starts in the body, and sometimes, as Anzaldúa writes, begins as a "cactus needle embedded in flesh." Whether testimonio and/or acts of the imagination, the release through language and crafting this release helps it become something else, and that is creation. For me, this contributes to my existing with a greater sense of dignity, through remembering but equipped now with something I didn't know before, whether a revelation or even something seemingly small such as a new metaphor or a turn of phrase, which I believe is part of the process of soul-making Anzaldúa talks about in her work. I want to mention that creation is also the hands-on activist work that I admire so much, here in the Valley especially. These community-based organizations and individuals help keep hope alive. They spur on policy changes, see them through, and start again and again. They also help keep communities informed beyond what we read or hear in the news. I am inspired by their work.

For poets and writers, publishing is an important part of documenting the creation process, though there are other ways. Creation is not always a solitary act, and many of us do want to come together and speak/perform our art together as another form of collective creation and action. Recently, I co-organized, with Arnulfo Segovia and Alejandro Sánchez, a reading with local poets at part of the existing border wall here that was built after the so-called Secure Fence Act of 2006. Soon we will have individual videos with the poem texts of each reader to share online. The theme of the gathering: "What would you like to tell the world about your home?" This is where DIY comes in: we want to document our collective resistance beyond traditional publication and in more accessible ways. We are not waiting for news teams outside of the community to come find and/or validate these particular borderland stories and voices, and yet the work helps demonstrate that residents lead complex, varied lives beyond stereotypes, that a lot of people live here on both sides of the border, that it's not this tiny place, and that many have always resisted and will continue to do so. (*On social media, follow us with "Resistencia en la frontera: Poets Against Border Walls" and #poetsagainstwalls.*)

BOWLES: In Mesoamerican thought, order/creation was the flipside to chaos/destruction. In the face of one of the most chaotic and destructive political movements since Jim Crow, our primary tool must be creative in nature, must bring together the broken pieces of our hearts and [forge] them in mosaics that are stronger for the welding. Poetry, novels, essays, art of all types ... creation allows us to assert our existence in defiance of those who would erase us.

The Nahuas (Aztecs) had the perfect word: "chīhualoyān." *A time for making*. That's how we should see this moment of crisis.

SANDOVAL: Creating in a climate of political instability means privilege, it means having a voice and understanding the responsibility that comes through the narratives we choose to tell. As poets and scholars, we are present to capture and tell the truth about what is happening to us as a whole, and to our people. Creating means being able to ensure that what matters remains in focus, that what's important isn't erased to talking points and disembodied statistics on evening news graphs. As poets and scholars creating isn't just the poems we write, and the articles we publish, it is also in those spaces we make possible for others. The spaces we create where people can gather to talk, to write, to paint, to eat, to laugh, to feel safe; where we teach, where we learn, where we share of ourselves and our times to build communities, to make allyships. Creation is kin to resistance, kin to hope, kin to love, and in a climate of political instability, it will be our drive as creators that will that keep us connected to each other, keep us grounded, keep us building and working towards a more just world.

GOMEZ: I see creation now as an act of preservation: discovering what I have not known before, or rediscovering what I have known, and then protecting it through the act of poetry. It is not too much to imagine how easily entire histories and peoples can be erased. It has happened before. Erasure is happening now, in courthouses and legislatures all over the U.S., and their difference from erasures in the past is a difference of degree, not of kind. Creation needs also be awakening. Not only in myself, but in others. It must be a constant, vigorous voice. // Creation is the instability of the soul. If the soul sleeps, it does not create. As an artist, I see my self as contiguous with the community, seeing what the community sees, feeling what the community feels. With the election of a race-baiting misogynist who has vowed to inflict a permanent wound along the Río Grande, the intensity of violence upon the body of the community has been exposed as more than potentiality—it has been born as a living, breathing animal. By necessity, the embedded self creates, and what I create is an act of defiance, and survival, and hunger.

RODRÍGUEZ: In the current climate, which I see as an uncovering of an ever-present American ethos, rather than some new aberration, creation of art feels small sometimes. Writing a poem at times feels inadequate to the task, given the urgency of the situations in which so many find themselves with regard to document status, for example. But this is how I know to contribute, as an artist. As a community member, I see the classroom as a manifestation of that community or as a space for community, so I strive to create a safe space, a space free of bullying where real growth can happen. Beyond the classroom, I look for ways to stand in solidarity with the oppressed and the marginalized, while at the same time acknowledging that as a brown queer immigrant, I intersect with those communities, in spite of the welcoming professional space I may inhabit.

NOTES

1. Irene Lara Silva and Dan Vera, eds., *Imaniman: Poets Writing in the Anzaldúan Borderlands* (San Francisco: Aunt Lute Books, 2016).

2. Gloria Anzalduá, *Borderlands/La Frontera: The New Mestiza*. 4th ed. (San Francisco: Aunt Lute Books, 2012), 25.

3. "In Lak'ech" has been a poem central to the culture wars in Arizona public schools.

4. Luis Valdez, "In Lak'ech: You Are My Other Me," *Voices in Urban Education*, http://vue.annenberginstitute.org/perspectives/lak%E2%80%99ech-you-are-my-other.

Eirik Steinhoff

A Fiery Flying Roule first ignited and took flight in early November 2011 when the writing of my dissertation was so rudely interrupted by rioting in the streets of downtown Oakland, the city in which I worked, and where a number of my friends lived, some of whom had been arrested on the morning of October 25, 2011 in the course of the Police Department's first eviction of the Oakland Commune, that encampment also known as "Occupy Oakland" arrayed alongside a sprawling oak planted by Jack London's widow in the plaza in front of City Hall that had been renamed by the people camping there after Oscar Grant, Jr., a young black man shot to death while under arrest in the Fruitvale BART station by a transit cop early New Year's Day 2009. My writing concerned the sense of chance in the English Renaissance and was long overdue, thanks in part to a distracting sequence of uprisings earlier that year, actions at a distance variously articulating a general antagonism—in Egypt, in Wisconsin, in London. When it kicked off across the Bay from where I lived in San Francisco, it was, as Philip Sidney puts it in another context, "no hard matter to consider": I added the commune to my commute.

*

If you came to Oscar Grant Plaza at midday on a Sunday in late 2011 and walked around the elaborate encampment, chances are you would have encountered a motley crew arranged loosely on the staircase facing the entrance to the BART station at 14th and Broadway across the street from the Rite Aid, an intersection that had been the scene of repeated confrontations with the police, most notably the fusillade of teargas and flashbangs that dominated the evening of October 25 following the first clearance of the plaza. On the Sundays I'm remembering, though, that area was where something called "Poetry for the People" transpired: an improvised collective performance that took place each week of the occupation and continued to the end of the year following the second eviction in mid-November.

The invitation was general and the idea was simple: to read to one another from the radical tradition, however broadly or narrowly conceived, including your own poems or the poems of your friends, to read sometimes with the assistance of proper amplification, sometimes (if you so desired) through the people's mic, but usually with your own voice unenhanced. Duncan, di Prima, Whitman, Blake, Waldman, Retallack, Neruda, Baraka, Shelley, Dickinson, Oppen, Howe: such might be the ad hoc set list on any given Sunday. Poetry for the People—P4P for short and named after the arts/activism program founded by poet & Berkeley professor June Jordan—supplied an opportunity to congregate under the sign of poetry and populism conjoined in an effort to refashion both. We gathered and performed a supply of shapely words, planted seeds that took root and sprouted in unexpected forms: arguments, alliances, romances. It was a de facto affinity group's laboratory and seminar, a means of making itself visible to itself by doing things to and with each other with words. A rhizomatic effervescence was in effect. The thing was open-ended, apt to the moment, and often contagious. Unsuspecting passersby frequently tarried and often joined in.

I rode my bike the first time I went, from a sublet on the north side of Bernal Heights, a San Francisco neighborhood whose longstanding working-class character was being extirpated before our very eyes by a rampant real estate market accelerated by the employees of Google and Facebook who, we were told, appreciated easy access to the highway down to Silicon Valley. I remember reading, with the human microphone, first forwards, and then in reverse, some lines from Susan Howe's *Souls of the Labadie Tract* that would later be printed on the first page of the third *Roule*. "'Here we are.'" Here we are. "You can't hear us." You can't hear us. "Without having to be us." Without having to be us. "Knowing everything we know." Knowing everything we know. "You know you can't." You know you can't.

And there we were. A General Assembly was to follow the poetry on the other end of the plaza, but I skipped it for a late lunch with David Brazil and Sara Larsen, two of the driving forces behind P4P. I remember bright sunlight on empty Chinatown streets. We drank green tea, ate eggplant curry, and spoke about the ancient Greek idea of timing known as kairos. I pointed out that the word contained "Cairo," where earlier that year just a few weeks of occupying Tahrir Square had succeeded in toppling the regime (or so at least we could then still almost believe). David mentioned the entry on kairos in *The Origins of European Thought* by Richard Onians, which I looked up when I got home to discover a wealth of material gathered and framed, ranging from the ephemeral artifacts of poetry and oratory, on the one hand (Pindar: "I have lighted upon many themes, hitting the kairos with no false word"), to the more concrete practices of weaving and archery, on the other:

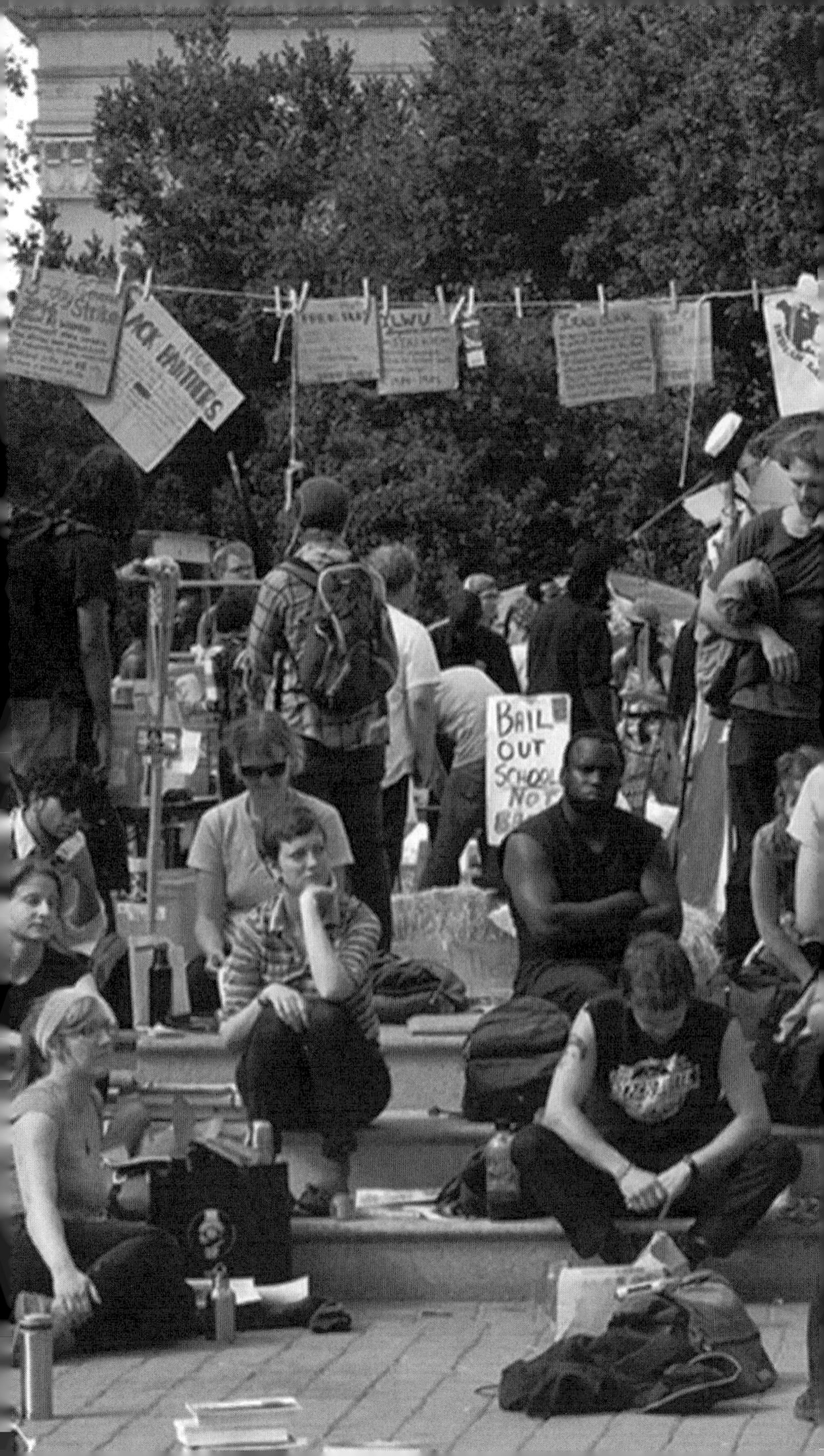
ILWU
BAIL
OUT
SCHOOL
NO

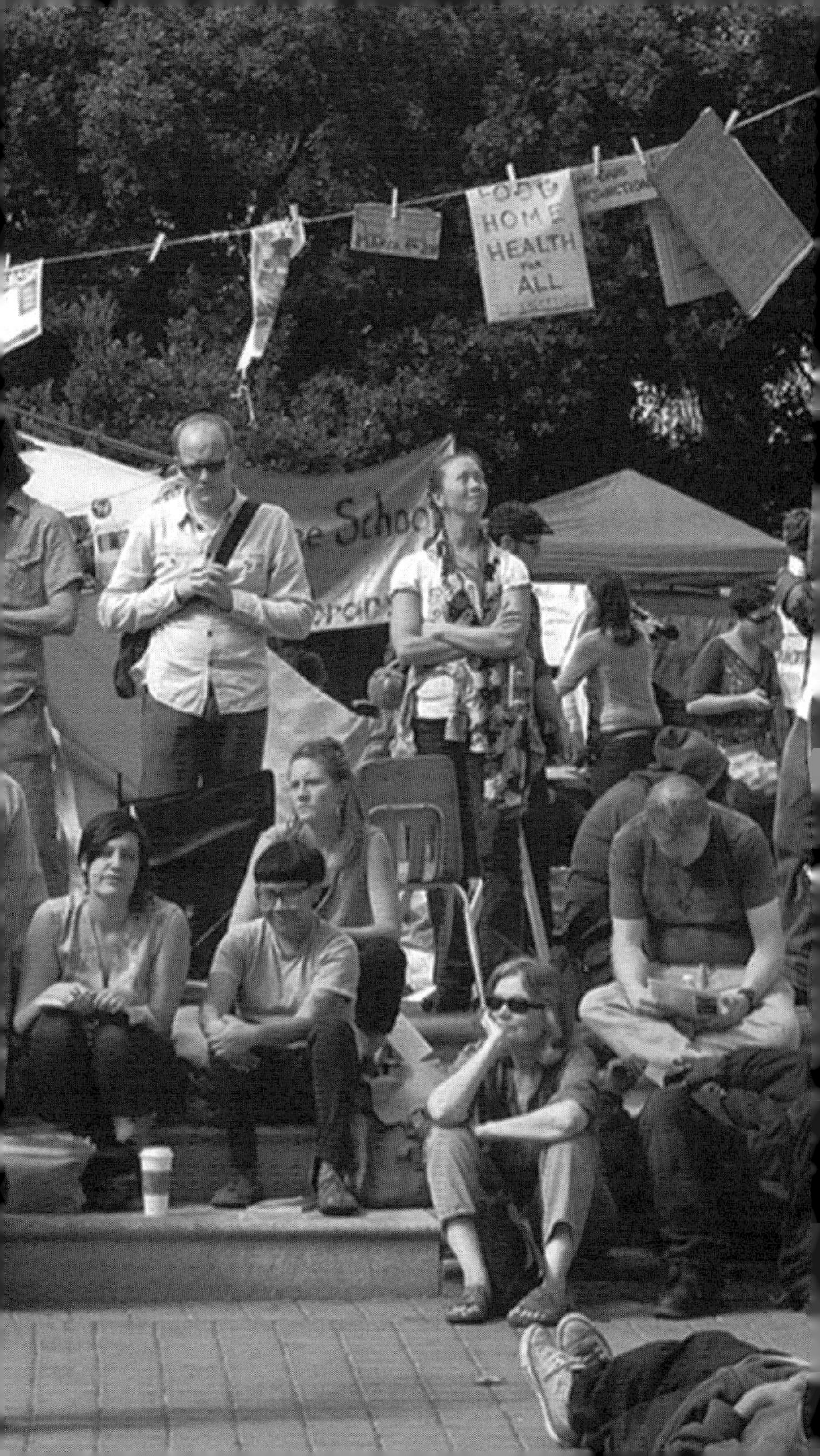
HOME
HEALTH
ALL

> [Kairos] is generally taken to mean the row of thrums which draw the odd warp-threads away from the even, making in the warp a triangular opening, a series of triangles, together forming a passage for the woof. [...] Through the opening, the passage through the warp, should be the path of the shuttle with the woof, as the proper path for the arrow was through a series of apertures. [...] The use in weaving will better explain the sense 'critical time,' 'opportunity' [...]; for there the opening in the warp lasts only a limited time, and the 'shot' must be made while it is open.[1]

Did Emily Dickinson know this philology?

> Pain contracts the Time—
> Occupied with Shot
> Gammuts of Eternities
> Are as they were not[2]

Gwendolyn Brooks certainly performs it in "the Second Sermon on the Warpland" (see *Roule* 21):

> The time
> cracks into furious flower.

The feeling those days, in any event, was very "Future is now" (as Nina Hagen has it).

A "General Strike," whose centerpiece was to be a colossal blockade of the Port, had been called by Occupy Oakland's general assembly for the coming Wednesday, November 2, in response to the clearance of the plaza the week before. Onians reports that Euripedes uses kairos to "refer to the part of the body where a weapon can penetrate to the life within" (343). Could the closure of the Port do that? "The root meaning of porta," Onians explains, "is entrance, 'passage through'" (348). Who put the "port" in opportunity? "The system has got to die | Hella hella Occupy" was one of the couplets chanted in the streets. "This description of the places where penetration was most easy the Romans appear to have translated literally [...] by their word for what was the common meaning of kairos in their day, tempus, whence our 'temple'" (344). The Wednesday before (October 25; "Pain contracts the Time") the police had grievously wounded Marine veteran Scott Olsen with a drag-stabilized bean bag filled with lead shot illegally aimed at his forehead—his temple, to be precise. Would it be possible to reverse the vector of that attack, to bypass the police and the corrupt politicians who fail to control them, to interfere directly with the circuitry of capital itself? It felt like we could glimpse the nick between the row of thrums.

The restaurant did not take plastic. Since I had barely enough cash for the ferry ride home, Sarah and David paid for the meal. "We believe in the gift economy," David said simply. I think I still owe them.

*

Asphalt is easier on the knees than concrete. Over the course of Occupy's six-month season I saw more of Oakland walking with strangers and friends on unpermitted marches down the center of city streets than I had as a pedestrian on the sidewalk. Two and a half miles on the hoof with tens of thousands

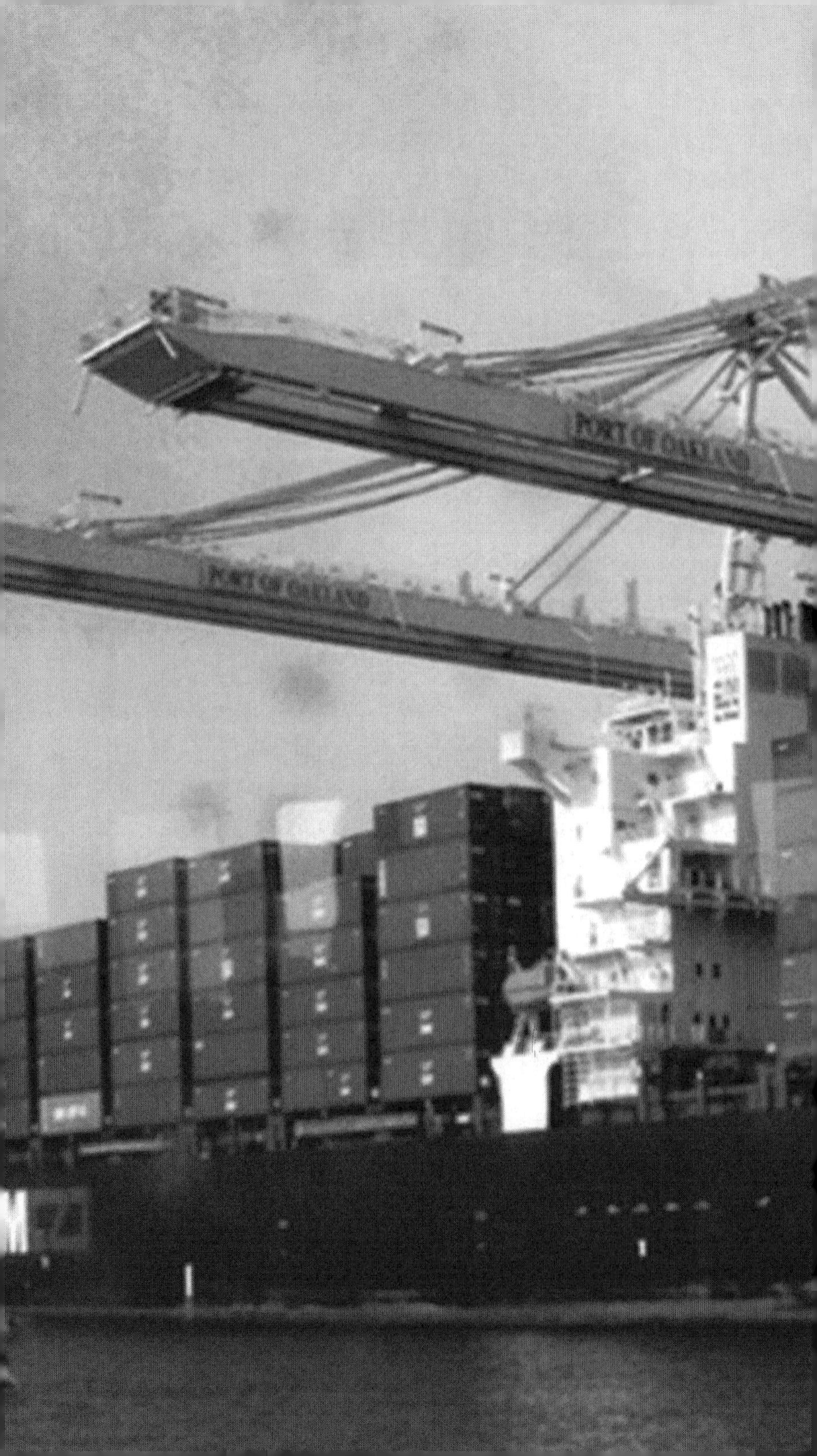
PORT OF OAKLAND
PORT OF OAKLAND

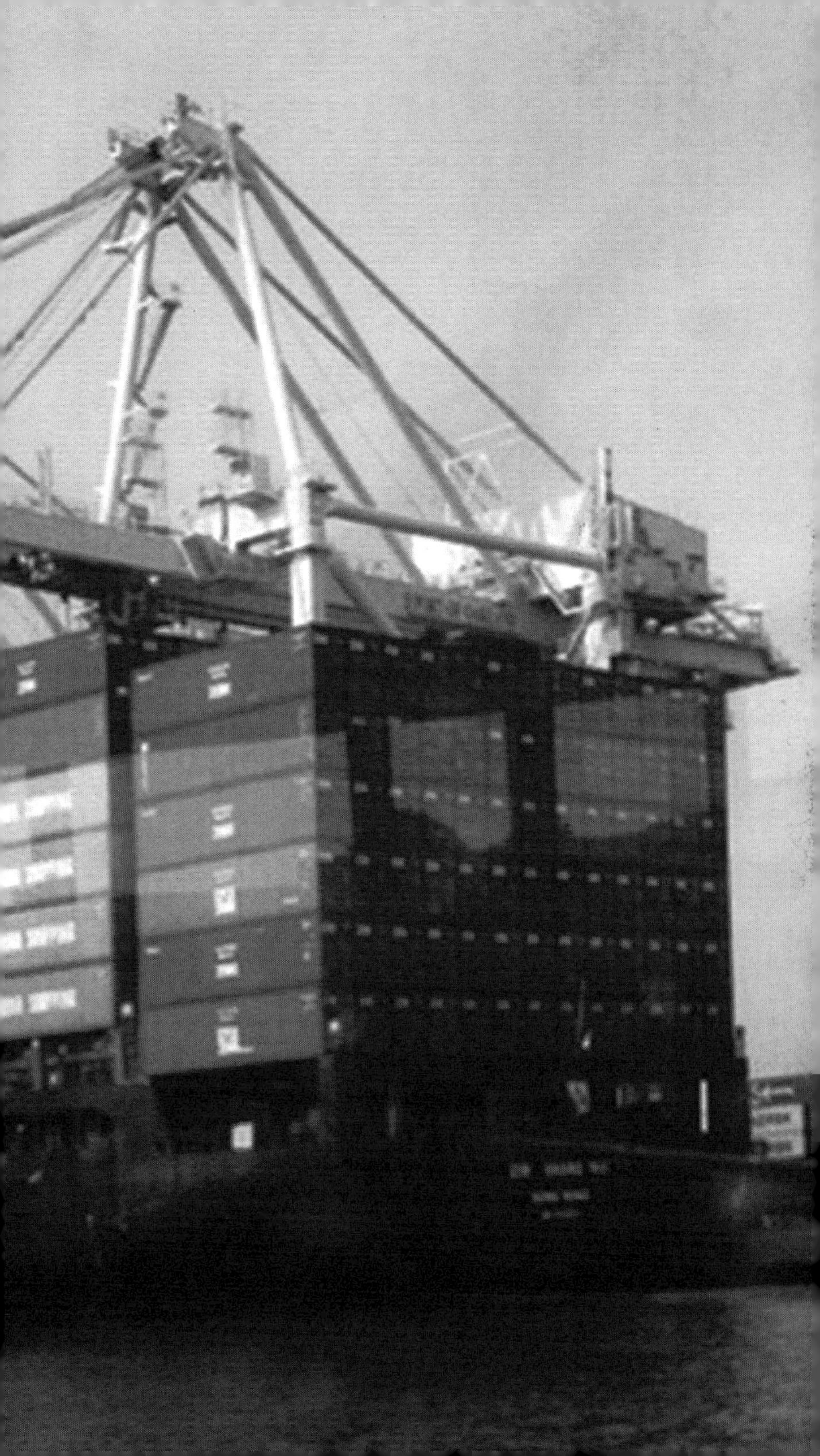

(estimates vary) from Oscar Grant Plaza (OGP) to the Port of Oakland the afternoon of November 2 (see the first *Roule*). A couple of miles in the rain around downtown Oakland on Veterans Day (November 11) with Veterans for Peace, pausing in front of Obama's re-election campaign office before continuing to the Oakland Police Department's headquarters to chant "Stop beating veterans! Stop beating everyone!" (see *Roule* 7 and 9). We got ferried in by busses early on the morning of the West Coast Port Shutdown on December 12 (see *Roule* 16 and 17), but one friend estimated that we logged several miles doing laps from curb to curb on the picket at Hanjin Terminal 55-56; as the sun rose the riot-suited Oakland Police Department initiated a sequence of gratuitous, menacing maneuvers, only to be interrupted by a "portable horde" (see *Roule* 20) arriving on foot in the rosy-fingered dawn from the West Oakland BART two miles away flying flags to the beat of a rabble-rousing drum corps. (Some of us spent that afternoon icing our hips.) Three-and-a-half miles from OGP to the Fruitvale BART station on New Year's Day 2012, the third anniversary of Oscar Grant's murder (see *Roule* 18). How many miles on Move-In Day, January 28 (see *Roule* 19)? I have no idea—I do know we had to run for part of it, and I was long gone in bed watching it on the livestream by the time the cops finally got their kettle to work (see *Roule* 21 and 22).

"What made Oakland different?" I've been asked this question more than once. It bears repeating, not least since it reflects the accurate impression that Occupy's brand changed shape and acquired a more militant flavor once a franchise was inaugurated on la contra costa of the San Francisco Bay. The Mayor of Oakland, for instance, sought to disaffiliate Occupy Oakland from the larger movement ("Mayor Jean Quan wants

OWS to disown Occupy Oakland," read one headline in early 2012); visitors from Occupy Wall Street, for their part, were impressed by the phalanx of latterday hoplites equipped with corrugated metal shields and trash can lids who turned up on January 28 for Move-In Day. David Graeber, in town on a reading junket for *Debt: The First Five Thousand Years*, tweeted a snapshot of these defensive measures, observing: "Much more militant style than we can get away with in NYC." A style suggestive of particular substance, we might add, and uniquely expressive of the larger form.

It can be easy to misunderestimate (if I may use that ex- presidential verb) the material significance of this municipality across the Bay from an imperial city named after a saint (San Francisco) and south of the town named after a university named after an idealist philosopher (Berkeley). In addition to being the sometime hometown of such various writers as Jack London, Gertrude Stein, Robert Duncan, Philip K. Dick, Maxine Hong Kingston, and Ishmael Reed, Oakland was the site of the Oakland Work holiday of 1946, one of the last city-wide general strikes in the United States. Twenty years later Oakland was the birthplace of the Black Panther Party for Self Defense, whose armed militancy and free breakfasts so successfully transformed the conditions of possibility for direct action and resistance against what they theorized as an internal colonization—"the racist military police occupies our community," Bobby Seale observed, "just like the foreign American troops in Vietnam"—that before long they were targeted by "an unparalleled campaign of repression and vilification" ruthlessly administered by the FBI's COINTELPRO,[3] whose tactics of "snitch-jacketing" and the like, designed to divide movements with threatening momentum, were being reprised, some suspected, against activists involved with Occupy.

Oakland was also the site, in 1967, of the less-well- remembered "draft board riots," a.k.a. "Stop the Draft Week," at the height of which "ten thousand demonstrators surrounded the induction center":

> Many were dressed for conflict with the police, wearing helmets and shields. they painted the streets and built barricades using benches, large potted trees, parking meters, garbage cans, cars, and trucks. [...] the confrontation grew into a violent melee that soon spread over a twenty-block area of downtown Oakland.[4]

These agitations injected into the aftermath of the 1965 Berkeley Free Speech movement a heated debate over physical confrontation with the cops, targeted strategic property damage, vanguardism, and the like—debates that were reprised in the same city in the age of Occupy under the rubrics of "black bloc" and "diversity of tactics" (see *Roule* 6 and 11).

These struggles in the streets of Oakland were immediately contemporaneous with a new way of moving cargo through the city's port, a new way stimulated by the confluent imperatives of commerce and war. the conversion from the labor-intensive piecemeal unloading of ships known as "break-bulk stevedoring" to the process of semi-automated mechanization—which gives us the lumbering cargo cranes along the Oakland waterfront and the colorful TEU containers we see pulled by freight trains and tractor-trailers—can be recognized in retrospect as a great leap forward into the ceaseless, seemingly effortless transmission of commodities that characterizes a globalized circuit of production and consumption whose watchwords are "logistics," "just-in- time delivery," and "intermodal transport." But at the time this metamorphosis was considered an ill-conceived venture; the Port of San Francisco, for instance, whose labor conditions sparked the bloody General Strike of 1934 and gave birth to the International Longshore and Warehouse Union (ILWU), refused to take the bait, and congratulated itself for having dodged a bullet. Oakland, situated further from the San Andreas Fault but more prone to other forms of risk, was at the leading edge of an automation gamble that by the end of the 1960s had made it into "the second busiest container port in the world."[5]

Oakland's unlikely emergence as a port on this scale would not have been possible without the U.S. Army's decision to ship most of its war materiel to Vietnam in containers through the Port of Oakland. Moreover, funding for the Port's expansion and conversion came by way of an arranged marriage with the nascent Bay Area Rapid transit system. As Marc Levinson explains, "In return for permission to tunnel beneath port property, the rail agency agreed to clear abandoned buildings along the embankment, construct a 9,100-foot dike, and fill the enclosed area with dirt excavated in tunnel construction."[6] Five million cubic yards of spoil displaced by the BART tunnel under the Bay were used to fill in 140 acres of wetlands in order to build twelve berths lined with gantry cranes and easy access to both railroad and highway: a central switching point between all three modes of transport. the construction of the 7th Street terminal, whose entrances we blockaded first on November 2 and again on December 12, 2011, was thus enabled on the fiscal hand by BART's federally subsidized deep pockets, and on the physical hand by Army cargo

INSIDE: THE

THE DAYS WE SEIZED THE STREETS IN OAKLAND

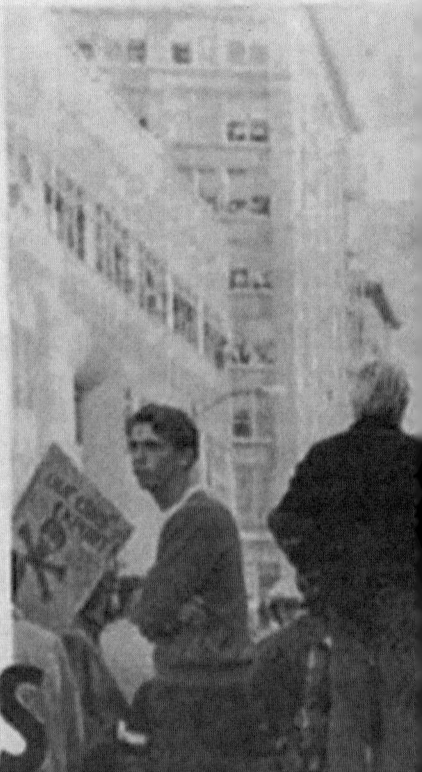

20¢

THE MOVEMENT

Affiliated with SNCC and SDS

NOVEMBER 1967 VOL. 3 NO. 11

ORY OF STOP THE DRAFT WEEK

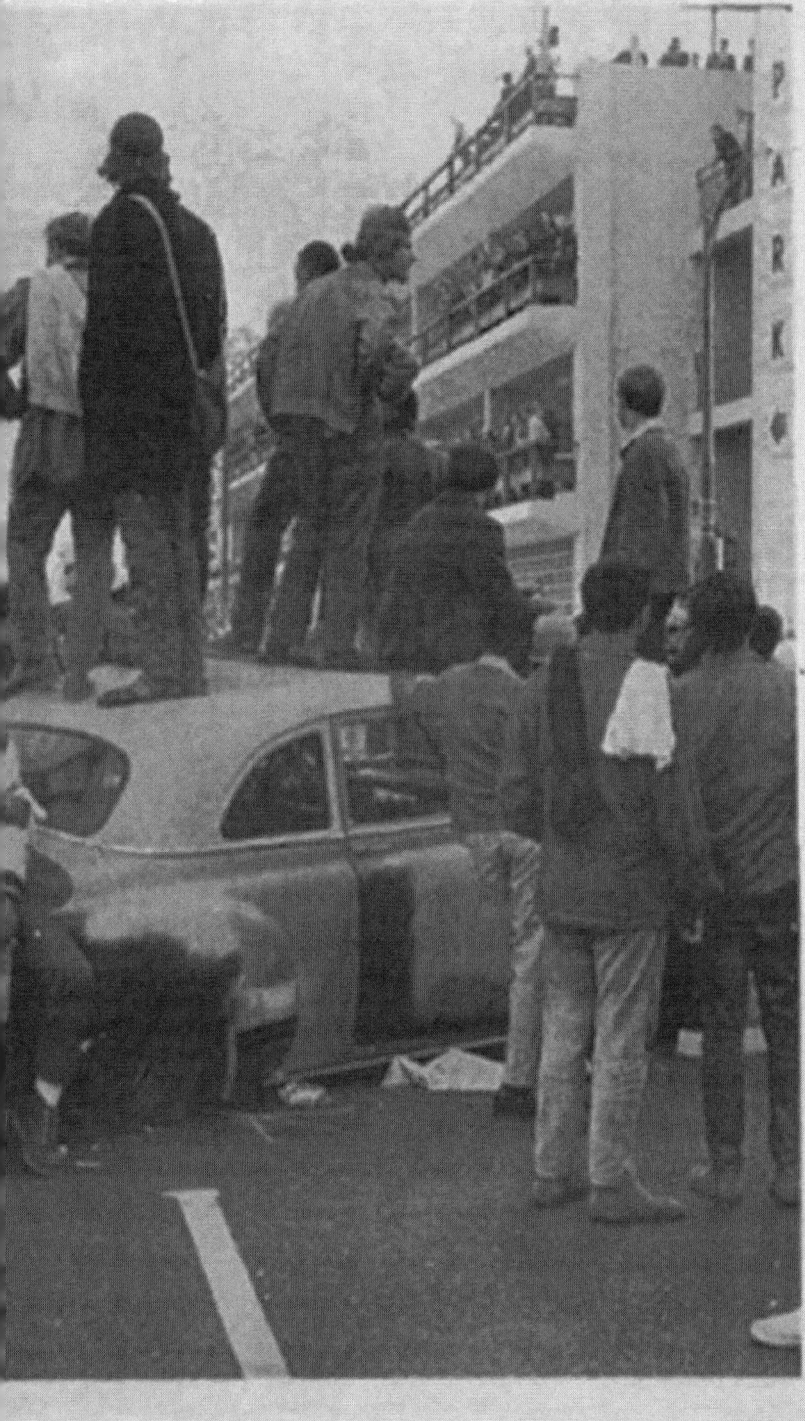

loaded by the ILWU, who under Harry Bridges' charismatic leadership had controversially conceded to mechanization.[7] So one way of reckoning Oakland's contribution to the political temper of late 2011 would be to observe that as a consequence of its proximity to what is now the fifth largest port in the country, Occupy Oakland was able to transform the largely symbolic disruptions performed by the Occupy encampments elsewhere in the country into a tourniquet directly strangulating the physical flow of capital. When tens of thousands of us marched from a Plaza that had been re-named after a person murdered by BART police to shut down a Port built by an imperial armed force in collusion with BART and with very little benefit to the surrounding community, it felt like things, for once, were moving in the right direction—a seemingly inexorable momentum stopped cold in its smelly tracks, however briefly, by collective action. When we learned that the Port takes in $4 million on a bad day and $8 million on a good one (see *Roule* 17), it seemed like we'd dealt a body blow to capitalism. On the ground in Oakland, Occupy became more than an inconvenience: it was now engaged in a coordinated and collective interference with capital's mobility. Bernard Harcourt has tried to theorize the activities of Occupy Wall Street as a form of "political disobedience," but what we saw at the Port in Oakland was something that felt more primary and fundamental still, something we might call *economic disobedience*: a popular desire to disrupt the circulations demanded by the dominant value form, and to do so on a scale and in a fashion unprecedented on these shores, and pretty well unanalyzed since.[8] We were translating our expression of a general antagonism into a concrete disruption of the general metabolism.

The first of these pamphlets was produced for that first blockade of the Port on November 2, 2011. I didn't know I would make more than one. Nor did I know all that much of the history I've just rehearsed when I made it.

I confess to having been inspired by a more recent and more ephemeral innovation.

NOTES

1. Richard Onians, *The Origins of European Thought* (Cambridge: Cambridge University Press, 1951), 346.

2. From "My life had stood—a Loaded Gun," cited by Susan Howe in *My Emily Dickinson* (Berkeley: North Atlantic Books 1985), 114.

3. Joshua Bloom and Waldo E. Martin, *Black Against Empire: The History and Politics of the Black Panther Party* (Berkeley and Los Angeles: University of California Press, 2013), 83, 5.

4. Bloom and Martin, *Black Against Empire*, 103.

5. "Between 1965 and 1969," Robert O. Self reports, "the cargo tonnage handled in Oakland waters increased ten times." *American Babylon: Race and the Struggle for Postwar Oakland* (Princeton, NJ: Princeton University Press, 2003), 154 (his emphasis).

6. Marc Levinson, *The Box: How the Shipping Container Made the World Smaller and the World Economy Bigger* (Princeton, NJ: Princeton University Press, 2006), 195. See also Marc Rosenstein's thesis "The Rise of Maritime Containerization in the Port of Oakland: 1950-1970," (M.A. Thesis, New York University, 2000).

7. See Stan Weir, "Effects of Automation in the Lives of Longshoremen," in *Singlejack Solidarity* (Minneapolis: Minnesota University Press, 2004).

8. Bernard E. Harcourt, "Political Disobedience," *Critical Inquiry* 39, no. 1 (Autumn 2012): 33-55.

IMAGES (IN ORDER OF APPEARANCE)

Untitled photo by Andrew Kenower.

Untitled photo by Sasha Berkman Tupac Spahr.

Untitled.

Takáts Márk

PECULIARITY

We meet according to the all-agreed-on customs
We go through all the genocides that our ancestors committed

We compare, disect and analyze the things we do according to similarity and difference

We discuss the words we have for making love
We discuss the words we have for fucking
We discuss our definition of being human

After all the comparing, disecting and analyzing
In my exhaustion I tend to curl up to a goofball
And roll the conversation over

Matthew Whitley

THE PHANTOM OF HEILBRONN

> Police in Germany have admitted that a woman they had been hunting for more than 15 years never in fact existed.
>
> *Dubbed the "phantom of Heilbronn," often alternatively referred to as the "Woman Without a Face," she was described by police as the country's most dangerous female criminal. Investigators had connected her to six murders and an unsolved death based on DNA traces found at the crime scenes. Police now acknowledge that swabs used to collect DNA samples were contaminated by an innocent worker in a factory in Bavari.*
>
> —BBC News

the difference between searching for a woman and an apparatus
lies in a simple question most can answer:

how were you born?

it's a natural operation, fucking,
but how many can say instead:
    from a phthisic cough that scattered manhunts
    across 60 feet of the conveyor belt
    and colored a decade with Motherly crime,
    across an unmarked border and two Cardinal Points
    a cough that saluted the factory floor
    concentrating entire mobs at the tip of a cotton swab

by one Taylorist pirouette
Germany imported a fame that cannot be located
a dangerous kind of star power
capable of making the nightly news without an excited call from Auntie Gren

ten women for a particular shape of cotton
ten carefully differentiated motions ten time cards ten uniforms
ten workers cast in two available roles – cipher or abomination

the former jealous of the latter
the former still without a face
like aerobic, like paycheck, like movement

only the police were surprised
only the ministers

for the ones who still make without authorship
they'll remember the prayer:
"by a q-tip I am multitudes"–
you'd laugh if I said it was an old prayer
but prayers can age months in days, years in weeks
and grow old in congress with the tired breath of their penitents

Contributors

Jeff Alessandrelli is a writer living in the United States of America.

Mitch Anzuoni is an author and editor living in New York. He is a founding editor of Inpatient Press, an independent imprint with a focus on esoteric and eclectic printed works from the past and present.

Justin Blinder is a Brooklyn-based artist, technologist, and researcher. His work examines how data has shaped our claims of ownership, criteria for an object's value, and social interactions in the built environment. Justin's work has been exhibited internationally, including at MoMA, New York, NY; Haus der Kulturen der Welt, Berlin, Germany; the Collection Museum, Lincoln, England; Urban Institute of Contemporary Arts, Grand Rapids, MI; and Eyebeam Art and Technology Center, New York, NY. Selected personal projects of his have been featured in publications such as *The New York Times*, *Washington Post*, *Atlantic*, *BBC*, *Guardian*, and *New York Magazine*.

David Bowles has lived most of his life in South Texas, where he presently teaches at the University of Texas Río Grande Valley. His most recent release is a short story collection titled *Chupacabra Vengeance* (Broken River Books, 2017).

Catherine Chen is the author of *Manifesto, or: Hysteria* (Big Lucks) and *Other Monsters of Love* (Container), both published in 2019. Their work has appeared in *Slate*, *The Rumpus*, *Apogee*, *Hobart*, among others. They have been awarded fellowships and awards from Poets House, Millay Colony, Lambda Literary, Sundress Academy for the Arts (SAFTA), and Art Farm.

Jackie Clark is a poet living in Jersey City. She is the author of *Aphoria* (Brooklyn Arts Press) and the chapbooks *Office Work* (Greying Ghost), *I Live Here Now* (Lame House Press), *Sympathetic Nervous System* (Bloof Books), and *Depression Parts* (dancing girl press). Her writing has appeared in or is forthcoming from *The Brooklyn Rail*, *Fence*, *The Elephants*, and *The Tiny*. She works at Eugene Lang College for Liberal Arts at The New School and teaches writing in New Jersey.

DJ Ashtrae (Joshua Escobar) is the author of *Caljforkya Voltage* (No, Dear/Small Anchor Press) and *XXOX FM* (DoubleCross Press, 2019). *Bareback Nightfall*, his first full-length collection, is forthcoming in 2020 from Noemi Press and Letras Latinas. A CantoMundo fellow, he publishes *Orange Mercury* and lives in San Bernardino.

Ted Dodson is the author of *At the National Monument/Always Today* (Pioneer Works, 2016) and *Pop! in Spring* (Diez, 2013). He does editorial work for *BOMB* and Futurepoem and is a former editor of the *Poetry Project Newsletter*.

Shou Jie Eng is an architectural designer and artist. His practice is rooted in frictional rituals, material politics, and the poetics of geometry. He lives and works in Hartford, Connecticut. His work has been published in, among others, *Paprika!* and *We Begin When We Finish We Begin*, and exhibited at the National Museum of Wildlife Art in Jackson, Wyoming, and Wayfarers Gallery in Brooklyn.

Future Host (Kang Kang and Tingying Ma) is a performance ensemble named after an epithet bestowed to children in official socialism, who are always already ready to create the world with ecstatic optimism and absolute urgency. Future Host conceptualizes the experience of post-socialist bodies to activate alternative fugitivity and resistance. The ongoing choreography and lecture series *Studies* proposes Qigong as both an art of not being governed and a cybernetic system of controlled freedom where, enabled by epistemological transgressions of Qi, the historical body's rearrangement of authority threatens and emancipates the real.

Rodney Gomez is the author of the chapbooks *Mouth Filled with Night* and *Spine*. He lives and works in the lower Río Grande Valley.

Jeremy Hoevenaar is the author of *Cold Mountain Mirror Displacement* (American Books, 2013), *Our Insolvency* (Resolving Host, 2016), and *Insolvency, Insolvency!* (Ugly Duckling Presse, 2017). His work has variously appeared in *The Recluse*, *The Brooklyn Rail*, *A Perimeter*, *6x6*, *Elderly*, *'Pider*, *Across the Margin*, and other publications. He lives in New York City with his beautiful family.

Mia Kang is an Oregon-born, Texas-raised writer, named the 2017 winner of *Boston Review's* Annual Poetry Contest by Mónica de la Torre. Her poetry has recently appeared in journals including *Rattle Poets Respond*, *Poetry Northwest*, *Sugar House Review*, and the *PEN Poetry Series*. A Brooklyn Poets Fellow and runner-up for the 2017 Discovery/*Boston Review* Poetry Contest, she is a recipient of the Academy of American Poets' 2016 Catalina Páez and Seumas MacManus Award, among others. Mia is a Ph.D. student in the history of art at Yale University, where she studies contemporary art, constitutive outsides, and impasse.

Josef Kaplan is the author of *Poem Without Suffering* (Wonder, 2015), *All Nightmare: Introductions, 2011-2012* (Ugly Duckling Presse, 2014), *Kill List* (Cars Are Real, 2013), and *Democracy Is Not for the People* (Truck Books, 2012). His new book, *Loser*, is forthcoming from Les Figues Presse.

Rebecca Keith's poetry and prose have appeared in *Narrative*, *Joyland*, *Vol. 1 Brooklyn*, *The Rumpus*, *BOMBlog*, *Best New Poets*, and elsewhere. She holds an MFA from Sarah Lawrence, hosts the MIXER Reading & Music Series, and sings/plays with her bands, Little Hustle and the Roulettes.

Matthew Kosinski is a socialist, poet, and occultist from New Jersey. He holds an MFA from The New School. His poems in this anthology are part of an as yet unpublished manuscript, *Put on Your Human Shape*, which reinterprets the seventeenth-century grimoire *The Lesser Key of Solomon* as a site of poetic generation. His self-published chapbook, *I Made a Map of Where We Used to Live*, is available on his website: matthewkosinski.com. His work has appeared or is forthcoming in *No, Dear*; *Always Crashing*; *Right Hand Pointing*; *A Bad Penny Review*; and elsewhere.

Krystal Languell lives in Chicago, where she works for the Poetry Foundation. She is the author of three books: *Call the Catastrophists* (BlazeVox, 2011), *Gray Market* (1913 Press, 2016), and *Quite Apart* (University of Akron Press, 2019). A NYSCA/NYFA 2017 Artist Fellowship Finalist in Poetry, she previously completed a Lower Manhattan Cultural Council workspace residency in 2014-15 and a Poetry Project Emerge-Surface-Be fellowship in 2013-14. Since 2010, she has helped coordinate the activities of Belladonna* Collaborative while publishing the feminist poetry journal *Bone Bouquet*. New and recent work can be found in *American Poetry Review*, *Boston Review*, *Fence*, and elsewhere.

Amy Lawless is the author of the poetry collections *My Dead* and *Broadax* (both from Octopus Books). With Chris Cheney, she co-authored the hybrid book *I Cry: The Desire to Be Rejected* from Pioneer Works Press' Groundworks Series. Her chapbook *A Woman Alone* is out from Sixth Finch. She received a NYFA Poetry Fellowship in 2011, teaches writing workshops, and lives in Brooklyn.

Matt Longabucco is the author of the chapbooks *Heroic Dose* (Inpatient, 2019), *Athens Notebook* (Imp, 2017), *The Sober Day* (DoubleCross Press, 2016), and *Everybody Suffers: The Selected Poems of Juan García Madero* (O'Clock Press, 2014). Other work has recently appeared in *Folder*, *Lana Turner*, and *The Poetry Project Newsletter*. He teaches at New York University and Bard College, and lives in Brooklyn.

Cameron Quan Louie lives in Tucson, where he serves on the board of directors with *POG: Poetry in Action*. He received his MFA from the University of Washington, has worked with Wave Books, and was a Multiplying Mediums Fellow in 2016. His work has been nominated for a Pushcart Prize, and he received the McLeod-Grobe Prize for Poetry in 2017. His poems, nonfiction, and erasures have appeared in *Duende*, *The Gravity of the Thing*, *Sonora Review*, *Quarterly West*, *Hobart*, *jubilat*, and elsewhere.

Takáts Márk lives in Budapest, Hungary. His work explores collective consciousness through mythology and folklore. He is the author of *This is Where I Fell* (2017) and *From All the Rot that He Created* (2019), both published by the Pillanat Art Foundation, and hosts poetry and performance programs in Budapest.

Miranda Mellis is the author of *Demystifications* (forthcoming from Solid Objects), *The Spokes*, *None of This Is Real*, *The Quarry*, *Materialisms*, and *The Revisionist*. She co-authored *The Instead*, a book-length conversation with Emily Abendroth, and co-edited *The Encyclopedia Project*. She lives in the woods in the Pacific Northwest where she teaches at Evergreen State College.

Feliz Lucia Molina's books and chapbooks include *Undercastle* (Magic Helicopter Press), *The Wes Letters* (Outpost19), *Crystal Marys* (Scary Topiary Press), and Roulette (forthcoming from Make Now Books). Her poems have appeared in *Open Space*, *PEN America*, *Night Papers*, Poetry Foundation, and elsewhere.

Devin N. Morris is a Baltimore-born, Brooklyn-based artist who is interested in abstracting American life and subverting traditional value systems through the exploration of racial and sexual identity in mixed media painting, photography, writing, and video. His works prioritize displays of personal innocence and acts of kindness within surreal landscapes and elaborately draped environments that reimagine the social boundaries imposed on male interactions, platonic and otherwise. The use of gestural kindnesses between real and imagined characters are inspired by his various experiences growing as a black boy in Baltimore, MD, and his later experiences navigating the world as a black queer man.

Laura Mullen is the author of eight books: *Complicated Grief*, *Enduring Freedom: A Little Book of Mechanical Brides*, *The Surface*, *After I Was Dead*, *Subject*, *Dark Archive*, *The Tales of Horror*, and *Murmur*. Recognitions for her poetry include Ironwood's Stanford Prize, a National Endowment for the Arts Fellowship, and a Rona Jaffe Award. Recent poems have been published in *The Nation*, *Poetry*, and *Lana Turner*. Her translation of Veronique Pittolo's *Hero* was just published by Black Square in 2019.

Sarah Passino's work has appeared in *DIAGRAM*, *Poetry Daily*, and *Boston Review*'s collection "What Nature." She has poems forthcoming in *The Brooklyn Rail* and *Berkeley Poetry Review*. She received the Rachel Wetzsteon Poetry Prize from the 92nd Street Y and was a 2018 Poets House Fellow. She teaches at Bard and right now is experimenting with collaborative book projects and a long-distance transcription collective.

Emmy Pérez is the author of the poetry collections *With the River on Our Face* and *Solstice*. Originally from Santa Ana, CA, Emmy has lived on the Texas-Mexico border since 2000 and currently teaches at the University of Texas Río Grande Valley.

Daniel Poppick is the author of *Fear of Description* (Penguin, 2019), selected for the National Poetry Series, and *The Police* (Omnidawn, 2017). His poetry appears in *The New Republic*, *BOMB Magazine*, *Granta*, *Bennington Review*, and the PEN Poetry Series. A graduate of the Iowa Writers' Workshop, he currently lives in Brooklyn, where he works as a copywriter and co-edits the Catenary Press.

José Antonio Rodríguez is the author of the poetry collections *The Shallow End of Sleep* and *Backlit Hour*. He currently teaches at the University of Texas Río Grande Valley.

Judah Rubin is a poet living in Queens, NY.

Veronica Sandoval aka Lady Mariposa is a poet sCHOLAr from the Río Grande Valley. She is currently an academic chola getting her PhD at Washington State University.

Danniel Schoonebeek is the author of *American Barricade* (YesYes Books, 2014) and *Trébuchet*, a 2015 National Poetry Series selection (University of Georgia Press, 2016). A recipient of a 2015 Ruth Lilly and Dorothy Sargent Rosenberg Poetry Fellowship from the Poetry Foundation, his recent work has appeared in *Poetry*, *The New Yorker*, *American Poetry Review*, and elsewhere.

Cam Scott is a poet, essayist, and improvising non-musician from Winnipeg, Canada, Treaty One territory. *WRESTLERS*, a visual suite, was published by Greying Ghost in 2017.

Shelby Shaw is a multidisciplinary writer based in New York. Her work has been commissioned byor appears via *The Believer*, MIT List Visual Arts Center, *The Brooklyn Rail*, and others, and she was the Managing Editor of *Storyfile*, a biannually printed journal of art and literature. She has been an invited Researcher at Images Festival (Toronto, Canada), works with the programmers at the IFC Center (New York), and is the Program Assistant to Projections at the New York Film Festival. Her current research debates whether or not images archive or manifest existence.

Josh Silver is a graduate student in architecture at the University of Toronto, a writer, multidisciplinary artist, and designer. His work explores the intersection of everyday life with literary and architectural constraint systems, along with the narratives embedded in trash, leftovers, and process detritus. This research allows his work to cross mediums, from the production of text-based works, to the development of publications, to construction of small-scale urban projects and image-making processes. Josh's work has been featured in multiple international and domestic publications and exhibited both locally and internationally.

Maya Sisneros is the Marketing Director at Aunt Lute Books, a nonprofit, feminist publishing press based in San Francisco. She lives in Oakland, CA.

Eirik Steinhoff is a co-editor of *Black Box: A Record of the Catastrophe*. He lives in Olympia, WA, where he co-teaches interdisciplinary classes with names like "Words/Woods" and "A New Middle East?" at The Evergreen State College. *A Fiery Flying Roule* is available in book form from Publication Studio Hudson.

Celina Su was born in São Paulo, Brazil, and lives in Brooklyn. Her first book of poetry, *Landia*, was published by Belladonna* in 2018. Her writing also includes two poetry chapbooks, three books on the politics of social policy and civil society, and pieces in journals such as *n+1*, *Harper's*, and *Boston Review*. Su is the Marilyn J. Gittell Chair in Urban Studies and a Professor of Political Science at the City University of New York.

Deirtra Thompson studied at the Rhode Island School of Design, the Maryland Institute of Art, and Bard College, where she received her MFA. Thompson has also attended the Skowhegan School of Painting and Sculpture in Skowhegan, Maine. Her films and drawings have been exhibited internationally, including at the Baltimore Museum of Art. She is the host and author of the podcast and book *Freeze Forensics*, forthcoming from Cashimotos Press. Thompson lives, works, and teaches in New York.

David Whelan is an artist living and working between Brooklyn, New York, and Athens, Greece. He holds degrees from Lyme Academy College of Fine Art (BFA, Painting) and Yale University School of Art (MFA, Painting and Printmaking). He is a recipient of the Toby Devan Lewis Fellowship, MacDowell Colony Fellowship, and completed a Fulbright Scholarship in 2017. Whelan is also a writer whose texts have appeared in publications such as *Flaneur Magazine*, *Precog Magazine*, and *Effects Journal*.

Matthew Whitley is an NYC-based writer, anarchist organizer, and anthropologist-in-training. His work has appeared in various publications including *N+1*, *The Brooklyn Rail*, *Vanitas*, *Matter*, *Translit* (St. Petersburg), and *Gigantic Sequins*. In 2018, Commune Editions released his chapbook *Do You Like the Word Crisis?* His writing has also appeared in exhibition and conference contexts, most recently in *Vertical Reach: Political Violence & Militant Aesthetics* organized under Yale University's "Utopia after Utopia" research initiative. He currently co-edits the radical artists' imprint Cicada Press, serves on the steering committee of the Emergency Committee for Rojava, and organizes with the Metropolitan Anarchist Coordinating Council (MACC).

Rachael Guynn Wilson is a writer living in Brooklyn. Her work has appeared in *The Brooklyn Rail*, *Elderly*, *Evening Will Come*, *Free Spirit News*, *Jacket2*, *Textual Practice*, and the Reanimation Library's *Word Processor* series. She is co-founder of the Organism for Poetic Research and Managing Editor at Litmus Press. She previously collaborated with Wendy's Subway as a contributor to the A + WS Reading Room at NADA New York in 2015. She holds a Ph.D. in English from New York University. She formerly co-authored an arts blog, *Most Perfect World*.

RITUAL AND CAPITAL

Series: BGCX
Bard Graduate Center Director of Public Programs: Emily Reilly
Managing Editor: Sarah McEachern
Editorial Committee: Sarah McEachern, Rami Karim, Gabe Kruis, Matt Longabucco,
Cam Scott, Rachel Valinsky
Book Design: Gerardo Madera
Cover Design: Erik Freer
Cover Image: Maryam Hoseini, *Women With Green Lies*, 2018. Acrylic, ink and pencil on wood panel, 30 x 24 inches. Courtesy the Artist and Rachel Uffner Gallery, New York.
Proofreader: Kathleen Hefty
Typeface: Fournier

Published by Bard Graduate Center and Wendy's Subway
Printed by McNaughton & Gunn, Michigan
Distributed by University of Chicago Press

ISBN: 978-1-941792-19-3

Library of Congress Control Number: 2019022987

ACKNOWLEDGEMENTS

Catherine Chen's "A Manifesto, or: Hysteria" first appeared in "Queer/Trans/Asian Folio," edited by Yanyi, in *Nat. Brut 8* (Spring 2017).

Feliz Lucia Molina's "Hello Kitty Virgin Mary" was previously published in the PoetryNow Series by the Poetry Foundation in 2018. "The Pigs in the Bahamas are Dispersed" and "Marriage: a fragment" were published in *Aurochs* 1 (2018).

Daniel Poppick's "Rumors" was originally published in *The Fanzine*, November 12, 2017.

Danniel Schoonebeek's "Poem with a Gun to Its Head" was originally published in *American Poetry Review* 46, No. 2 (March-April 2017).

Maya Sisneros's "A Time for Making: An Interview with Poets in the Borderlands" was originally published in *Medium*, May 4, 2017.

Eirik Steinhoff's "A Fiery Flying Roule" is adapted from *A Fiery Flying Route: To all the Inhabitants of the Earth; Specially the Rich Ones* (Troy, NY: Publication Studio, 2018).

Celina Su's "Notes on the Shape of Absence" was previously published in a modified form in *EDNA* 4 (2013): 101-109.

David Whelan's "Conjunctives" was previously published in Is *This Your House?* (The Seeld Library, 2015).

BGCX SERIES

The BGCX series, is a publication series designed to extend the learning period around time-based programming so that it may continue after the events themselves have ended. Taking the spontaneous alchemy of conversation, performance, and hands-on engagement as their starting points, these experimental publishing projects provide space for continued reflection and research in a form that is particularly inclusive of artists and makers.

BARD GRADUATE CENTER

Bard Graduate Center is devoted to the study of decorative arts, design history, and material culture through research, advanced degrees, exhibitions, publications, and public events. Our community encourages creative investigation of objects, from the everyday to the esoteric.

WENDY'S SUBWAY

Wendy's Subway is a nonprofit library, writing space, and independent publisher located in Bushwick, Brooklyn. Since 2013, it has provided a versatile platform for expanding modes of reading, writing, and publishing. Wendy's Subway is dedicated to encouraging creative, critical, and discursive engagement with arts and literature with the belief that collaborative practice and equitable access to reading are catalysts for social transformation. The Wendy's Subway Reading Room has been installed at the Museum of Modern Art, Brooklyn Academy of Music, Bard Graduate Center, White Columns, NADA New York, Brown University, and the Carnegie Mellon University School of the Arts.

FUNDING CREDITS

This anthology was published on the occasion of the Wendy's Subway Reading Room at the Bard Graduate Center, New York, on view from March 24 to July 30, 2017, coinciding with the exhibitions, *Design by the Book: Chinese Ritual Objects and the Sanli tu and New York Crystal Palace 1853.*

Design by the Book: Chinese Ritual Objects and the Sanli tu was organized by Bard Graduate Center and curated by François Louis, Associate Professor, History of Chinese Design and Visual Culture, with the collaboration of seminar participants: Cabelle Ahn, Julie Bellemare, Martina d'Amato, Anna-Mikaela Ekstrand, Susan Hunter, Cindy Kok, Olga Panova, Lanzhen Wang, Xiaoyi Yan, and Zhonglin Zhang. Support for the exhibition was provided by donors to Bard Graduate Center.

New York Crystal Palace 1853 was organized by Bard Graduate Center and curated by the late David Jaffee, Professor and Head of New Media Research, with the collaboration of seminar participants: Clara Boesch, Alexandra Beuscher, Ana Estrades, Margaret Frick, Roberta Gorin, Jessica Kitz, Sheila Moloney, Elizabeth Muir, Caroline O'Connell, Rebecca Sadtler, Lara Schilling, Garrett Swanson, and Andrew Taggart. Support for the exhibition was generously provided by the Henry Luce Foundation and other donors to Bard Graduate Center.

Bard Graduate Center
18 West 86th Street
New York, NY 10024
bgc.bard.edu

Wendy's Subway
379 Bushwick Avenue
Brooklyn, NY 11206
wendyssubway.com